Robert Vennell works as a Collection Manager in the Natural Science department at Auckland Museum — Tāmaki Paenga Hira, where he collects and prepares specimens for the natural science galleries. His background is in ecology and he has spent many hours wandering through the bush, eating wild berries and studying the impact of wild pigs on native flora and fauna. *The Meaning of Trees* is his first book.

THE MEANING OF TREES

ROBERT VENNELL

Harper
Collins

HarperCollins_Publishers_

First published in 2019
by HarperCollinsPublishers (New Zealand) Limited
Unit D1, 63 Apollo Drive, Rosedale, Auckland 0632, New Zealand
harpercollins.co.nz

HarperCollins_Publishers_
Unit D1, 63 Apollo Drive, Rosedale, Auckland 0632, New Zealand
Level 13, 201 Elizabeth Street, Sydney NSW 2000
A 53, Sector 57, Noida, UP, India
1 London Bridge Street, London, SE1 9GF, United Kingdom
Bay Adelaide Centre, East Tower, 22 Adelaide Street West, 41st floor, Toronto,
    Ontario M5H 4E3, Canada
195 Broadway, New York NY 10007, USA

A catalogue record for this book is available from the National Library of New Zealand.

ISBN: 978 17755 4130 1 (hardback)

Cover and internal design by Hazel Lam, HarperCollins Design Studio
Front cover illustrations: Rewarewa by Martha King (Alexander Turnbull Library, A-005-014), Kotukutuku by Martha King (Alexander Turnbull Library, A-005-005), _Phormium cookianum_ by Fanny Osborne (Auckland Museum)
Back cover illustrations: Lancewood by Martha King (Alexander Turnbull Library, A-005-036), Tutu by Martha King (Alexander Turnbull Library, PUBL-0011-14-1), Supplejack by Martha King (Alexander Turnbull Library, A-005-034), _Knightia excelsa_ by Fanny Osborne (Auckland Museum)
Layout by Jane Waterhouse
Printed and bound in China by RR Donnelley on 140gsm woodfree

8   23

For Lizzy

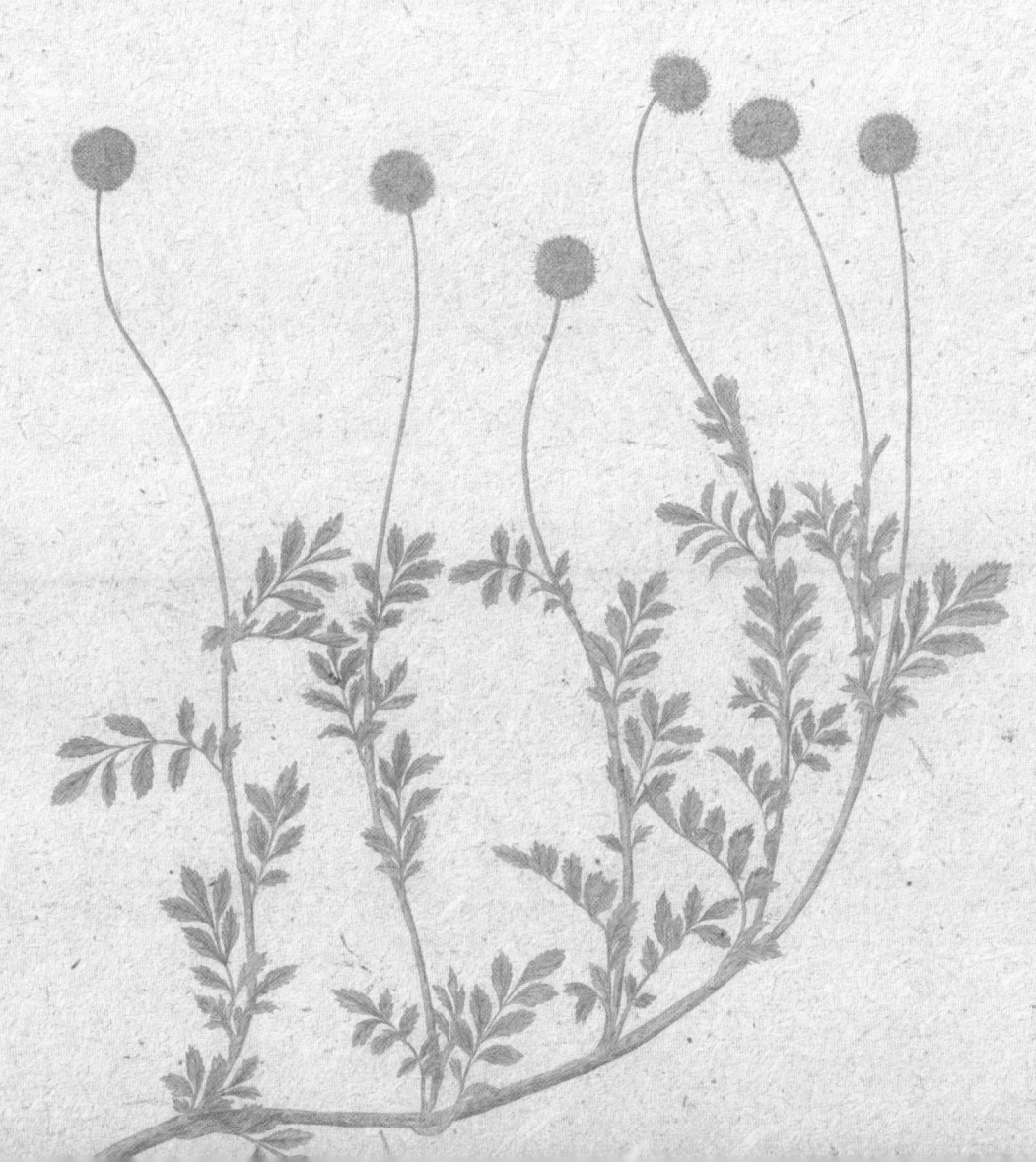

CONTENTS

PREFACE

I have always loved New Zealand's plants. As a child I would spend hours with friends
wandering through small patches of forest trying to get lost, building forts out of nīkau
fronds, and trying to catch eels with spears crafted out of lancewood. Sometimes we
would try to survive off the bush, drinking the nectar of harakeke flowers and chewing
the salty beads of Neptune's necklace between our teeth. Then came the ultimate
test: to see whether our survival shelters could withstand an enemy raid. We armed
ourselves with the strongest and longest flax sticks we could find, and waged a campaign
of guerrilla warfare on rivals' camps. After our enemies had been vanquished, the
battlefield was littered with hundreds of broken flax sticks strewn in our wake.

   The seeds of this book were first planted later on in life, when I set myself
a challenge: to eat my way through the New Zealand forest. Equipped with
Andrew Crowe's fantastic *A Field Guide to the Native Edible Plants
of New Zealand*, I would head into the forest on treasure hunts to
locate and eat all of the edible leaves, berries, shoots and roots I
could find. Wandering far off track and sleeping out in the bush,
I have managed to eat almost every edible plant in New Zealand,
except for a few poisonous or endangered species.

   While some of our native plants taste great, many leave a
lot to be desired, and so I would often challenge myself to make
delicious gourmet plant feasts. A typical menu might consist of
a sampling platter of native berries followed by a main course
of mock kererū — chicken marinated in miro (*Prumnopitys
ferruginea*) berries — and sautéed wood-ear fungus with a salad
of roasted mamaku and bush asparagus. Then to top it off,
a dessert of upside-down pudding with kahakaha berries
and a horopito hot chocolate.

When I first started this journey to eat all of the native plants of New Zealand, the forest was mostly a blur of overlapping shades of green. Other than the iconic plants I already knew and loved, most of the trees were still a mystery to me. So I set to work familiarising myself with all the fascinating and interesting ways New Zealand plants have been used throughout history. Very soon, the forest began to come alive. Bushwalks became like trips to the library or the museum, and the plants became characters from history, all with a story of their own to tell.

Bursting with excitement for these incredible creatures, I decided to share what I had learned. In between my lectures at university I set up a blog called *The Meaning of Trees* (www.meaningoftrees.com), where I wrote about the history and uses of our native plants. At the time, I did not expect anyone beyond a few friends to read it. But slowly it began to develop a name for itself, with a following from New Zealand and around the world. Pretty soon even my lecturers began referencing it in class. I was absolutely blown away by the response, and it confirmed my belief that there is a real thirst and interest out there for learning about the natural world — you just need to show why it matters.

This book is a compilation of everything I have learned from my research and experimentation with native plants. My goal in writing it is to get more people excited about and interested in our native flora. For me, learning about the history and uses of our native plants opened up the forest and made it come alive with meaning. I hope this book will do the same for you.

Robert Vennell
July 2018

HOW THIS BOOK IS ORGANISED

The book begins with a brief introduction to the story of plants in New Zealand, looking at how they have shaped our history and our identity. It then delves into the plants themselves: how they have been used, how they have been viewed, and the origins of and meanings behind their names. I have grouped the plants based on their most interesting features, the dominant way they have been used by people, or where you are most likely to find them. Many of the plants could justifiably belong to several of these groups, but I aimed to place them in the group that seemed the most fitting. This is just one lens to view the forest; there are of course many others.

- Rongoā rākau: Plants that have been used for medicine and healing
- Bush kai: Plants that have been important sources of food
- Jurassic giants: Kauri and the podocarps, ancient plant families with a long history in New Zealand
- Trees of the gods: Plants that serve as powerful symbols or have had important ceremonial uses
- Traveller beware: Climbing, sticking and stinging plants that frustrate and annoy
- Fringe dwellers: Plants commonly found around the coast and seashore
- Botanical oddballs: Weird and unusual-looking plants with bizarre flowers and growth forms

When deciding which plants to include, I prioritised the interesting and unusual, and preferred to focus on plants that have the most diverse, exciting stories to tell. The process of selection was quite organic and informed by my research. Many of the plants I thought would be in the book dropped out for one reason or another, while a number I had no intention of including have become my new favourite plants. I have had to play fast and loose with the definitions — I realised pretty early on that I could not limit myself to just trees and expanded my search to include any and all interesting plants that I discovered. There is even a chapter on bull kelp, which is on the outer limits of what we might typically call a plant, but I found it so fascinating that I couldn't resist. I avoided those plants that were too similar to ones already included; mānuka and pōhutukawa made the cut for instance, while kānuka and rātā missed out. I apologise if your favourite plant didn't make it in, but rest assured that many of the plants that do not feature here will eventually find their way onto the blog. I must also apologise to those readers who cringe when they read the many botanical puns in these pages. At first, I tried to remove these when I spotted them, but they began to crop up all over the place. Rather than try to *weed* them out, I have left them in the text as another reminder of just how integral plants are to the way we think and speak.

A NOTE ON TAXONOMY

Each entry includes two box features, one on the taxonomy (classification) of the plant and the other on the etymology (origins) of its scientific and common names. The classifications and scientific names can sometimes be a little intimidating to the uninitiated, but they really don't have to be. All living things are grouped together in a hierarchical family tree based on how closely they are related to one another. The categories in this classification are kingdom, phylum, class, order, family, genus and species. A neat way to remember these categories is by the mnemonic 'Kiwi's Play Cricket On Flat Green Surfaces'.

One of the most interesting levels for studying connections between different plants is the level of family. Many of these will be familiar already, as they encompass the major flower shapes and structures (for example the rose family, Rosaceae, or the daisy family, Asteraceae). Getting more specific, the genus is a cluster of related plants in the same family. For instance, within the rose family the genus *Rubus* contains all of the raspberry and blackberry plants. Finally, the species name helps to narrow it down and tells you exactly which organism you are referring to. *Rubus cissoides*, for example, is the name of the native New Zealand blackberry or bush lawyer.

A BRIEF WARNING

While this book contains a record of how plants have been used in the past, this does not necessarily mean that they are safe to use now. For example, the fronds of bracken were once readily eaten, but are now known to be carcinogenic. Please never put anything in your mouth unless you are 100 per cent confident that it is safe to eat. A similar warning goes for the medical treatments listed here. I have simply listed what the plants were used for in the past, but I have not attempted to establish their efficacy. It is important to remember that just because something is 'natural' does not mean it is harmless. If you are not sure if something is safe, do not make yourself a guinea pig.

INTRODUCTION

A brief history of plants

History books are full of tales about kings and queens, terrible battles and incredible inventions, and yet they leave out one of the most important characters of all — plants.

Without plants, human life as we know it could not exist. Plants produce the air we breathe, the food we eat, and the raw materials for our houses, clothes and tools. They are the spices in our food, the beans in our coffee, the cotton in our clothes and the basis for almost all of our drugs and medicines. And it does not stop there. Not content to observe events from the sidelines, plants often step directly into our lives and shape the course of human history. They have carried us across oceans to discover new lands, fought alongside us in battle, and allowed us to communicate our ideas across the world. They have inspired great works of art and epic voyages of discovery. They have been a source of conflict and war, and of spirituality and worship.

The same is true in Aotearoa New Zealand. From the very first moment humans arrived, plants have been shaping the human story. New Zealand's plant life has found its way into every facet of human life: food, shelter, medicine, transport, hunting, warfare, science and spirituality. The roles plants have played have constantly shifted, depending on the time, place and people. Plants have been viewed as enemies, friends and even family. They have been treated as scientific oddities and valuable commodities. They have been seen as links to a forgotten past and keys to the future. In order to fully understand our own history, it is important we understand this shared history with plants.

PLANTS AND MĀORI

Around 750 years ago, Polynesian explorers landed on the shores of Aotearoa New Zealand. What they discovered was a land of forest, far larger than all of the islands in Polynesia put together. Every square inch of land, from the sea to the towering mountain tops, was brimming with plants. Along the coastline, scarlet-red pōhutukawa blossoms would have lit up the forest canopy like wildfire, while the shiny green leaves of harakeke waved at the explorers from the shoreline. As they paddled further along the coast they would have seen flocks of kererū gorging on orange karaka berries, and heard the deafening sound of a thousand tūī, each defending its own golden kōwhai tree. As they ventured into the dark forest interior, they would have seen a curious assortment of shrubs competing fiercely for sunlight, carpets of moss dripping with water, giant tree ferns shading the forest floor, and herds of moa grazing the forest understorey. Above them all were the podocarps, ancient forest giants that towered over the canopy and lived for thousands of years. In the north, they would have encountered the mighty kauri trees, gargantuan columns of wood that seemed to touch the heavens themselves.

Making a new home among this strange wilderness of plants could not have been easy. With its much colder and unforgiving climate, Aotearoa was very different from tropical Polynesia. Many of the treasured plants the travellers would have brought with them across the Pacific — banana, coconut, sugar cane and breadfruit — would not grow here. Those that did survive the journey — the kūmara, taro, gourd, paper mulberry, yam and Pacific island cabbage tree — could be grown only in the north of the country, and even then never grew as well as they did in the tropics.

The strange and unusual plants the travellers discovered here therefore held the key to survival in New Zealand. If they were going to make a life here, they would need to learn the secrets of these new plants. So these groups of early Polynesian explorers became the first scientists in Aotearoa. With hard-won knowledge they learned which berries and roots were safe to eat, and which were deadly poisonous. They experimented with different weaving materials and techniques to create warmer clothes that could withstand the colder weather. They applied herbal medicines and studied their effects. They developed new crops of native plants and refined the best methods for growing them.

By adapting to this new land and the creatures that inhabited it, the Polynesians began to develop a distinct culture and worldview that we now know as Te Ao Māori. Plants would be central to this change. In fact, they became so closely intertwined with Māori culture that it is difficult to talk about one without the other. From the very first moment a child entered the world, they were wrapped in the leaves and fibres of plants. Throughout the rest of their lives Te Wao Nui o Tāne (the great forest of Tāne) provided everything that was needed to sustain life. It was a supermarket, chemist, garden centre, hunting ground, hardware store and playground rolled into one.

The flowering of native plants provided the rhythm for daily life. Flowers were carefully studied to know when to plant crops and when to hunt and fish. For the expert tohunga, the forest represented a pharmacopoeia, a storehouse of herbal medicine (rongoā). When combined with karakia and ritual, these herbal remedies could heal practically any ailment. And when a person passed from this life to the next, their loved ones wore plants over their heads as a sign of their sorrow. Even the spirits of the dead

Early Spring; or, A Narrow of the Waikato River, 1881, Auckland, by Kennett Watkins. (Te Papa, 2000-0022-1)

A Māori village in a kauri forest along the Waihou River. (Alexander Turnbull Library, PUBL-0015-08)

used plants, carrying the treasured plants of their homeland with them as they made their spiritual journey back to Hawaiki.

Not only did plants provide all of the materials for daily life, but they became an integral part of the way Māori understood the world. A central concept in Māori thought is whakapapa — a vast genealogical tree that links everything together in a network of relatedness. Plants, animals, humans, rocks and minerals can all be traced back to the primordial gods or atua — the sky father Ranginui and the earth mother Papatūānuku. Those early Polynesian ancestors of the Māori people would have held similar beliefs, but their world was dominated by the vast seas of the Pacific Ocean. In Polynesian tradition, it is often Tangaroa, atua of the oceans, that rules supreme among the children of Rangi and Papa.

For Māori living among the great forests of Aotearoa, it was Tāne Mahuta, atua of the forest and birds, who was the most revered. Tāne Mahuta was seen as the physical embodiment of trees of the forest, the model of manhood and righteousness; steadfast, strong and brave. It was Tāne, with his back to the earth and his feet to the sky, who wrenched Ranginui and Papatūānuku from their primordial embrace and allowed light to flood into the world; Tāne who placed the stars, moon and sun across the sky; Tāne who travelled to the heavens and brought back knowledge for humankind. In some traditions it is even Tāne who brought human life into the world. It is told that Tāne was looking for *te ira tangata* — the essence of humanity — and mated with many female atua, hoping to produce human offspring. The result of these couplings were the chiefly trees of the forest kauri and tōtara, the hardwoods pūriri and maire, the climbing plants such as rātā and supplejack, and the shrubs such as karamū and horopito. In this way Tāne was able to clothe the naked body of Papatūānuku, who had been left exposed by the violent separation from her husband. It was only when Tāne moulded a female from mud and breathed life into her that humans were created. In this traditional understanding, plants were not simply a resource; they were relatives. In fact, because plants were created before humankind, Māori saw them as older siblings (tuākana), with seniority over humankind. It was essential, therefore, that trees were to be treated with respect and reverence, and great ceremony always attended their harvest. If humans did possess any privileged status it was as kaitiaki (guardians), whose role was to ensure the mana and mauri of the forest. In just a few hundred years of settlement, these plants, which had never before been seen by human eyes, had become family, an integral part of human society, and vital to the understanding of the world.

PĀKEHĀ ARRIVE

When the next wave of human explorers arrived on New Zealand's shores, plants again played a decisive role. While Abel Tasman had encountered the west coast of New Zealand in 1642, it was not until 1769 that Europeans would get the chance to set foot on Aotearoa and meet its plants face to face. As Lieutenant James Cook and his crew aboard the *Endeavour* travelled around the country, they marvelled at the tall groves of kahikatea along the banks of the Waihou River, and traded with local Māori for the tools and clothing they had made from plants of the forest. They carried away boatloads of scurvy grass and New Zealand celery to ward off disease, brewed tea from mānuka and kānuka leaves, and fed on the heart of the nīkau palm.

An early settler's camp made from native timber and woven raupō leaves. *(Alexander Turnbull Library, A-234-012)*

For the naturalists Joseph Banks and Daniel Solander, every spare moment was spent botanising on shore. The pair must have been like kids in a candy shop — every new plant they found was a new discovery for Western science. While Māori had a deep and special connection with the plants of New Zealand, they did not quite know what to make of these visiting botanists. Te Horeta te Taniwha, who observed the *Endeavour* arrive in Whitianga harbour, could not work out why they were collecting grasses from the cliffs and pressing them between sheets of paper. He decided they must be goblins. But he laughed along with them anyway, and helped bring them more plants for their collection.

For millions of years, New Zealand's plants had remained in isolation from the rest of the world. But after the arrival of the *Endeavour*, they went global. They were archived in the herbariums of Europe, grown in overseas gardens and British glasshouses, and Māori plant 'curiosities' were displayed in museums around the world. Botanists scrutinised and studied their floral characteristics, and attempted to piece together a new kind of whakapapa based on taxonomy, linking New Zealand plants with their overseas relatives. Once word got out about New Zealand's plant life, the lure of these plants was so great that they inspired more voyages of discovery. Captivated by the glowing reports from the journals of the *Endeavour*, entrepreneurs set sail for New Zealand eager to capitalise on the vast supplies of timber and flax. Traders collected kahikatea spars along the banks of the Waihou River and bartered with local Māori for harakeke fibre. Not only had plants drawn these explorers from the other side of

Kororāreka in the Bay of Islands, in the early days of European settlement. *(Te Papa, 1992-0035-1819)*

the planet, but they were the backdrop to some of the earliest and most extensive interactions between Pākehā and Māori.

Plants brought Māori to the wider world as well, willing or not. In 1793, Lieutenant Hanson arrived in Doubtless Bay on the ship *Daedalus*, and lured the tohunga Tukitahua and the rangatira Hurukokoti onto his boat with the promise of trade. Then he pulled anchor and set sail for Norfolk Island. On Norfolk a penal colony had been established, and convicts were forced to process harakeke into rope. However, they could not achieve the highly refined product of Māori weavers. When they arrived in Norfolk, Tuki and Huru were made to teach the prisoners everything they knew about processing flax. It turned out to be almost nothing, since flax weaving was generally carried out by women. Nonetheless they were the first Māori to live among Europeans in a foreign land, and much was learned about both cultures during this time. Later on, Māori entrepreneurs back in Aotearoa would develop a thriving harakeke industry of their own. They sold tonnes of processed harakeke fibre to Australia, and traded harakeke to buy European goods, tools and muskets.

When Europeans began to permanently settle in New Zealand, their reactions to the plants were polarising. For some settlers, native plants were treated with open hostility. Many had been sold on a promise that New Zealand was an agricultural paradise of rolling pastures and meadows — a little Britain of the South Seas. Arriving in a dark, damp and forbidding rainforest full of unfamiliar flora, many viewed native plants with fear and hostility. It was believed the best way to deal with the forest was to get it under grass as soon as possible. Much of the settlers' time was therefore spent

A pioneering Pākehā family carving a life for themselves among the Kauri trees. *(Te Papa, 2006-0020-2)*

clearing and burning native plants so they could scratch out a living in this new home on the other side of the world.

But not all Pākehā felt this way. Like Māori before them, plants provided Pākehā with the essential requirements for survival in New Zealand. Settlers learned how to utilise the plants of the forest, constructing huts out of nīkau and raupō leaves, making beds out of bushman's mattress (mangemange, *Lygodium articulatum*), treating illness with bushman's painkiller (horopito, *Pseudowintera colorata*), and resorting to bushman's toilet paper (rangiora, *Brachyglottis repanda*) in emergencies. The immense kauri giants and podocarps of the forest provided the material to build the new colony, and were used to construct houses, churches and government buildings. Missionaries were early adopters of native plants. They quenched their thirst for tea with kawakawa and piripiri leaves, brewed beer from the roots of cabbage trees and distilled wine from tutu berries.

All the while, botanists and naturalists continued to roam the New Zealand wilderness, making new discoveries in every corner they travelled. While on an adventure in the Ruahine Ranges, the missionary William Colenso collected so many new plant species that he was forced to tear off his shirt and fashion it into a carry-bag.

PLANTS OF WAR

When Pākehā and Māori clashed in bitter struggles over land, plants became a central player in the conflicts. Plants helped Māori hold their own against arguably the most powerful industrial nation on the planet. Māori could traverse tangled rainforest with ease, and directed British soldiers into the bush where they held a clear advantage. They built remarkable fortified palisades out of pūriri and woven flax that could resist the might of British cannon fire. They dug pits and concealed themselves with the leaves of raupō, lying in wait to spring ambushes on unsuspecting soldiers. They stitched musket wounds back together with harakeke and hauled away the wounded with loops of supplejack.

For British and colonial forces, on the other hand, the forest was a terrifying place. It was filled with vines that tripped them up and caught their bayonets, and their bright red coats made them sitting ducks for Māori musket fire. During the Land Wars, the need to adapt to forest warfare was so great that the army put together an élite unit of Forest Rangers. They were trained in the art of back-country tramping, taught how to fire off rounds while ducking between trees, and equipped with short swords and kilts for easier movement in the bush.

A NEW LEAF

Just as plants became deeply woven into the Māori worldview, the same was true of Pākehā settlers. New generations born in New Zealand grew up alongside the plants, which became powerful symbols of what it means to live in New Zealand, from the lonely, stoic cabbage tree on the farm to the primeval kauri forests of Northland and the dripping-wet beech forests of Fiordland.

Conservation movements began to argue that our forests should be protected and preserved, not just so they could be cut down at a later date, but because they had spiritual, scientific and cultural value all of their own. Scientists, iwi and conservationists campaigned for greater recognition of the value of our plants, and environmentalists rallied to save the forests of Manapouri and put their lives on the line to protect the giant trees of Pureora and Whirinaki. With the growing realisation of the damage that introduced mammals have caused, forest sanctuaries have sprung up all around the country, and pests have been eradicated or controlled to allow native plants to regenerate. Millions of native plants have been replanted along motorways and rivers, farmland and sanctuaries, converting grass and pastureland back to forests.

Plants continue to be a feature of modern life in New Zealand. We sing and write poetry about them, we breed them and trade them around the world — we even tattoo them onto our skin. They are on our postcards and artwork, worn by our sports teams and our soldiers, and feature on our government institutions and our money.

And while we might not always pay them much notice, they are ever present throughout our lives. From the summer holiday spent under a shady pōhutukawa at the beach, to the bush-bash out to a back-country hut, plants have permeated our culture and become integral to a shared New Zealand identity. And their appeal continues to grow. Native plants are finding their way into trendy tea shops, cafés,

The death of the forest ranger Gustavus Von Tempsky during a bush assault on Te Ngutu o te manu. *(Puke Ariki, A66.590)*

and classy restaurants. Rongoā Māori is undergoing a revitalisation with a huge surge of interest in Māori medicinal plants. And native plants are attracting increasing attention from scientists, with New Zealand plants being investigated to find new medicines, foods, alcohols and cosmetics.

Despite this growing interest, New Zealand's native plants are not out of the woods yet. They are still facing down hordes of introduced pests, weeds and disease. Kauri dieback threatens our ancient kauri forests, and myrtle rust has arrived to threaten our mānuka and pōhutukawa. While the road ahead is not easy, the first step is realising what we have got. New Zealand plants are truly remarkable. They have a unique and fascinating history. And, if we stop and listen, they still have many incredible stories left to tell.

Pōhutukawa
(*Metrosideros excelsa*)
by Fanny Osborne
(*Auckland War
Memorial Museum,
CCBY*)

RONGOĀ RĀKAU

Medicinal plants

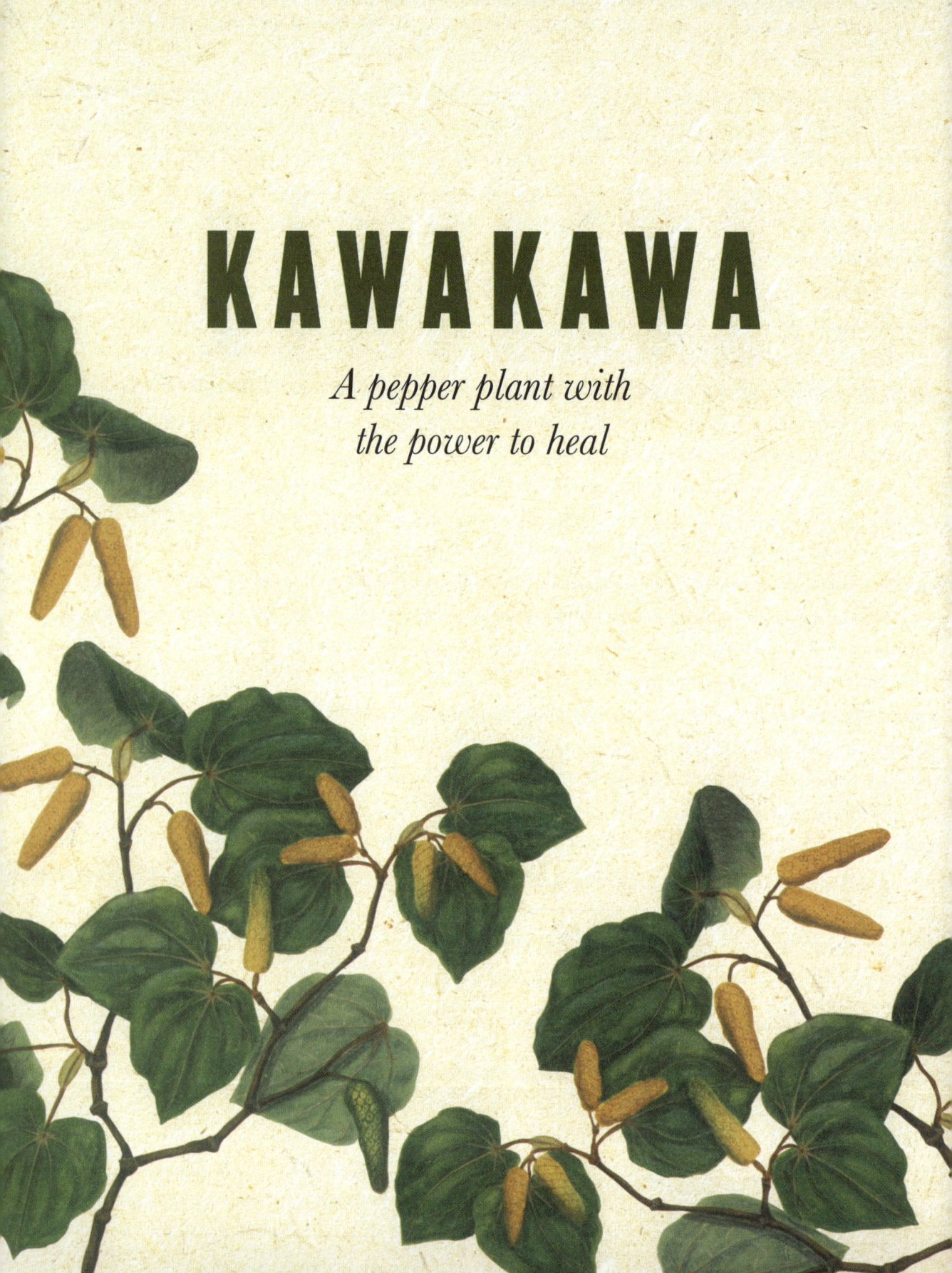

KAWAKAWA

*A pepper plant with
the power to heal*

For those early Polynesian explorers encountering the lost world of Aotearoa for the first time, the heart-shaped leaves of kawakawa must have been a welcome sight. The plant bears a striking resemblance to its close cousin kava, a powerful sedative that is esteemed throughout the Pacific. While it lacks kava's strongly intoxicating properties, kawakawa would come to occupy an equally vital role in the Māori world.

For many, the relationship with the plant began at conception, when Māori parents might place a sprig of kawakawa under the bed during intercourse as a good luck charm. From there, it remained an ever-present symbol throughout life. It was present during the birth and naming of children, and it was used when welcoming guests and blessing food and to bless war parties with strength before they departed for battle. When laid on the marae it was seen as an omen of death, and it took on an important role at end-of-life ceremonies as well. When it was time for a loved one to depart this world and return to Hawaiki, mourners of the dead would carry kawakawa leaves and wrap them around their heads as a sign of their loss.

HERBAL HERO

Perhaps the greatest value of kawakawa was as a potent plant medicine, and it was used to treat almost any ailment. Kawakawa leaves and roots were boiled in water to produce a refreshing tonic that was considered an aphrodisiac. The tasty beverage was drunk as a treatment for gonorrhoea, worms and problems with the chest, kidneys and bladder. Skin complaints, boils and bruises were treated by placing the patient in a soothing bath of kawakawa leaves, where compounds from the leaves would infuse into the

Kawakawa leaves were used as a healing tonic and chewed to relieve toothache. (*Edin Whitehead*)

water. Bleeding cuts and wounds could be wrapped in kawakawa bandages, which were said to aid the healing process. The bitter, peppery leaves produce a numbing sensation in the mouth like that of kava, and were often chewed to ease toothache and sore throats. Māori mothers would even rub the leaves on their breasts to help wean their children off breast milk faster.

Myristicin is one of the bioactive molecules in kawakawa, and may be responsible for its remarkable healing properties, as it is a known anti-inflammatory, antimicrobial and insecticide and helps prevent damage to the liver. It is also a known psychoactive, and is the compound responsible for the psychedelic properties in nutmeg. A few recreational drug enthusiasts have attempted to smoke kawakawa leaves and roots, with mixed results other than mild numbing effects. Needless to say, experimentation is not advised. The side-effects from consuming too much myristicin from nutmeg are incredibly unpleasant and potentially life-threatening.

INSECT KILLER

In Māori tradition, kūmara was stolen from the god Whānui and brought to earth for humans to use. Filled with rage, Whānui decided to punish humans by sending the kūmara moth (*Agrius convolvuli*) to lay waste to the kūmara crop. The caterpillar of this species ravishes the kūmara leaves and greatly reduces the harvest. Fortunately, Māori gardeners discovered they could use kawakawa to fight back against the attack. The leaves of kawakawa contain a potent insecticide that protects them from hungry insects. Māori would burn rows of kawakawa branches among their kūmara plantations to help ward off kūmara moths and other insects that might damage the crop.

There is one insect, however, that is unaffected by this defence. The kawakawa looper moth (*Cleora scriptaria*) has adapted to the insecticide and has made kawakawa its preferred host plant. The caterpillars of the kawakawa looper are responsible for the leaves that are riddled with holes and bite marks. Māori believed that the leaves covered in holes were the best for rongoā, as the caterpillars selected the leaves with the highest concentration of medicine. It is possible there may be a scientific basis behind the tradition, as leaves that have been attacked are triggered into changing their chemical composition, and may increase concentrations of certain bioactive compounds.

The holes seen on these kawakawa leaves were made by feeding caterpillars of the kawakawa looper moth, *Cleora scriptaria*. (Edin Whitehead)

CULINARY DELIGHT

The value of kawakawa was not lost on European settlers either, who were quick to experiment with brewing native plants into teas. One writer in the 1800s even boasted that, between kawakawa and mānuka tea, New Zealand had no need for tea from China. Others have used the leaves to brew beer, and the result is said to be most refreshing. Kawakawa tea has recently hit the mainstream big time, and can be seen in trendy tea shops, upmarket cafés and gourmet supermarkets.

The leaves were used in traditional Māori cuisine as a kīnaki, or relish, cooked in a hāngī, and served with meat such as muttonbird. Kawakawa leaves have begun to have something of a modern culinary renaissance as well, being increasingly used in both sweet and savoury dishes, where they take on peppery, basil-like flavours. Chef Charles Royal has been at the forefront of this revival of native foods, and has pioneered the use of kawakawa in cooking. His recipes use kawakawa leaves dried as a spice, sautéed in oil, baked into shortbread, meringues and biscuits, and made into ice cream.

The orange-yellow fruit was eaten by Māori, and used as a diuretic. It is sweet and delicious, with a taste that is slightly reminiscent of pawpaw. When eating the fruit, care must be taken not to crush the small peppery seeds, as this releases a pungent aroma that can spoil the taste. Forager Johanna Knox recommends the fruits dipped in chocolate, made into a sauce, or added to fruit salad. Kawakawa is also a close relative of black pepper, and the dried fruit can be roasted to make peppercorns, ground as a spice, or infused into alcohol.

Birds such as this silvereye are quick to eat kawakawa fruits as soon as they ripen. *(Edin Whitehead)*

HOROPITO

The bushman's spicy painkiller

Horopito is known as 'pepper tree', and it certainly lives up to the name. Chewing on the red mottled leaves produces an intense, numbing spice. It has a different kind of heat to chilli and takes some getting used to, as it can knock out taste buds and leave everything tasting rather strange. A common trick to play on friends — or enemies — is to introduce them to horopito as the delicious 'ice-cream plant' and then watch them recoil in horror as their mouth is engulfed in spice.

Māori were aware of the hot, spicy leaves, which were considered one of the stars of traditional Māori medicine. People suffering from a sore mouth and teeth chewed the leaves, as the numbing spice helped to ease the pain. Māori mothers also used horopito to wean their children off breastfeeding, by rubbing the hot, peppery leaves on their breasts. Hot baths of horopito leaves and bark were used to treat a wide range of complaints, including skin disease, ringworm, gonorrhoea, chafed skin, wounds, burns, bruises or cuts.

EFFECTIVE TREATMENT

Pākehā bushmen learned of the value of horopito medicine from Māori, and dubbed it 'Māori painkiller', or 'bushman's painkiller'. It made a useful on-the-go medicine when out travelling the country, and they brewed its leaves into a warming aromatic 'tea' and drank it when suffering from stomach ache, headaches, fever or diarrhoea. The leaves were also chewed and placed on wounds and cuts to aid in healing, although it is reported that the skin sometimes heals with a slightly blue tinge.

The leaves of horopito pack a powerful, peppery punch. (Robert Vennell)

Lowland horopito (*Pseudowintera axillaris*) by Sarah Featon. (Biodiversity Heritage Library)

Modern researchers have found that the substance responsible for the spicy red leaves, polygodial, has many other intriguing effects as well. It has been found to have anti-fungal, antibacterial, anti-inflammatory and anti-allergic properties. Horopito extracts have been shown to be particularly effective at killing the yeast infection *Candida albicans*, which is responsible for oral and vaginal thrush. Horopito is currently marketed in New Zealand and overseas in creams for treating yeast infection, and as a tea for treating a sore mouth or throat.

DEER DETERRENT

The spicy leaves provide a huge advantage for horopito. Deer cannot stand the taste, so in some areas of the country horopito has become the dominant understorey plant, while all of its competitors have been eaten away. The leaves are also able to repel insects, and contain oil glands full of polygodial. When insects chew through these oil glands, the compound is released, killing the insect and also damaging the plant tissue itself, leading to the blotchy red patches found across the leaf surface. Researchers have found that this red patterning serves as a warning signal to insects: the redder the leaves, the more polygodial they contain.

The signal is so effective that other plants appear to be copying it. The unrelated small toropapa (*Alseuosmia pusilla*) bears a striking resemblance to horopito, with many plants containing the same red blotchy colour patterning across their leaves, but without the anti-insect compounds. When the two plants grow in the same environment they can be almost indistinguishable, and the similarity between the plants remains constant in different environments. This has led researchers to propose that this may be a rare case of Batesian mimicry — when a harmless species takes on the appearance of a harmful one — in the plant world. By mimicking horopito and pretending it is well defended, the small toropapa might be able to avoid being eaten. Exactly what animal toropapa might be trying to avoid is not exactly clear; it could be trying to protect itself from herbivorous insects or may have evolved as a response to browsing from moa. You can tell whether or not the plant you are looking at is horopito

Horopito can become the dominant plant in some forests, as deer will avoid eating it.
(Edin Whitehead)

by turning over the leaves — horopito has a pale white or blue underside, whereas small toropapa leaves are pale green underneath.

A VERSATILE FLAVOURING

The use of horopito in food is now unequivocally mainstream: the ground dried leaves are used in fancy restaurants, sold as gourmet teas, and are available in sauces and dressings. Horopito can be used wherever black pepper or chilli is normally used, for a bit of an extra kick and depth of flavour. It shares similarities with culinary vegetables from Japanese cuisine such as the Japanese water pepper (*Persicaria hydropiper*), which also contains polygodial.

Horopito makes an excellent marinade to rub into meats, fish and vegetables, and can be infused into oils before cooking or used as an ingredient in condiments such as aioli, mustard and hummus. The leaves have been used to flavour spirits and brew beer, and have even been incorporated into desserts, baked into biscuits and used as a topping on ice cream.

KOROMIKO

A diarrhoea remedy and
a flavouring for moa

Koromiko is one of the most revered medicinal plants in the New Zealand flora, and its greatest power lies in its ability to combat diarrhoea and dysentery. For early Māori chronic diarrhoea could be a death sentence, and it remains a leading cause of death in developing parts of the world. To ease the symptoms, Māori would chew the growing leaf buds, or boil them into a soothing tea with astringent properties. Pākehā learned of this use from Māori, and many early settlers, bushmen and gumdiggers came to rely on it as a valuable source of medicine. The leaves were even used by some farmers to cure bouts of diarrhoea among their cattle.

Dried koromiko leaves were sold by chemists for a time, under names such as 'Koromiko Cordial' and 'Monk's Herbal Extract' and were taken by explorers when travelling overseas. This was so successful that people even began selling knock-off imitations, which claimed to be koromiko cures but did not use any of the leaves.

Over the past century, the value of this diarrhoea remedy has been proven time and again. During the First World War, dried parcels and jars of koromiko leaves were sent to the Māori Battalion in Egypt and readily shared out among the troops, who swore by its effect. When an outbreak of diarrhoea struck Christchurch Hospital in the 1920s, doctors and medical supplies were overwhelmed, so staff resorted to treating patients with koromiko leaves instead. By the Second World War, koromiko was used extensively by New Zealand soldiers throughout North Africa and the Middle East, and the New Zealand army initiated trials to test its drug potential. The Russian army was even interested in koromiko, and requested seeds from the Christchurch Botanic Gardens so they could grow the plant and test it on their troops.

TAXONOMY

The name 'koromiko' can refer to a number of different species in the *Veronica* genus but is perhaps most commonly applied to *Veronica stricta*, which occurs from the coast to lower montane areas throughout the North Island and in northern areas of the South Island. There are over 100 species of *Veronica* in New Zealand, including many rare and threatened plants. They belong to the Plantaginaceae, which includes the plantains (*Plantago* spp.), common weeds of lawns and parks that also have a long history of medicinal use.

BALMS AND MAKEUP

As well as treating diarrhoea, koromiko was useful in other rongoā remedies. The young growing buds and leaves were harvested and stored in gourds for later use. The leaves were then bruised and applied to treat ulcers, boils, rheumatism and skin diseases. They were particularly useful to mothers, who after childbirth might bathe in a cold stream and press leaves of koromiko between their legs to prevent haemorrhaging. In the care of a baby, chewed-up koromiko leaves served the same purpose as talcum powder, and were applied to chafes and rashes.

The sticky substance that exudes from the young leaf buds could also be used to adorn the face, and was mixed with the blue pollen of tree fuchsia to form a type of makeup. Jacky Marmon, the notorious Pākehā-Māori who joined Hongi Hika's war expeditions, used dry koromiko leaves as a substitute for tobacco when living in Māori communities, but it is difficult to imagine that this was very effective.

THE FAT OF THE MOA

Koromiko had some use in Māori cuisine as well. The leaves were used to line hāngī, and imparted a pleasant flavour to the cooked meat. There is even a tradition that koromiko wood was used when cooking the meat of the extinct moa. Moa flesh was said to be incredibly tough, and most other woods only warmed the flesh, but twigs of koromiko cooked it right through. The name of a creek near Oamaru, Te Awa-kokomuka, was said to be the site of extensive moa ovens, with abundant koromiko plants nearby used for cooking. Because of this use, the juice that exudes from the branches was known as *te ngako o te moa* — the fat of the moa.

A watercolour painting of koromiko by Martha King made in 1842. (Alexander Turnbull Library, A-005-032)

ETYMOLOGY

The genus is named *Veronica* after the legendary Saint Veronica, who wiped the brow of Jesus with her veil as he carried his cross through the streets of Jerusalem. The species name *stricta* comes from the Latin *strictus* and means 'stiff' and 'upright'. The old name *Hebe* is still used occasionally, and was named for the Greek goddess of youth. Koromiko as a plant name appears to have originated in Aotearoa, and other names for the plant include kōkoromiko, koromuka, kōkoromuka and korohiko.

BRANCHING OUT

For a long time, koromiko were thought to belong to a plant group known as the Hebes, as they have distinct woody stems, groups of tubular flowers, and opposite pairs of leaves at right angles. However, a range of evidence from morphology, chemistry and genetics points to them being unusual members of the larger *Veronica* group. This was something of a shock when it was first proposed, as the name 'hebe' had become firmly engrained, and it is still commonly used to describe the plants.

It is thought that *Veronica* made it's way to New Zealand from Australia. Once here, it underwent a massive adaptive radiation — a rapid evolutionary branching event, where a single plant group splits into multiple different species. This was probably due to the diverse range of habitats New Zealand provided, which allowed these opportunistic plants a wide variety of niches and ways of life.

There are thought to be over 100 species of *Veronica* in New Zealand, more than any other plant genera. They are found all over New Zealand, from down at the coast right up to 2800 metres above sea level — possibly the highest known altitude for a flowering plant in New Zealand. Because they occur in a vast diversity of habitats, they adopt a wide range of different shapes, from small scale-leaves in alpine environments to larger, fleshy leaves by the coast. But they are all united by a regular repeating pattern of opposite leaves. New Zealand *Veronica* remain incredibly popular garden plants, and the diversity of shapes, sizes and colours means there is one suited to almost every requirement. They have been extensively bred and cultivated, and are traded and planted around the world.

Koromiko and its relatives in the *Veronica* genus have adapted to almost every available habitat in New Zealand. (Robert Vennell)

Folio C Nᵒ 32.

KŌWHAI

Magic yellow flowers and
an 'Invincible' cure

The typical native flower is pale, white and inconspicuous. Little wonder, then, that the flashy yellow blooms of the kōwhai have become ingrained in the New Zealand consciousness. They hold unofficial status as our national flower and are a common icon of artwork and nationhood — depictions of kōwhai have been used on postage stamps and coins.

'Kōwhai' is the Māori word for 'yellow', and is used for a number of endemic species from the *Sophora* genus — all with strikingly bright, golden flowers. Many kōwhai are semi-deciduous, losing most of their leaves in the wintertime, another feature that sets these plants apart from most other natives. The eruption of sunny yellow flowers from the barren branches was a sign for Māori of the last frost of the winter and signalled it was time to plant kūmara or to seek out kina.

A legend from Te Arawa explains that the blossoming of the kōwhai tree was the handiwork of a powerful young tohunga. Sitting under the lifeless branches of a kōwhai tree, he asked his lover for her hand in marriage. At first she resisted his advances, claiming that she would only marry a man who could perform a wondrous deed. So the man mustered all of his magical power and applied it to the lifeless branches of the kōwhai tree. The tree erupted in a dazzling display of golden yellow flowers, and as a grand finale he made a crown of kōwhai flowers to adorn the young girl's dark hair. Ever since, the flowers have burst forth from the barren branches.

Kowhai (Sophora microphylla) by Fanny Osborne (Auckland War Memorial Museum, CCBY)

RONGOĀ MĀORI

Kōwhai was an important medicinal tree for many iwi, and was used to treat a dizzying array of diseases and ailments. The bark was perhaps the most important part, and care was taken to always harvest it from the sunny side of the tree. It was then soaked in water to produce a healing infusion — wai kōwhai — that could be used to treat anything from skin disease, scabies, dandruff and itchy skin to wounds, cuts, bruises, sprains, gonorrhoea and various aches and pains. Those with broken bones were made to bathe in wai kōwhai, as it was believed to help stitch the bones together. Travellers weary after a day of walking were known to soak tender feet in the potion, which helped toughen up the feet but also left a yellow stain.

One account recalls a man who had an unfortunate encounter with a kekeno — fur seal — where his face was bitten. A treatment of wai kōwhai was applied to his face, which is reported to have healed in a matter of days. A small amount of the brew could also be drunk as a purgative to relieve constipation; the effects were said to be rather dramatic.

MIRACULOUS PROPERTIES

One kōwhai cure has become part of New Zealand legend. In 1925 tragedy struck for George Nepia, the most famous member of the 'Invincibles' All Blacks team that had toured the United Kingdom and won every game. A bad tackle threatened to end George's career when an elbow struck his thigh and burst a blood vessel in his leg. Subsequent weeks of physiotherapy had no effect, and when the blood began to congeal doctors wanted to operate immediately to avoid blood poisoning. But George opted for a kōwhai cure instead. Heading out with a teammate's mother, they collected kōwhai bark and filled a bath with two large sacks of it. After bathing in the potion, George's leg responded remarkably fast, and he was back on the field the next week, leading Hawke's Bay to a 28–3 victory over Taranaki.

Kōwhai was believed to have remarkable healing properties and was used to treat skin problems, wounds, diseases and even broken bones. *(Robert Vennell)*

However, the apparently miraculous properties of kōwhai have sometimes been taken to the extreme. During the battle of Ōrākau, the prophet Penetiti readied a Tūhoe war party for battle. Praying over the men, he gave each of them a small vessel of water mixed with the bark of kōwhai and other plants. He convinced some of the troops that this was life-saving rongoā, and that if they drank it on the day of battle it would turn away bullets. Unfortunately, the kōwhai cure does not appear to have worked in this instance, and many in the battle lost their lives.

For Māori, the eruption of yellow blossoms from the barren kowhai branches marked the best time to plant kūmara. (Robert Vennell)

POISONOUS AND PURGATIVE

Despite its medicinal uses, however, it is strongly recommended that no part of kōwhai be consumed, as it contains the toxin cytisine.[1] There are reports of people becoming very ill simply from eating with cutlery made from kōwhai wood. There are even reports of people having violent headaches from eating kererū that have fed on kōwhai leaves, and the birds' flesh was said to have an unpleasant smell.

The poisonous power of kōwhai is demonstrated by the following cautionary tale of an old barrel-maker in Bluff who used to manufacture beer from the roots of cabbage trees. One day while he was out, a group of whaling men helped themselves to his beer, smashed his possessions and stole as much grog as they could carry back to the ship. When he found out, the old man was furious, and made a plan for a revenge. He waited until the whaling ship was arriving back in port, and then boiled up kōwhai leaves and flowers and added it to his home brew. Then he packed up his store and took all his valuables, leaving only a few drinking cups. Sure enough, several men entered his shop and helped themselves. When they failed to return to their ship on time their officers went out looking for them and finally found them in a state of violent purging; for 12 hours straight they had been erupting from both ends.

TUI OR PARSON BIRD.
PROSTHEMADERA NOVÆ ZEALANDIÆ
(ADULT AND YOUNG.)

A PLANT OF MANY USES

Kōwhai is most probably a fairly recent arrival on New Zealand shores, sometime in the past 2 million years. It comes from a group of plants that have hardy, buoyant seed pods that resist salt water, which have allowed them to colonise a range of islands across Europe, America, Asia and the South Pacific. This distribution fascinated Charles Darwin, who performed experiments with kōwhai seeds to test his theories about plant dispersal.

ETYMOLOGY

The name *Sophora* is thought to derive from the Arabic name 'sufayra' for a tree in the pea family. The specific names refer to various attributes of each species. For example, 'microphylla' refers to the little leaves of this species whereas 'tetraptera' refers to the four wings of the seed pod. The word 'kōwhai' derives from the ancient Polynesian word *koofai*, used for pod-bearing plants, and similar words, *ofai* and *kohai*, are used in the Pacific for plants in the pea family. Kōwhai is also used in te reo Māori as a word for yellow.

Many places where kōwhai occurs today are likely to be the result of deliberate plantings by Māori, and kōwhai is often common around old pā sites and sacred areas. Its occurrence in Wellington is possibly the result of an invasion by Waikato and Taranaki tribes who used the plant for a variety of spiritual and medicinal purposes.

The timber was an important resource for both Māori and Europeans, as it is tough, dense and durable. It has been used for tools, machinery, wood-splitting wedges, houses, cabinets, fencing and ship-building. The branches are also quite flexible, which made them useful as bird snares. The spectacular flowers were used to produce a pigment for yellow dye, the seed pods could be used to produce a paler yellow, and the twigs and bark made a dull yellow colour.

Today, kōwhai are planted widely in parks and gardens because they provide abundant nectar for birds such as the bellbird and kākā. Tūī in particular are very attracted to kōwhai, and will fly great distances in search of it, and aggressively defend it from other birds.

Adult and juvenile tui sitting on a branch of kōwhai (*Sophora microphylla*) by John Keulemans, 1888. *(Alexander Turnbull Library, PUBL-0012-10)*

MĀNUKA

*A scrubby fire-starter full of
medicine and honey*

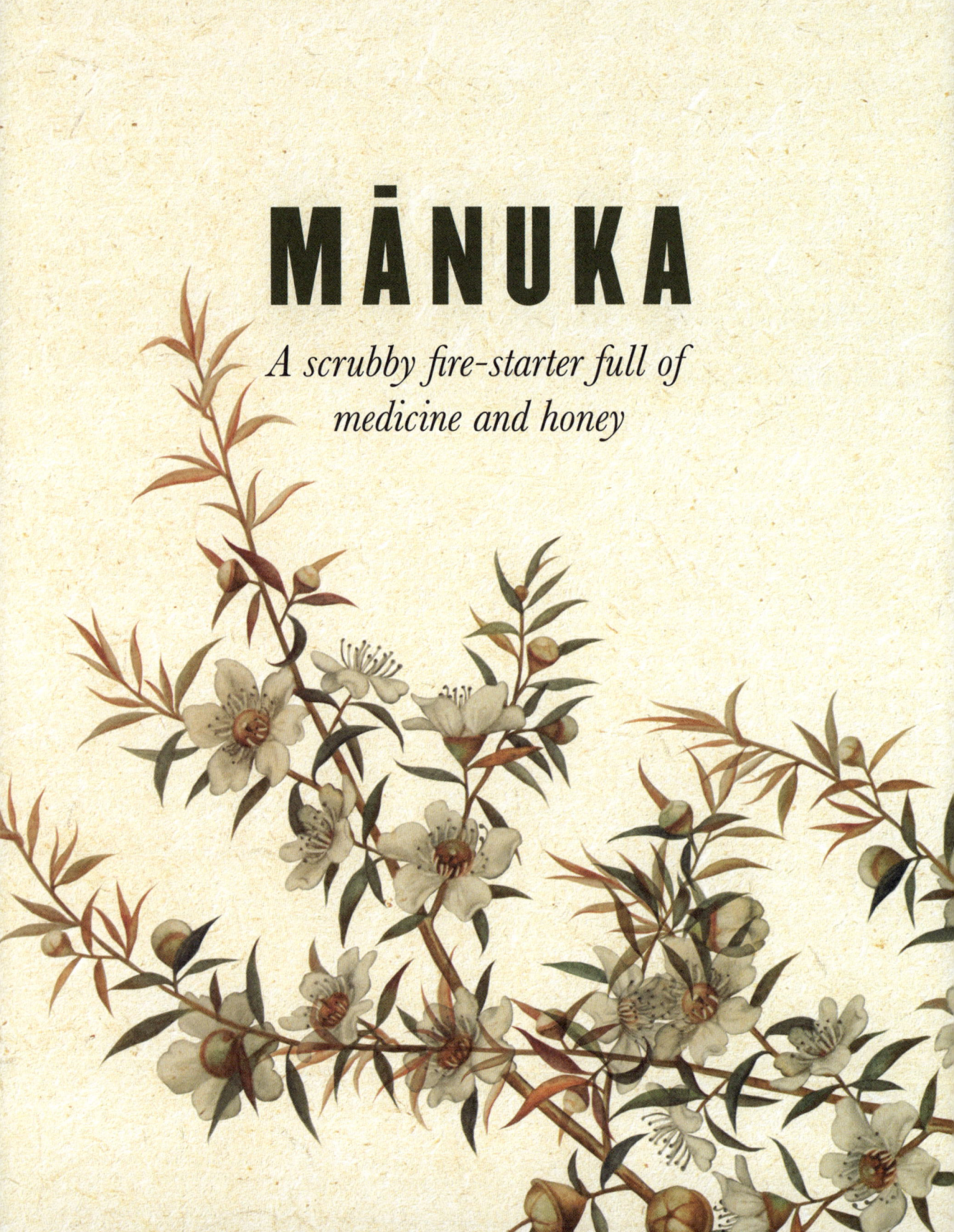

There is perhaps no more polarising plant in New Zealand than our native mānuka. Throughout its history it has gone through a turbulent relationship with the New Zealand people, at one moment treasured as a vital taonga, at another viciously maligned and removed from the landscape.

This rocky relationship stretches back to the very first people who set foot on New Zealand's shores. For the early Polynesian settlers in New Zealand, fire was a critical tool used for carving out a space to live and opening up land for crops and hunting. But prior to the arrival of humans, fire was incredibly rare in New Zealand forests, and very few native plants have evolved adaptations to cope with it. Mānuka, however, is different. It is actually a relatively recent migrant to our shores; its seeds probably blew over from Australia several million years ago. Like many of its Australian counterparts, mānuka has a fire ecology where its life cycle is adapted to the extreme conditions of forest fires. It contains volatile oils that help fires burn hotter and more intensely, and its woody capsules will often spring open when exposed to heat and smoke, scattering their seeds on the recently cleared ground.

When the ancestors of Māori brought an ignition source, plants like mānuka and kānuka took off, rapidly expanding their range. This set in motion a major feedback loop: these fire-loving plants made bigger and more intense fires, creating the perfect conditions for the growth of even more fire-loving plants. The New Zealand landscape would never be the same again. Mānuka benefited greatly from the new regime and is now one of the most common plants in New Zealand, occurring almost everywhere from the coast to the mountains, from wetlands to dry hills, and extending from Cape Reinga to Stewart Island/Rakiura.

MĀORI AND MĀNUKA

This omnipresent tree became a valuable material for Māori, who found a staggering amount of uses for the hard, straight-grained wood and aromatic leaves and seeds. It was a typical material for building small temporary whare, thatched with raupō or nīkau leaves. It could be used to make delicate articles such as combs or needles for piercing babies' ears. It could provide practical tools, paddles, canoes and digging sticks. Mānuka was dug into rivers to form eel weirs, or used as a rake to dredge for mussels. The wood had a particular value in producing articles of war, and was crafted into spears and taiaha, and used to make palisade walls in the fortifications of pā.

Not only that, mānuka was a powerful source of rongoā as well. Infusions made with the leaves were used to reduce fevers and treat stomach and urinary problems. Decoctions from the bark were used as a sedative, a mouthwash and to treat fever. The seeds could be chewed to treat diarrhoea, and were said to be just as effective as koromiko. Gum is occasionally secreted from the branches, and this was highly valued as well. It was taken to alleviate coughs and used as a moisturiser for burns.

THE TEA TREE

Mānuka initially got off to a good start with Europeans as well. On Captain Cook's voyages of discovery around New Zealand, his crew boiled the leaves of mānuka to make tea. European settlers also adopted the practice, and mānuka was seen as a viable alternative to Chinese tea. Whaling and sealing gangs, left for many months in remote areas of the country, often drank no other beverage. The common name 'tea tree' is still used for mānuka and kānuka. Mānuka tea is highly palatable, although it is easy to overdo it. Because it produces a very clear-looking liquid, it can be tempting to add more and more leaves to the pot in search of the traditional distinctive-looking 'tea' colour, but the result is an intensely bitter drop.

Cook also brewed a beer using mānuka and rimu leaves, and found it 'exceedingly palatable and esteemed by every one on board'.[2] He wrote the recipe down in his journals, and the brew was replicated by other sailors and explorers, who greatly relished it, some even comparing it to champagne. In recent times, a number of craft beer outlets have attempted to replicate the beer recipe, and mānuka-leaf teas and tonics have become an increasingly regular sight in tea shops, cafés and health stores.

DEATH TO THE SCRUB

As Europeans settled the country and began clearing vegetation for agriculture, mānuka posed a problem. Because of its vigorous growth and ability to colonise open pasture, mānuka was perceived as a noxious, scrubby weed. Farmers, especially, loathed the mānuka scrub, viewing it as a costly nuisance that prevented them from developing areas of hill country. When a black sooty mould fungus caused widespread devastation of mānuka, it was seen as a cause for celebration. Infected trees were used as a biological control agent, and were bought and sold to help spread the disease. However, mānuka managed to overcome the mould, in part because the scale insect that caused the problem, *Eriococcus orariensis*, was attacked by its own parasitic fungus. Nowadays, the unsightly black mould is often seen on mānuka trees, but rarely has much of an impact on the population.

TAXONOMY

There is only one species of mānuka (*Leptospermum scoparium*) currently recognised in New Zealand, but it is thought that it might separate into a number of regional varieties or species. Despite its superficial similarity, the other tea tree, kānuka, actually belongs to an entirely different genus, *Kunzea*, of which there are around 10 species in New Zealand. Both trees belong to the myrtle family, Myrtaceae, which includes natives such as pōhutukawa, rōhutu and ramarama, and exotics such as feijoa and eucalyptus.

Portrait of Captain James Cook by John Webber, c. 1780. (*Te Papa, 1960-0013-1*)

The plant was not without its uses to settlers, however. It provided a practical and readily available timber source, used to construct fence posts, and was valued as a source of firewood. The sawdust from the wood is still commonly used to impart flavour when smoking fish and meat.

REDEMPTION

Following further research and understanding, New Zealanders have almost completely changed their attitude to mānuka, and it is now looked on as a medical and environmental saviour. Because of its ability to cope with harsh environmental conditions, mānuka plays a critical role in forest regeneration. By colonising disturbed, open environments, it helps provide shade and shelter to more sensitive natives, eventually nurturing this next generation of plants as it grows into a future forest. Because of this ability, it has been widely adopted for use in all kinds of conservation projects, improving ecologically degraded areas and promoting natural regeneration.

Another reason for this reversal of attitudes has been the changing fortunes of mānuka honey. It may seem difficult to believe now, but there was a time when mānuka honey was dirt-cheap and barely anyone wanted to buy it. People generally preferred the lighter, milder taste of clover honey to the strong, astringent taste of mānuka. It was primarily used in cooking, and there were even trials underway to dilute and treat it to remove its colour and flavour.

Today, however, mānuka honey is worth a fortune — a tiny jar of high-quality mānuka honey can cost hundreds of dollars. The change came about with a realisation

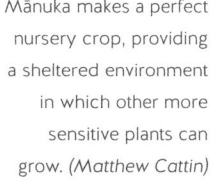

Mānuka makes a perfect nursery crop, providing a sheltered environment in which other more sensitive plants can grow. *(Matthew Cattin)*

S. Featon

MANUKA — Leptospermum scoparium

of the remarkable antibiotic properties of mānuka honey. Honey in general is antibiotic, the result of a chemical reaction that produces hydrogen peroxide and kills bacteria and fungi. Mānuka honey, however, has extra antibiotic agents that are incredibly effective, and which have been shown to inhibit strep throat and periodontal bacteria. But its most important use has been for healing wounds, and it has been employed by hospitals around the world to treat skin infections and burns that have not healed using other treatments.

Essential oils from the leaves are now also being recognised as having an important antibacterial, anti-fungal and antiviral effect as well, and mānuka oil currently forms the basis of a variety of medicinal and cosmetic products. The New Zealand parakeet kākāriki (*Cyanoramphus* spp.) has been observed chewing up the leaves and bark of mānuka and using the oil when preening itself to help remove lice, mites and other parasites.

Mānuka's leaves, bark, oils and honey have all been used medicinally. (*Matthew Cattin*)

Mānuka (*Leptospermum scoparium*) by Sarah Featon, c. 1885. (*Te Papa, 1992-0035-227713*)

KŪMARAHOU

A soapy shrub used for coughs and colds

For most of the year kūmarahou is a rather unremarkable-looking plant, often hiding in plain sight with its dull-green velvety leaves. In late spring, however, the plant bursts forth with clusters of creamy-yellow flowers, colouring the landscape in sunny blossoms. For Māori, this brief flush of yellow was an important event in the natural calendar, and the signal that it was time to plant kūmara. The flowering blossoms also synchronised with the main spawning time of the toheroa — a former seafood delicacy of New Zealand — and gave the signal that the harvest should stop to allow stocks to regenerate. The brief golden blossoms last around three weeks, and then disappear as quickly as they appeared, with kūmarahou retreating into obscurity once more.

BUSH SOAP

Kūmarahou is a hardy pioneer, able to cope with some of the most barren and inhospitable soils, leading some Europeans to give it the name 'poverty weed'. This is probably why it became so strongly associated with the gum fields of Auckland and Northland, where it grew prolifically on the fire-scarred landscape of former kauri forests. Its other common name — gumdigger's soap — relates to a curious property of its flowers that led to its adoption by kauri gumdiggers. These men were hardy pioneers as well, living a rough existence in barren scrublands, hoping to make their fortunes with a strike of kauri gum. Living off the land, they discovered that by rubbing the flower heads of kūmarahou with a little water they could create a soapy lather. Far away from civilisation, this soap must have provided a brief moment of luxury. It is surprisingly effective at removing mud and filth, and was particularly useful at removing kauri resin, which sticks to the hands and clothes. This soap is the result of compounds called saponins, which are sometimes found in modern detergents. More recently, kūmarahou flowers have been used by farmers and motorists who have broken down on the roadside as an emergency soap to clean greasy, oily hands.

TAXONOMY

Kūmarahou (*Pomaderris kumeraho*) is found in the north of the country, sprouting in regenerating bush and along roadside banks. There are a number of other *Pomaderris* species in New Zealand, including tauhinu (*P. amoena*) and the pale-flowered kūmarahou (*P. hamiltonii*). The majority of the diversity in the genus *Pomaderris* is found in Australia. *Pomaderris* species belong to the Buckthorn family, Rhamnaceae, which includes *Rhamnus* species and the jujube fruit (*Ziziphus jujuba*).

COUGH REMEDY

The plant is greatly admired by both Māori and Pākehā for its medicinal qualities, and kūmarahou played an important role in traditional rongoā. An infusion of kūmarahou leaves was used as a general tonic to treat a variety of ailments, but was considered especially good at healing chest complaints: coughs, colds, bronchitis, pulmonary tuberculosis, heartburn and asthma. Gumdiggers used to gargle the leaves in the throat to help treat coughs and colds, and the leaves were soaked in water and applied to wounds and skin irritations to speed the healing process. It is thought that the saponins that provide the soapy texture of the flowers are also responsible for its expectorant properties, helping to remove mucus from the throat.

Kūmarahou-leaf tea infusion remains a popular herbal remedy today. It produces a deep amber-coloured liquid, which becomes darker the longer the leaves are left to steep. The tea is a rather strong and bitter brew, and honey is often required to sweeten it. Using the young tender leaves is generally advised, as these are more palatable than older leaves. Kūmarahou has been readily adopted into the world of organic teas and herbal remedies, and is currently being incorporated into face cleansers and makeup removers.

Despite the growing interest in kūmarahou, the bulk of the medicinal research on native plants has been on the stars of the rongoā world — mānuka, kawakawa and horopito. The quiet, unassuming kūmarahou may have more fascinating secrets to reveal once scientists focus their gaze on it.

ETYMOLOGY

The name *Pomaderris* means 'membraneous lid', and refers to the covering of the seeds possessed by members of this genus. The species name *kumeraho* is a Latinisation of the Māori name kūmarahou. The Māori word is itself a composite of two words, 'kūmara' (sweet potato) and 'hou' (new), as the flowering of this plant was used to signal the time to plant kūmara. The name could also relate to a very ancient Māori legend, which says that kūmarahou is a kūmara from Raro, a mystical mother figure from the underworld. The yellow blooms inspired the English name 'golden tainui'. (The names 'gumdigger's soap' and 'poverty weed' are discussed on page 49.)

The striking, sunny blossoms of kūmarahou make it easy to spot along tracks and roadsides. *(Jacqui Geux)*

Kūmarahou leaves and flowers have been used for tonics, teas, soaps and beer. (Robert Vennell)

The bitter taste of kūmarahou tea has led to its use in alcoholic beverages as well. Prior to the arrival of Pākehā, Māori were among the few traditional societies in the world that did not have an established culture of alcohol use. The arrival of European liquor spurred a newfound interest in developing native brews, and Māori made the kūmarahou tonic into a type of home brew called paikaka. Pākehā settlers and missionaries were also on the lookout for innovative new alcohol recipes, and found that the bitter leaves made a good substitute for hops when brewing beer.

This dazzling floral display only lasts for a few weeks and then disappears. (*Jacqui Geux*)

PUKATEA

*The giant burial tree with
medicinal bark*

The trunk of a mighty pukatea tree, held in place by strong-walled buttress roots.
(Beren Allen)

Pukatea (*Laurelia novae-zelandiae*) by Walter Hood Fitch, 1853 (Biodiversity Heritage Library)

Pukatea rises from wet and swampy ground to tower among the giants of the forest. To achieve this amazing feat, it builds itself walled buttress roots, a trait more commonly seen in tropical rainforest trees. The tall, twining roots help prop it up in soggy soil and keep it from falling over. In very wet conditions, pukatea has the ability to grow pneumatophores — small snorkel-like structures covered in pores that allow the roots to breathe above water. Its leaves have a characteristic toothed, sharp edge, but they can be difficult to spot on older trees, which often become swamped in mosses, ferns and climbers.

NUMBING PAIN

The bark of pukatea contains a powerful painkiller, which played an important role in Māori medicine. Application of pukatea causes an instant numbing effect that soothes stabbing pain. It could be infused with water and rubbed on sores, ulcers, tubercular lesions and eczema. This infusion was also drunk as a tonic to combat sexually transmitted diseases and soothe sore mouths and ulcers. Chewing the bark has a similar effect.

Researchers have isolated the compound responsible for these properties, 'pukateine', an alkaloid with similar effect and potency to morphine but which does not appear to have the same negative side-effects. Experiments in the 1930s found that when patients were administered doses of pukateine, they reported feeling sleepy and free of pain and there were no instances of nausea or vomiting.

Modern research has highlighted a number of exciting areas where the antioxidant compound may be applied medicinally, from Parkinson's disease to hypertension to tuberculosis, but more research is needed to find out exactly how to get the most out of pukateine.

Reports of the 'morphine-like' effects of this compound have also inspired recreational drug enthusiasts to chase a pukateine high, smoking, drinking and consuming the bark in various ways. Few people have reported anything significant beyond a numb tongue and throat. Needless to say, self-experimentation is not advised.

There is an early report that pukateine causes convulsions in rabbits, and research that involved feeding the bark to sheep and rats found it to be poisonous in high doses.

WATERLOGGED WOOD

Māori also found a number of uses for pukatea timber, crafting it into bowls, clubs, paddles and the figureheads of canoes. However, the light wood can become waterlogged, making it undesirable as a material for building waka, where tōtara was preferred. In Māori proverbial wisdom, the different properties of these two woods were used as an analogy for youth and old age. It was said that while the tōtara floats, the pukatea lies in deep water. The proverb suggests that young people can move and travel with freedom, while the elderly are like the pukatea, weighed down by its waterlogged wood. Another whakataukī compares the wood of pukatea with that of kohekohe:

> *Te waka pukatea; te waka kohekohe.*
> The waka made of pukatea; the waka
> made of kohekohe.[3]

The timber of both of these trees suffers from soft wood that becomes waterlogged. The proverb is said to have a double meaning, and is used against cowards who are not made of the right material and will easily fail when put to the test.

Pākehā found uses for the wood as well, in boat-building and the making of ornamental furniture, and as wharf piles, as it is resistant to marine borer.

HOLLOW TREE OF DEATH

When pukatea trees age, they often leave cavernous hollows in the centre of the trunk. These hollows were sometimes used to hide the dead bodies of relatives to save them from being discovered during enemy raids. A large pukatea tree near Ōpōtiki called Te Ahoroa served as a burial tree for local people for a long time. The bodies of the dead

Sunshine highlights the attractive, distinctively jagged leaves of pukatea. *(Robert Vennell)*

were hoisted up the tree and pushed through a hole in the trunk some 15 metres off the ground. In the late 1800s the tree rotted through and burst, exposing hundreds of skeletons. Captain Gilbert Mair visited the tree and recalled the impressive sight:

> An enormous pukatea tree, some 22f. in girth, had fallen against the hillside, and, splitting open, disclosed cartloads of skeletons. I counted 397 perfect skulls, but an equal number, probably, had crumbled away, or been broken up by the trampling of cattle …[4]

Some individual pukatea trees were said to possess the power to help women conceive. A young woman wishing to have a baby would visit these special trees with a tohunga, who would recite karakia and request that the woman become pregnant.

HAKA PUPPET

A giant pukatea tree presided over one of the most significant battles of the New Zealand Wars. In the 1860s, the great military general Riwha Tītokowaru waged a fierce war against colonial forces to prevent the confiscation of land in south Taranaki. At the height of his power, he constructed Tauranga-Ika, a military fortress described as the most impressive pā structure built in New Zealand. Rising above the stockade at the front of the pā was a 5-metre-tall marionette fashioned out of a large pukatea tree and carved to resemble a great warrior. When the government forces laid siege to the pā, the defenders pulled on ropes to manipulate the arms of the puppet, making it look as if it was performing a haka. Presumably the giant puppet was meant as an intimidation tactic, or to draw some of the enemy's fire. Nevertheless, the battle was ultimately lost. Tītokowaru's people abandoned him en masse, and the pā was taken.

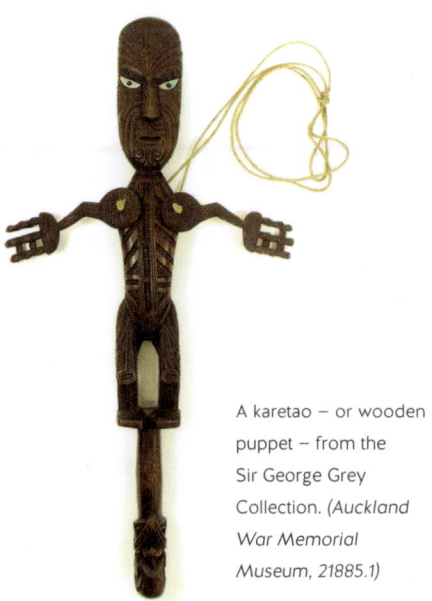

ETYMOLOGY

The name *Laurelia* refers to the similarity the plants have with the members of the Lauraceae family. The species name *novae-zelandiae* refers to its status as a New Zealand native. The origin of the name 'pukatea' is a difficult one to untangle. The names 'puka' and 'pukapuka' are given to a number of diverse plants, including large-leaved trees (*Meryta sinclairii*), epiphytes (*Griselinia lucida*), tree daisies (*Brachyglottis repanda*), vines (*Muehlenbeckia australis*), and a swamp myrtle (*Syzygium maire*). It is not entirely clear what, if any, characteristics these plants share. The words 'puka' and 'pukatea' are used across Polynesia for the lantern tree (*Hernandia nymphaeifolia*) and the grand devil's-claws (*Pisonia grandis*), neither of which seems to bear any strong resemblance to the New Zealand pukatea.

A karetao – or wooden puppet – from the Sir George Grey Collection. (Auckland War Memorial Museum, 21885.1)

BUSH KAI

Food from the forest

BRACKEN

The food that never fails

The dry, crunchy fronds of bracken may not be much to look at, but this has easily been one of the most important plants in all of Aotearoa. Digging beneath the soil reveals the real treasure, a starchy edible 'root' known as 'aruhe' — the food that never fails. It was often the primary source of carbohydrate in the traditional Māori diet, especially further south where Polynesian food crops would not grow. Māori men would sing as they dug for this root in straight lines with wooden digging sticks, chanting for a good harvest:

> *He aha te kai e ora ai te tangata?*
> *He pipi, he aruhe, ko te aka o tuwhenua*
> *Ko te kai e ora ai te tangata.*

> What is the food that will satisfy man?
> It is shellfish, and fern root,
> such are the foods that satisfy man.[5]

Once the roots had been harvested they underwent extensive processing to render them edible, and were beaten for a long time before being roasted. Even then the roots are incredibly fibrous, and the strands were typically spat out while eating. For babies who could not do this, nursing mothers would chew them up first. The roots could be eaten plain, or mixed with the nectar of harakeke and mashed into a type of porridge, or cooked along with meats such as fish and eel, shark, inanga, kiore and tītī.

Bracken root being pounded on rocks to soften it before eating. *(Alexander Turnbull Library, PUBL-0015-03)*

Pteridium esculentum by Sydney Parkinson, artist on Cook's HMS *Endeavour. (Te Papa, 1992-0035-2353/1917)*

PRESTIGE PLANT

The importance of bracken is underscored by the hundreds of names that have been recorded for it. There are names for the shoots, roots and fronds, names for different varieties and qualities of the plant, names for the best and worst areas to dig for it, names for the tools used to pound it, and names for the sites where it was stored. A man who was good at digging bracken root, it was said, had no difficulty in getting a wife. His prestige was considered higher even than an expert bird-catcher or fisherman, as he could supply a food source that was always abundant and never failed.

In Māori tradition, bracken (rārahu) was actually the hair of Haumia-tiketike, the god of wild food crops. When Ranginui and Papatūānuku were locked together in their embrace, Haumia grew as hair on Rangi's back. When Tāne Mahuta separated the two parents, Haumia fell from his father's side and buried himself in the bosom of Papatūānuku. However, Haumia's hair — the fronds of rārahu — stuck up above the ground, allowing him to be spotted. Tūmatauenga, the war god, captured these fronds and roasted the roots for food, providing the model for the harvest of aruhe for future generations.

TAXONOMY

Bracken (*Pteridium esculentum*) is a widely distributed species, occurring across New Zealand, and is also native to a number of countries in South-East Asia, Australia and the Pacific. It is a relative of one of the most abundant ferns in the world, the common bracken (*Pteridium aquilinum*), and belongs to the large bracken family of fern, Dennstaedtiaceae.

Bracken was so highly valued, that a good bracken digger had no trouble getting a wife. *(Jacqui Geux)*

BATTLE RATIONS

Bracken was often contrasted with the other staple food crop, the kūmara. Kūmara was a food of peace, and came under the dominion of Rongo-mā-Tāne, the god of cultivated foods. It needed extensive preparation and care, and therefore was only suitable for times of extended peace. Bracken, on the other hand, was a food of war. It was simple to grow, and vast amounts could be dried and kept in storehouses. This provided excellent food for warriors on the move, and was very nourishing, keeping them full and alert for longer. It was a common food for Māori during the New Zealand Wars, when they were shifted off their land and could not access other food sources. The warrior Te Kooti and his troops frequently ate bracken root to avoid starvation while hiding out in the bush. Kūpapa Māori, seeking out Te Kooti's forces for the British, also resorted to eating the roots when their rations of bacon and biscuits ran out, digging them up with their bayonets.

THE PĀKEHĀ VIEW

Many Europeans struggled to comprehend the Māori love of bracken. There was a general view that Nature had been very unkind to Māori and the thought of living off bracken — which grows in England as a pasture weed — seemed to be the height of desperation. The botanist Georg Forster, on board Cook's second voyage to New Zealand, wrote: 'That wretched article of New Zealand diet, the common fern-root

… consists of nothing but insipid sticks'.[6] Thomas Edgar, the master of HMS *Discovery* on Cook's third voyage, in 1777, remarked: 'They have no thing by way of Bread but the Fern Root which is intolerably bad and which they are obliged to beat a long time before they can eat it.'[7] And perhaps unkinder still, a Taranaki surveyor in 1841 suggested: 'A very good imitation might be made with a rotten stick, especially if slightly pounded, to which it bears a striking resemblance, both in taste and smell.'[8]

Later when Pākehā began to settle the country, bracken frequently stood in the way of breaking in the land. This scrubby weed continued to reclaim farmland, and the young fronds could poison stock, causing internal bleeding in sheep, horses and cattle. Bracken was frequently burned and removed by farmers; some even used farm pigs to root it up.

Yet Pākehā did not universally condemn the plant. Others described the taste of bracken root as pleasant and sweet, one writer even comparing it to ships' biscuits. Bishop George Selwyn became a huge a fan of bracken root, and carried it with him wherever he went, nibbling on it as a source of nourishment. Some of these divergent views may stem in part from the fact that bracken root is highly variable between plants, and in soft, fertile soil it grows much larger and is more palatable.

ETYMOLOGY

The name *Pteridium* means 'resembling *Pteris*', a fern known to the ancient Greeks that had feathery fronds (*pteron* means 'wing'). The species name *esculentum* means edible, and refers to the use of the plant as food. The plant was called 'bracken' by the British, due to the similarity between this plant and common bracken (*Pteridium aquilinum*), which is abundant in the moorlands of Britain. The whole plant was known to Māori by various names, such as rārahu, rarauhe and rahurahu. The edible part was commonly referred to by Europeans as 'fern root', although it is more accurate to call it a rhizome. The name 'aruhe' derives from the Pacific, where similar words are used for a number of different fern species, but in Aotearoa it refers specifically to the edible rhizome. The fronds were referred to as 'rauaruhe', the leaf of aruhe; the newly emerged shoots were known as 'mōkehu'; and once harvested the rhizome was known as 'roi'.

SPIRITUAL HEALING AND CUSTOMS

Due to its importance in Māori culture, bracken was seen as a medium for contacting the atua, and so was incorporated into a wide variety of fascinating customs. Bracken root was worn around the neck as a type of charm, used to ward away headaches and colds, and was carried on waka journeys as an antidote for seasickness. A person who had broken tapu might be thrown into a river tied to a piece of bracken root. In the water they would attempt to untie themselves from the root, and once removed it floated away, carrying off all of the evil. It was also used in trying to woo a lover: the root was blessed and then buried where a love interest might walk over it, such as at the entrance to a whare. Occasionally when digging bracken root, the voices of the fairy folk — the patupaiarehe — were heard, and digging had to stop immediately and an offering of bracken root be placed aside for them.

Bracken fronds (mōkehu) were said to give rise to mosquitoes and sandflies, which do sometimes shelter among the fronds. In some traditions these pesky insects are sent by Haumia to punish humankind for harvesting Haumia's children. Thankfully the bruised fronds of the bracken also offer a good remedy for itchy bites, providing instant relief.

The fronds were also a favourite habitat for freshwater crayfish (kōura), which Māori fishermen used to their advantage. Bundles of dried bracken fronds were placed on the bottom of lakes and rivers, where kōura swarmed into them to rest. Then the fronds were delicately collected, making sure not to let any of the crayfish get away.

TOOTH DECAY AND CONSTIPATION

There were consequences to a diet of bracken. Bracken roots contain silica spicules, which over time grind the teeth to dust. Skull remains of early Māori in the South Island show teeth that have been almost completely worn away and would have been a major source of infection and disease, not to mention toothache.

The other disadvantage of a bracken diet is that it has strong constipating effects. In fact this effect is so well known that the plant was used by Māori to treat diarrhoea and dysentery. Sometimes bracken root was drunk along with the juice of tutu or the oil of the tītoki berry, which are mild diuretics. In severe cases, flax-root juice might be applied to the affected rear end.

Both the shoots and roots are now known to be carcinogens. While Māori preparation would have largely eliminated the ill effects, bracken can no longer be recommended as a food.

CABBAGE TREE

An immortal tree with a sweet root

Māori wisdom teaches us that humans are not like cabbage trees — *E hara i te tī e wana ake.*[9] When humans die, they die completely, but the cabbage tree is nearly immortal. When cabbage tree branches are cut, others immediately grow to take its place, like the snake heads of Medusa. Even if the whole trunk is severed down to ground level, new buds will rise again, bursting forth out of the corky bark.

These extraordinary undying trees were highly revered in Māori culture, and some were even thought to be possessed by spirits. They were said to be able to move from place to place when no one was looking; they could embrace other trees, and then disappear suddenly when approached. It was believed that cabbage trees had been brought over on the voyaging waka from Hawaiki, and within New Zealand they were planted around places of settlement and used to mark paths, boundaries and cemeteries.

A VITAL FOOD PLANT

Before the arrival of Europeans, cabbage trees were one of the most essential sources of wild food. While Māori had an abundance of protein in New Zealand, finding enough starchy, carbohydrate-rich foods in the native flora would have been challenging. Cabbage trees therefore became an important element of the diet, especially in the south of the country, where it was too cold to grow tropical food crops.

One part that was eaten was the cluster of undeveloped leaves, which resembles a white, fleshy artichoke heart and was known as 'koata'. This wholesome vegetable was a reliable food source right across the country. Koata contains saponins, soapy

A lone cabbage tree somewhere in the Nelson region. *(Te Papa, 1935-0005-67)*

Cordyline australis by Walter Hood Fitch, 1867 *(Biodiversity Heritage Library)*

compounds that help to break down fat — a particularly useful attribute for the traditional Māori diet, which consisted of rich, fatty meals of eels, muttonbird (tītī) and kererū.

Koata was also said to provide a medical benefit: it was used to cleanse the blood, and was fed to nursing mothers and to children with colic. Koata is still eaten today; modern recipes suggest it be stewed into a sauce, or sliced thinly, garnished with French dressing and served alongside pork or lamb.

Beneath the soil, however, was an even more important food source, a long tap-root like an overgrown carrot, known as 'kāuru'. This root has very high concentrations of fructose, and was harvested from small trees just before flowering to make the most of the stored sugar. It was eaten in a similar way to sugar cane: it was chewed in the mouth to extract the sugar, then the strands of fibrous material were spat out. Digging out the root was hard work, and it was considered a good day if just five tī roots were collected.

In the South Island gigantic ovens for cooking roots (umu tī) were constructed, and some of the largest were up to 2 metres deep and 20 metres across. The roots themselves are not large, and so these massive ovens serve as a testament to the immense quantity of kāuru that must have been cooked and consumed in days gone by. The roots could take up to a whole day to cook, and men and women were forbidden to have sexual intercourse during this time, as it was said it might spoil the meal. If the kāuru was found to be undercooked, then it was a sure sign someone had broken this commandment.

When the cooking was finished, those roots that were not eaten could be stored for the winter, and were a good food for travellers and war parties on the move. The explorer Thomas Brunner ate it with relish on his travels — pounded and soaked in water until it had the consistency of honey, and then smeared on cooked bracken root. The European settler James Hay fondly remembered chewing it as a boy, and used it to sweeten his tea.

CHAINED LIGHTNING

Cabbage-tree roots were the basis of some of the first native plant spirits brewed in New Zealand. In the 1850s, Owen McShane, a cooper who worked at whaling stations across Southland, began experimenting with brewing a liquor from the roots and selling it illicitly. The drink he produced has been described as a rum, a whisky or a brandy, and given the names Cooper's Schnapps and McShane's Chained Lightning. The taste has been described as hot and unpleasant, and disagreeable to the palate. Despite these disappointing reviews, the rum was said to be a favourite at Bluff Hotel in Bluff,

TAXONOMY

There are five species of native cabbage tree in New Zealand. The most familiar is tī kōuka (*Cordyline australis*), which is found from coastal to montane forest right across New Zealand. The group also includes the forest cabbage tree (*C. banksii*), the mountain cabbage tree (*C. indivisa*), the dwarf cabbage tree (*C. pumilio*) and the Three Kings cabbage tree (*C. obtecta*). There is also a cabbage tree that was introduced by the early Polynesians and known as tī pore (*C. fruticosa*), which was thought to be extinct in the wild but was recently rediscovered in Northland. Cabbage trees belong to the asparagus family, Asparagaceae, which includes *Agave* and *Yucca*.

Southland, where large barrels were placed on the table and the whalers and sailors were allowed to fill their cups as many times as they liked.

Owen McShane and other illegal distillers became so popular that the government initiated a crackdown on the trade. In 1860 one Waikouaiti trader who made tī kōuka whisky to sell to local Māori was forced to flee into the bush to escape the law, carrying his still on his back. European missionaries also experimented with making beer from the roots, and the result was said to be very pleasant. More recently, a number of PhD theses have focused on the commercial possibility of developing cabbage-tree liquor, and a range of spirits with similarities to rum and tequila has been produced.

IDEAL FOR WEAVING

In addition to cabbage tree's value as an article of food and liquor, its leaves are one of the finest weaving materials in New Zealand. The stiff, robust leaves are a useful alternative to flax, and because they do not shrink in water, they were used to make fishing nets and anchoring ropes to tie up waka.

Another species — tōī, or the mountain cabbage tree — has much broader leaves, and this was said to make the very best rain capes. To provide extra protection, an underlayer of overlapping leaves was applied, and the end result was surprisingly waterproof. It was once popular among Pākehā to wear hats of woven cabbage leaves, and racing toboggans (pānukunuku) made from cabbage tree leaves became a popular pastime for children.

Woven cabbage-tree leaves were also used in what must rank as some of New Zealand's greatest feats of endurance and survival. Ngāi Tahu bushmen would hike routes through the Southern Alps on foot, with little more than cabbage-tree leaves to

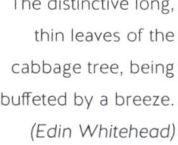

The distinctive long, thin leaves of the cabbage tree, being buffeted by a breeze. (Edin Whitehead)

protect them from the elements. They would weave cabbage-tree leaves into pāraerae (sandals) and wear cabbage-tree rain capes on their back. The terrain was so rough that these pāraerae sandals would typically wear out after a few days, and up to 20 pairs were carried at a time, so they could be replaced when needed.

A number of different types of pāraerae were made, and moss and other soft plants could be added to provide cushioning. Tall knee-sandals were made for wading through grassy country, while other sandals were woven for protection from spiky plants or for movement around the coast. Small mats of cabbage-tree or flax leaves were also used to aid in wading through heavy snow.

A rain cape, or kahu toi, made from cabbage tree leaves. *(Auckland War Memorial Museum, //5)*

GARDEN VARIETIES

Since the early days of European settlement, cabbage trees have been viewed as exotic and tropical-looking. They are widely admired overseas, and are commonly seen growing in gardens in America and the United Kingdom. In Britain cabbage tree is known as the Torbay or Torquay palm and is selected for its exotic, tropical look and its ability to withstand the cold climate.

This hardy nature also makes it useful for planting situations back in Aotearoa, and it is commonly used in restoration planting as a food source for birds and a habitat for a wide range of wildlife. Often found clinging to its branches are epiphytic plants: ferns, astelias, orchids, mosses, lichens, liverworts and fungi. Many insects are associated with the leaves, bark and soil, the most familiar being the cabbage tree moth (*Epiphryne* spp.). This moth is responsible for the holes that often dot the leaves, and its stripy brown patterning perfectly conceals it among the dead leaves. In the summer months, cabbage trees eject long stalks of delicate white flowers, which swell into hundreds of little pearls of white fruit. Tūī and kererū are fond of these fruits, and Māori would often use cabbage tree groves as sites to attract and snare birds.

ETYMOLOGY

The generic name *Cordyline* comes from the Greek word *kordyle* (club), and refers to the shape of the fleshy root. The species name *australis* is a Latin word for 'southern', and refers to the southern hemisphere. Tī is the generic Māori name for cabbage trees. The Polynesians brought the word 'tī', used for the Pacific cabbage tree, tī pore. While it is often claimed that the tree was called the 'cabbage tree' because Captain Cook's crew thought it tasted similar to cabbage, this actually appears to be a case of mistaken identity, and the plant the crew were referring to was the nīkau. However, the name 'cabbage palm' was widely used at the time for any plant that resembled a palm, and eventually the name 'cabbage tree' became so popular that it stuck.

The wings of the cabbage tree moth (*Epiphryne verriculata*) perfectly match the pattern on dead cabbage tree leaves. (*Landcare Research, CCBY*)

Cabbage trees are often covered with epiphytic plants and insects, and are an important source of food for birds. (*Right: Josie Galbraith. Far right: Robert Vennell*).

KARAKA

*A sacred Moriori plant
with the power to paralyse*

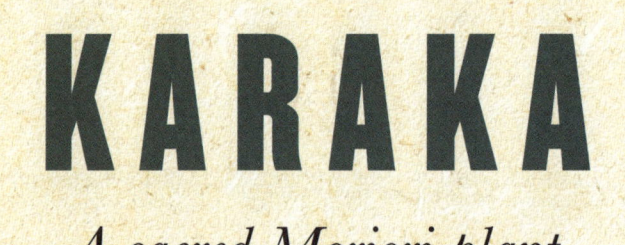

The karaka tree is an iconic feature of coastal New Zealand, where its glossy green leaves shine in the sunlight, and its seedlings carpet the forest floor. The most striking feature of karaka is its orange fruit, which in summertime covers the tree with large bunches of swollen orange berries. The image is so vivid that the the word 'karaka' is used to mean 'orange' in te reo Māori. The flesh of the berry — or drupe — is edible, and tastes somewhat like a cross between an apricot and a date. It does have a rather sickly-sweet taste that is not to everyone's liking.

TAXONOMY

Karaka (*Corynocarpus laevigatus*) is the only member of the tropical Corynocarpaceae family in New Zealand. The other species are found spread across New Guinea, New Caledonia, New South Wales and Vanuatu. Karaka's natural distribution is the coastal areas of the northern North Island, but it has been deliberately spread throughout lowland forest and to the offshore Kermadec and Chatham Islands.

However, extreme care must be taken when eating karaka, as the kernel inside the berry carries a toxic alkaloid, karakin, which is highly poisonous to humans. People who consume the raw kernels are known to convulse in violent spasms that leave them physically distorted and permanently paralysed.

The traditional Māori treatment for karaka poisoning was no picnic either. Because the poison relaxes the joints so they can bend the wrong way, it was important to keep a victim straight, otherwise their limbs could bend out of place or they might dislocate their neck. Victims might be gagged with flax, rolled up in mats and buried up to their neck. Another treatment involved relays of men trampling the limbs of the victim to straighten them out and prevent muscles from atrophying. It was essential that the toxin was removed from the system as soon as possible, and so in some cases water was forced down the victim's throat or they were hung upside down over a fire or held underwater until near drowned, in the hope that they would sweat out the poison or vomit it up.

Despite the considerable danger, the kernel was an important and revered food source for Māori prior to the arrival of Europeans. Through an extensive process of washing, steaming and heat treatment, Māori developed a way of removing the toxin, leaving a nourishing carbohydrate-rich meal. In fact, William Colenso, writing in the 19th century, believed the plant was of 'inestimable value' as a food item to Māori, third in importance after kūmara and bracken root. Once prepared, the kernels kept remarkably well and could be stored for use over winter or ground up into a type of flour for bread.

Karaka (*Corynocarpus laevigatus*) by Sarah Featon, c. 1885. (*Te Papa, 1992-0035-2277/63*)

SPREAD FAR AND WIDE

When the ancestors of Māori first arrived in New Zealand, karaka was confined to coastal areas in the north of the country. Today, however, karaka is found far inland, as far south as Banks Peninsula, and out on the offshore islands of Raoul, Three Kings, Kermadec and the Chathams. In the same way that the early Polynesian explorers brought their valuable 'canoe plants' across the Pacific, Māori took native karaka berries with them as they travelled around Aotearoa and the outer islands.

Karaka trees are particularly common in former pā, marae and settlement sites, and it is common to see them planted in straight lines, circles or groves. Historical records of vast karaka groves in Palmerston North and Wellington are thought to represent massive orchards, cultivated and cared for by Māori. Ownership of one of these large 'pā karaka' would have conferred a huge amount of mana and prestige.

It is even thought that in some places Māori were moving towards complete domestication of the karaka tree. The trees were often carefully tended to, being regularly cleaned of moss and mould. The sex ratios of the karaka plantations may have been managed, and it is thought that Māori gardeners actively selected for trees with larger berries, as berries found around former occupied sites are bigger than wild berries.

A CHATHAMS STAPLE

Nowhere was karaka more significant than in the Chatham Islands, where it was the most sacred taonga of Moriori, who know it by the name of 'kopi'. The ancestors of Moriori were Māori travellers from New Zealand, who around 1500 AD made the journey east to colonise the Chatham Islands — Rēkohu. Genetic and pollen data have shown that the karaka forests on the Chatham Islands are not native to the islands, and so seeds must have been taken there by these early travellers.

Without the karaka tree, it is highly likely that the settlement of the islands would have failed. The few hours of sunshine, thundering winds and generally cold climate meant that none of the tropical crops brought from Polynesia could survive. Instead, karaka came to form the main component of carbohydrates in the Moriori diet. As karaka is highly sensitive to winds, Moriori cultivated the seeds in the islands' interiors,

The delicate white flowers of karaka gradually swell into large, fleshy orange drupes. (Robert Vennell)

behind a screen of native vegetation that could serve as windbreaks. They spread the seeds far and wide, helped along by the native Chatham pigeon (*Hemiphaga chathamensis*), so that by the time of European arrival karaka was the dominant forest plant on the island and there was almost a compete monocrop of karaka in the forest interior. Moriori are even thought to have selectively bred the plant for bigger fruit, as the karaka berries on the Chathams are much larger than those found on mainland New Zealand.

Over time, as memory of New Zealand faded, a distinct Moriori culture and worldview emerged, in which karaka played a central role. Stories arose of how karaka was brought to Rēkohu from the ancestral homeland of Hawaiki, on the first voyaging waka. Ensuring the successful fruiting of the crop was vital, and during the summer months a special ceremony was held. Everyone would stand holding karaka branches bound with karaka kernels. They were led in a karakia invoking the gods' support for a good harvest, and raised the branches to the star Puanga, whose appearance marked the fruiting season.

Across the Chathams today, legacies of the Moriori relationship with karaka live on in fascinating dendroglyphs carved into living karaka trees, known as rākau momori, memorial trees. The carvings portray stylised images of humans, trees, fish, birds, seals,

Karaka, or kopi, was the main source of carbohydrates in the Moriori diet. (*Jacqui Geux*)

seaweed and crayfish. It is thought the human figures represented karapuna (ancestors) or atua, and served as memorials for loved ones who had passed away. While the style of the artwork shows Polynesian influences, the method of carving artwork on a living tree is unique in Polynesia and rare across the world.

A NATIVE WEED

However, karaka certainly is not welcome everywhere it has been introduced. Outside of its natural range, it has often become a weed, aggressively colonising an area and shading out the competition. As part of a re-forestation programme in Hawaii in the 1920s, thousands of karaka seeds were dropped from airplanes over the hinterland region of Kauai. They spread rapidly and now form a dense monoculture, shading out native vegetation and endangering native species such as as heau (*Exocarpos luteolus*), one of Hawaii's rarest species.

Even within New Zealand karaka has been perceived as a weed, such as in the lower North Island, where it competes with locally native species. It makes a rather effective weed because of its fast growth and shade-tolerant seedlings, and it is common to see a garden of karaka seedlings growing up under the shade of a parent tree.

COMMERCIAL POTENTIAL

Karaka leaves were used in medicine, and were applied to wounds and burns, being first warmed on the fire and then laid over the problem area. Only the upper glossy surface of the leaf was used, as the underside was said to have a harmful effect.

The wood is light, brittle and susceptible to rot, which meant it was not used as building material and its primary use was for firewood. In modern times the tree has become a popular garden and street plant. There are occasional calls for the plant's removal from public areas, however, because dogs have been known to be fatally poisoned after eating the fruit. Kiwi, too, have suffered from karaka poisoning. A little spotted kiwi named Flip Flop was found paralysed and convulsing on Kapiti Island, a nature reserve, and was rushed to the mainland for treatment. He was found to have a karaka berry stuck in his gizzard, and over many months was slowly nursed back to health. Sadly, Flip Flop never fully recovered, and eventually the decision was made to euthanise him.

A recent report looked at the commercial potential of karaka seed crops. As they are gluten-free, have a healthy nutritional profile and can be easily stored for a long time, they could be suitable for making a range of products, such as roast nuts, crumbs, flours, purées and beers. The main constraint would be the need to detoxify the kernels, but this is already done for other nuts, such as cashews. The berries have a high sugar content, and so have potential applications in juices, jams and liqueurs.

Fruiting karaka branch, watercolour by Martha King, 1842. (*Alexander Turnbull Library, A-005-019*)

Karaka.

Folio C. Nº 19.

KIEKIE

The sweetest fruit in the forest

In Māori tradition, kiekie and harakeke are regarded as long-lost brothers. While harakeke left home to live with Wainui, the mother of waters, kiekie stayed with Tāne, the lord of the forest, piggy-backing on his shoulders wherever he went. Today, this is where kiekie is most commonly found, suspended among the canopy of our mightiest trees. This lends a tropical look to the New Zealand forest, with tall trees covered in this scrambling climber. It has attractive green- and yellow-specked leaves, with white fleshy flower bracts and large, pineapple-like fruit. Where there are no suitable trees to climb, kiekie becomes an impassable mass of tangled roots, the bane of bushmen and trampers throughout the country.

Because both the large, fleshy flower bracts (tāwhara) and the fruit (ureure) can be eaten, kiekie was a prized food source for Māori, providing harvests twice a year. The bounty of food that kiekie yielded became a metaphor for living in an ideal environment overflowing with natural resources, as expressed in the whakataukī:

He wha tawhara ki wa, he kiko tamure ki tai.
The edible flower bracts of the kiekie of the land, and the flesh of the schnapper of the sea.[10]

TAXONOMY

Kiekie (*Freycinetia banksii*) is found from coastal to montane forest throughout lowland North Island forests and parts of the South Island. It is the only representative of the tropical screw pine family Pandanaceae in New Zealand, which includes the culturally significant *Pandanus* plants of the Pacific.

Kiekie (*Freycinetia banksii*) by Sarah Featon, c. 1885. *(Te Papa, 1992-0035-2277/10)*

Here kiekie can be seen winding its way up the trunk of a towering rimu tree. *(Beren Allen)*

This is also reflected in the naming of places around the country; for instance Tāwharanui on Auckland's east coast means 'the abundant flowers of the kiekie vine', while Maungakiekie, One Tree Hill, translates as 'mountain of kiekie'.

The kiekie harvest was strictly managed, and those with ancestral claim to a large crop of kiekie could place a rāhui over them, and put up a ceremonial pou so everyone would know it was off-limits. Kiekie were also a favourite food of the Polynesian rat (kiore), and so the flowers and fruit were protected by wrapping up the leaves and tying them together. This act of tying the leaves also helped identify them, and everyone knew whose kiekie belonged to who and only harvested from their own branch. When the plant was ready to eat, the rāhui was lifted and the harvest could begin. The flower petals were eaten raw, or made into a juice or jelly that is said to taste like strawberry jam. They have been described as one of our finest native foods, with the taste of a ripe apple, pear or pineapple, and the aroma of vanilla.

There are some tantalising reports that the flowers can cause intoxicating effects. In her autobiography, nurse and community leader Florence Harsant recalls speaking with a Māori woman who was acting strangely and claimed to be drunk from eating unripe tāwhara flowers. The overripe flowers seem more likely to produce this effect, as they can ferment over time and have a strong alcoholic smell. The politician Thomas Kelly observed Māori collecting large quantities of an unnamed flower in Taranaki and manufacturing a fermented liquor out of them, which surely must refer to the tāwhara.

The ureure fruit is rather unusual, with the rough skin needing to be peeled off to reveal the sweet pink pulp beneath. Views on the fruit vary. It has been described as medicated, earthy, unpalatable and bitter,[11] with one unenthusiastic reviewer suggesting that 'it might be eaten by Russian sailors on short allowance of rations'.[12] Others regarded it as something of a sweet delicacy, and some settlers even considered the possibility of cultivating it for sale on the British market. Unfortunately, possums and ship rats also developed a taste for kiekie, and the ripe flowers and fruit can be difficult to find outside of pest-controlled sanctuaries.

The fleshy white flower bracts were considered something of a delicacy, but are now difficult to find before rats and possums get to them. *(Robert Vennell)*

Without trees to climb, kiekie becomes a tangled mass that is *difficult to pass through.*
(Robert Vennell)

USING THE LEAVES

As well as being an important food source, kiekie was an incredibly useful weaving material, and a case could be made that it was the most valued weaving plant after harakeke. The sword-like leaves were generally stripped, boiled in water and dried in the sun, leaving them bleached white and easier to work. The leaves could then be dyed and woven to make clothing, kites, mats, belts, baskets, hats and tukutuku. For iwi living in heavily forested areas, such as Tūhoe, kiekie was a primary weaving material and was preferable to harakeke for some uses, as it is more durable in water. Kiekie leaves were sometimes woven into little pouches for carrying mokoroa grubs, which were used as bait when hunting eels.

In former times, saddleback would frequently make their nests at the base of kiekie leaves, and so the practice of weaving cloaks and rain capes out of kiekie was referred to as 'making a saddleback nest'. Kiekie remains an incredibly valuable taonga species for

ETYMOLOGY

Freycinetia is named after the 19th-century French explorer Louis de Freycinet, who led a number of expeditions around the Pacific. The genus was first described on one of these voyages. The species name *banskii* honours Sir Joseph Banks, the botanist on board the *Endeavour* and later the director of Kew Gardens in England. Early settlers described the plant as 'the New Zealand pineapple' on account of its tropical-looking fruit. The Māori name 'kiekie' is also given to a number of species in the *Freycinetia* genus throughout Polynesia, sometimes pronounced 'ie ie'. These plants were also used for weaving and made into fish traps. It has been suggested that the name of the delicious edible flower bracts, tāwhara, has a relationship with the ancient Polynesian word 'taa', used for 'banana'. The name of the fruit, ureure, appears to be related to the Māori name for penis (ure), and was presumably given this name for its phallic appearance.

many iwi, who keep alive the traditional art of weaving with kiekie. The aerial roots that sprout from the main growing vine provided another useful construction material, and were used to lash canoes together, make sails and create traps for fish, eels and lamprey.

A whariki (plaited mat) made from kiekie and pīngao leaves. (Auckland War Memorial Museum, 1990.111, 53494)

HĪNAU

A fertility tree used to make fruit cakes

The graceful hīnau tree, with its slender clusters of delicate white flowers, has become an enduring symbol of love and fertility. Māori believed that some hīnau trees contained the power to grant life and determine the sex of a child. In one tradition, the umbilical cord of a newborn baby was bound to a hīnau tree with vines, or hung from its branches, infusing it with the power of fertility. A woman who could not give birth naturally would approach one of these special hīnau trees with a tohunga, who would perform the necessary karakia. Closing her eyes, she would go to embrace the tree: if she grabbed hold of the side producing new green leaves, then she would conceive a child, but if not, she was doomed to remain barren.

HĪNAU CAKES

In autumn, the pretty white flowers swell into purplish-green drupes, like large olives. The berries were occasionally eaten raw in emergencies, and are said to taste like bitter custard powder. With proper preparation, however, these berries formed the basis of one of the most important dishes in traditional Māori cuisine — komeke hīnau, or hīnau cake. The missionary and botanist William Colenso ranked it as the third most important native plant food in traditional Māori society, and hīnau cakes were especially vital for iwi that lived in the mountainous interior without suitable land for crops.

In order to prepare these cakes, the ground was cleared beneath a particularly fruitful tree, and men would climb the branches and beat them. People gathered below would collect the fruit in large baskets of woven supplejack. The berries were then soaked and dried in the sun, and the flesh rubbed off between hands. This fruit pulp was mixed with water and then kneaded into a dark paste, after which it was wrapped in leaves such as rangiora, and steamed in an umu. A small cake might be ready to eat in a few hours, but larger cakes could weigh up to 15 kilograms and take up to two days to cook properly.

The resulting meal was like a dense fruit pudding, and could be served on kawakawa leaves. It could be eaten fresh or kept for several years using an unusual technique. To store it, the cake was placed in a supplejack basket and submerged in water. Over time, the outside of the cake would develop a dark mould. When it was time for a cake to be eaten, the cake was retrieved and the mould was scraped away.

Māori could take these cakes on adventures across the country, or use them as rations for war parties on the move. The komeke hīnau was seen as such a luxury in former times that it was celebrated in proverbs, where it was said, '*Kia whakaoho koe i taku moe, ko te whatu turei a Rua*',[13] meaning 'If you wake me from my sleep, let it be for hīnau cakes.' It has been suggested that this phrase may also be a cheeky sexual innuendo,

TAXONOMY

Hīnau (*Elaeocarpus dentatus*) is common in coastal and lowland forest in the North Island, and reaches its southern limit around Christchurch. Its close relative pōkākā (*E. hookerianus*) is similar-looking as an adult, but starts life as a divaricating shrub. Both belong to the Eleaocarpaceae, a mostly tropical family that also includes the native New Zealand wineberry (*Aristotelia serrata*).

Hinau (*Elaeocarpus dentatus*) by Fanny Osborne. (*Auckland War Memorial Museum, CCBY*)

The flowering hīnau tree had a strong association with women and fertility. *(Jacqui Geux)*

and that the speaker wishes only to be woken for the 'fruit of women'. Due to the strong connection hīnau has with women and fertility, this double entendre may have been much clearer to a traditional audience.

The rotten, musty old cake did not generally endear itself to Pākehā, however. George French Angas, the travelling painter of the 1840s, was positively repulsed by hīnau cake:

> The children soon afterwards began to cram themselves with hinau cakes — a black, filthy mass, consisting of the fruit of the hinau tree compressed together, and kept till quite rotten and musty, which they eat with avidity … one can hardly imagine anything more disgusting.[14]

But a few authors gave a more favourable view, describing the taste as similar to that of brown bread. William Colenso rather enjoyed it, and called it a 'cut-and-come-again' type of pudding.

ETYMOLOGY

The generic name *Elaeocarpus* means 'olive fruit', a reference to the olive-like drupes of this genus. The specific name *dentatus* means 'toothed', and is a reference to the serrated leaves. The common English name 'New Zealand olive' also recognises its olive-like fruit, and in the past hīnau was known as the 'lily-of-the-valley tree' due to the similarity of its delicate white flowers to those of *Convallaria majalis*. 'Hīnau' as a plant name appears to have originated in Aotearoa. In some places the word 'hangehange' is used to describe this plant, which is also the name for *Geniostoma* species in New Zealand and the Pacific.

MEDICINE, DYE AND TIMBER

Hīnau cakes alone could cement hīnau as one of our more important native plants, and yet the tree had a range of other uses. The leftovers from making komeke hīnau were used medicinally. They were repurposed into a type of gruel, which was fed to people recovering from illness as a nourishing meal that is easy on the stomach. For those suffering from diarrhoea, a hīnau cake was prepared using one part hīnau berries mixed with two parts pounded huhu beetle. The bark had medicinal value as well, and was soaked in hot water and used to cure the most severe cases of skin disease.

The timber was also considered valuable. Pākehā used the wood of hīnau to form bridges, furniture, cabinets, flooring, houses and boats. Māori crafted hīnau into small tools, canoe bailers, spears, wedges and palisades. The bark was useful in making carrying bags and water vessels, and younger hīnau trees were tied in a knot and allowed to grow, forming the perfect material for walking sticks.

Because the timber has such a high tannin content, it is perhaps the best native plant for fixing dye and making it permanent. The bark is stripped and beaten, and then mixed with a special black mud called 'paru', which is full of iron salts. The tannins react with the salts, creating a vivid and permanent black dye, which was used for dying clothing and wall panels, colouring the prow and stern of waka, and as the black pigment in tā moko. It has even on occasion been used as ink for writing letters.

A tree of many uses, hīnau not only provided food but was also a source of timber, medicine and dyes.
(Jacqui Geux)

POROPORO

A contraceptive shrub with
a fruit to die for

Poroporo is a relative of the tomato, and its bright orange fruit taste somewhat like a sweet acidic tomato. However, as with a number of plants in the Solanaceae family, the green unripe berries are poisonous. They are only safe to eat once fully ripe, and even then it is best to wait until they are so ripe the fruit is bursting and ready to fall off the plant. Poroporo fruit was a favourite of Māori children, and it was planted around villages and plantations. The leaves were used to line hāngī as a flavouring for food, and there is a tradition that it was used to impart flavour to the flesh of moa. Its use can no longer be recommended, however, as the leaves also carry poisonous alkaloids.

Pākehā settlers were quite enamoured of the fruit, and it was common to stew them into pies and jams. In the early days of settlement, the Taranaki Farmers' Club would host jovial meetings where they burst into song about the wonders of New Plymouth. Their most famous anthem included the lines:

> And as for fruit, the place is full
> Of that delicious bull-a-bull [poroporo].[15]

However, the strange acidic fruit was not everyone's cup of tea, with one settler describing the taste of the ripe fruit as somewhere between apple peel and a bad strawberry.[16]

A TROUBLESOME PLANT

In some traditional stories, poroporo was partly responsible for the Polynesian migration to New Zealand. In one version of the tale, the captain of the Te Arawa waka, Tamatekapua, raided the garden of the chief Uenuku, stealing the fruit from his poroporo trees. War broke out as a result, and Tamatekapua decided to leave his homeland and journey to Aotearoa. Stealing poroporo fruit seems like rather an unusual thing to do, as poroporo fruits prolifically and often springs up along roadsides and tracks like a weed. Other stories, however, say it was the kuru — the breadfruit — which was stolen, which makes a lot more sense. When Polynesians arrived, the kuru never grew in New Zealand, and so, as generations went by, the people telling these stories would never have seen a kuru themselves. Perhaps the storytellers, beset by questions from curious children, swapped it for a much more familiar fruit from the native bush.

Poroporo has caused a lot of trouble within New Zealand as well. A tohunga from Rotorua named Murirangaranga was once asked to conduct a birth ceremony for the rangatira's son Tūtānekai. After completing the ceremony, the tohunga was considered tapu, and was so sacred that he was not allowed to feed himself. However, he was spotted eating poroporo

TAXONOMY

Poroporo can refer to both *Solanum aviculare* and *Solanum laciniatum*. *Solanum aviculare* was once common 40 years ago but is now in serious decline, and scientists are not sure of the cause. There are a number of other *Solanum* species in New Zealand, including the black nightshades S. *americanum* and S. *opacum*, and the introduced S. *nigrum*. They belong to the nightshade family Solanaceae, which includes potato, tomato and deadly nightshade.

berries. This was a deadly insult, as bad as if he had cursed Tūtānekai himself. Filled with rage, the rangatira ordered Murirangaranga drowned in Lake Rotorua, and had his arm bone made into a flute. Some say it is this flute that was used in the legendary romance between Tūtānekai and the beautiful Hinemoa, who swam across the waters of Lake Rotorua to hear his enchanting music.[17]

MAKING MEDICINES

Poroporo had a number of medicinal uses. The leaves were used as plasters for ulcers, itchy skin or sores. When the leaves are boiled in water they form a reddish-yellow liquid, which has a pleasant cooling effect. It was useful in treating a condition known only as 'Māori itch', which spread rapidly in the gold diggings around Otago, with sores that erupted all over the body and would fester and run. It was also used to treat scab in sheep.

Poroporo juice could also be mixed with soot and used for a practice tattoo — those undergoing the process could look at their reflection in a pool of water and approve the pattern before committing to the permanent version.

ETYMOLOGY

The true origin of the name *Solanum* is unclear, but one common suggestion is that it means 'soothing' or 'comforting' and refers to the narcotic effects of some species. The species name *aviculare* means 'small bird', and Georg Forster was said to have given the species its name because it was eagerly sought after by native birds. The names 'poro' and 'poroporo' are used widely in New Zealand and the Pacific for plants in the genus *Solanum*. European settlers misheard the Māori name and called it 'bull-a-bull', or 'the Māori gooseberry'. The plant is also native to Australia, where it is known as the kangaroo apple.

In some areas of the country, Māori women used poroporo as a contraceptive, although this seems to be a fairly modern rongoā. The leaves were boiled and the water drunk just before menstruation to prevent pregnancy. It is not known how reliable this treatment was, and given the poisonous leaves it seems a rather risky procedure. But the practice may have some basis in science. The leaves contain the steroid precursor solasodine, which is used in contraceptives and in the relief of rheumatoid arthritis. In the late 1970s a factory was built near Taranaki in an attempt to start a poroporo industry to extract solasodine from the leaves. The former USSR was even interested in the plant, growing it in the Soviet Union and studying it for the potential to extract the steroid drug. However, the New Zealand venture was beset by problems, including frosts, wet weather and weeds, and variable yields made it difficult to make a profit. It closed several years later when a method for synthesising solasodine was discovered. Today, extracts of poroporo are sold as an anti-inflammatory skin cream for eczema and dandruff.

Poroporo was the basis of a small commercial industry in Taranaki and even attracted the attention of the Soviet Union. *(Jacqui Geux)*

MAMAKU

The saddest fern in the forest

Mamaku can grow up to 20 metres tall, reaching high into the canopy. (Edin Whitehead)

Mamaku (*Cyathea medullaris*) by Walter Hood Fitch, 1862. (*Biodiversity Heritage Library*)

Mamaku is the giant umbrella of the forest, our tallest tree fern, with immense fronds 6 metres wide shading out the forest understorey beneath them. To Māori, these drooping fronds seemed to represent a deep sadness, like a mourner bowing their head in grief.

One story explains this sorrow as the result of a tragic love story between Mamaku and Toroa. These two creatures were once human lovers, who would constantly bicker and argue. Eventually the sound of their arguing disturbed the gods, who warned them there would be consequences if they kept fighting. When they continued to argue, the gods turned Toroa into an albatross, sending him far across the sea, and they turned Mamaku into a tree fern, rooted to the spot so she could not chase her lover. Upon hearing their judgement, Mamaku's heart was filled with sadness and she bowed her head and pulled her hair over her face — the origin of Mamaku's drooping fronds.

In another tale, Mamaku once lived in the sea but was driven out by Tāwhaki, a demigod with powers of lightning. Mamaku retreated into the depths of the forest. However, Mamaku was not safe there either, transgressing tapu and offending the hakuturi, mysterious creatures that acted as guardians of the forest. In revenge, they sat on the rigid fronds of Mamaku causing them to sag and droop.

A LAST RESORT

Mamaku was a useful food source for travellers making their way in the bush. The white pith inside the trunk and the coiled fern frond (koru) are both edible. Mamaku was well liked, but the trunk was only taken in times of necessity as it does not regenerate. Māori would cut the trunk with an adze and let the thick red bitter goo ooze out first. Then they would chop the trunk into sections and cut away the tough, black outer covering. The pith could be baked or cut into thin strips and hung out to dry. The koru was first rubbed between the hands to remove the coating of hairs; it could then be eaten raw or baked. Koru produce a lot of sticky mucilage, which makes for a rather unusual eating experience.

Pākehā who tried the fronds generally liked them, comparing the taste to a potato or a turnip. The explorer Charles Heaphy, who is remembered for his arduous year-and-a-half-long journey from Nelson down the west coast of the South Island, was forced to resort to eating mamaku fronds when his rations of flour and potato expired, and complained bitterly about the vegetable in his

TAXONOMY

Mamaku (*Cyathea medullaris*) is found across the South West Pacific, and is native to a range of countries from Fiji to New Zealand. There are several *Cyathea* species in New Zealand, including ponga (*C. dealbata*), katote (*C. smithii*) and the gully tree fern (*C. cunninghamii*). The genus is found widely across the tropics, and gives its name to the scaly tree fern family *Cyatheaceae*.

diary, saying it wasn't worth carrying it. Later, however, Heaphy made a cooked spiced tart with mamaku and revised his earlier opinion, suggesting it tasted like baked apple.

Modern enthusiasts have found a range of culinary uses for mamaku. Rongoā practitioner Donna Kerridge suggests simmering it with berries to make jelly, stewing it with fruit for dessert, or making it into soothing vegetable juices and smoothies.

STRANGE MUCILAGE

The sticky red-brown mucus that exudes from the cut branches and trunks has a bitter taste, and Māori used it to produce a thick syrup, which has a pleasant bitter-sweet flavour and is deliciously cool.

Modern research has found that the mucilage expressed from the koru is a non-Newtonian fluid, which has curious properties, becoming more viscous under high pressure, similar to the way wet sand appears dry under foot. It has been speculated that this may be what allows this tree to keep itself upright in high winds despite not having a solid trunk.

The fluid has been the subject of much research, and may provide innovative uses in the food industry as a thickening agent, or as a medical treatment for people suffering dysphagia, who find it hard to swallow. It has even been suggested for use as an

The large coiled frond of mamaku is covered in scales, which need to be rubbed off before it can be eaten. (*Jacqui Geux*)

anorexiant in humans, to combat obesity. When mamaku gum was fed to rats in one study, it stopped their stomachs from contracting and emptying, and meant that the rats ate less food over the next 24 hours than those given just water.

However, while it is safe to eat from the plant, the pure form of the gum may be a health hazard, as its novel physical properties make it difficult to swallow.

A NEW SUCCESSION

We have only now begun to discover the important role that mamaku plays in forest regeneration. In wetter, steeper areas of the country, it often arrives first on the scene and quickly forms short-lived forests where it is almost the only canopy species. Underneath this dark umbrella, sensitive broad-leaved species such as kohekohe, pukatea, tawa and miro are able to develop, and eventually grow to replace it. Elsewhere, mānuka and kānuka are generally seen as the major primary successional plants, colonising open and disturbed environments and creating more suitable habitats for the establishment of sensitive forest trees. But mānuka and kānuka have only become ubiquitous in the landscape since the arrival of humans and fire. In the prehistoric period, when fire was very rare, mamaku may have played a much larger role in nurturing the forests of the future.

SOOTHING SUBSTANCES

As well as helping to promote forest regeneration, mamaku has nurturing qualities for humans. The pith was bruised and used as an eye mask for sore eyes, sore feet and sore breasts. It was considered useful for skin conditions, rashes and ulcers. The strange gum was particularly useful as well, and could be rubbed on poisoned and inflamed hands, and saddle sores on horses. It was eaten to cure internal parasites and used to soothe a sore throat. The koru could be boiled and the water drunk to assist with the removal of the placenta, or mashed and applied to boils.

Occasionally, the rough black bark was used to make a Māori musical instrument, the rōria. It was scraped very thin and pushed against the teeth and plucked as songs and words were spoken, giving them an eerie musical quality.

Mamaku helps to repair the landscape after disturbance, and has soothing medicinal qualities for humans as well. (*Jacqui Geux*)

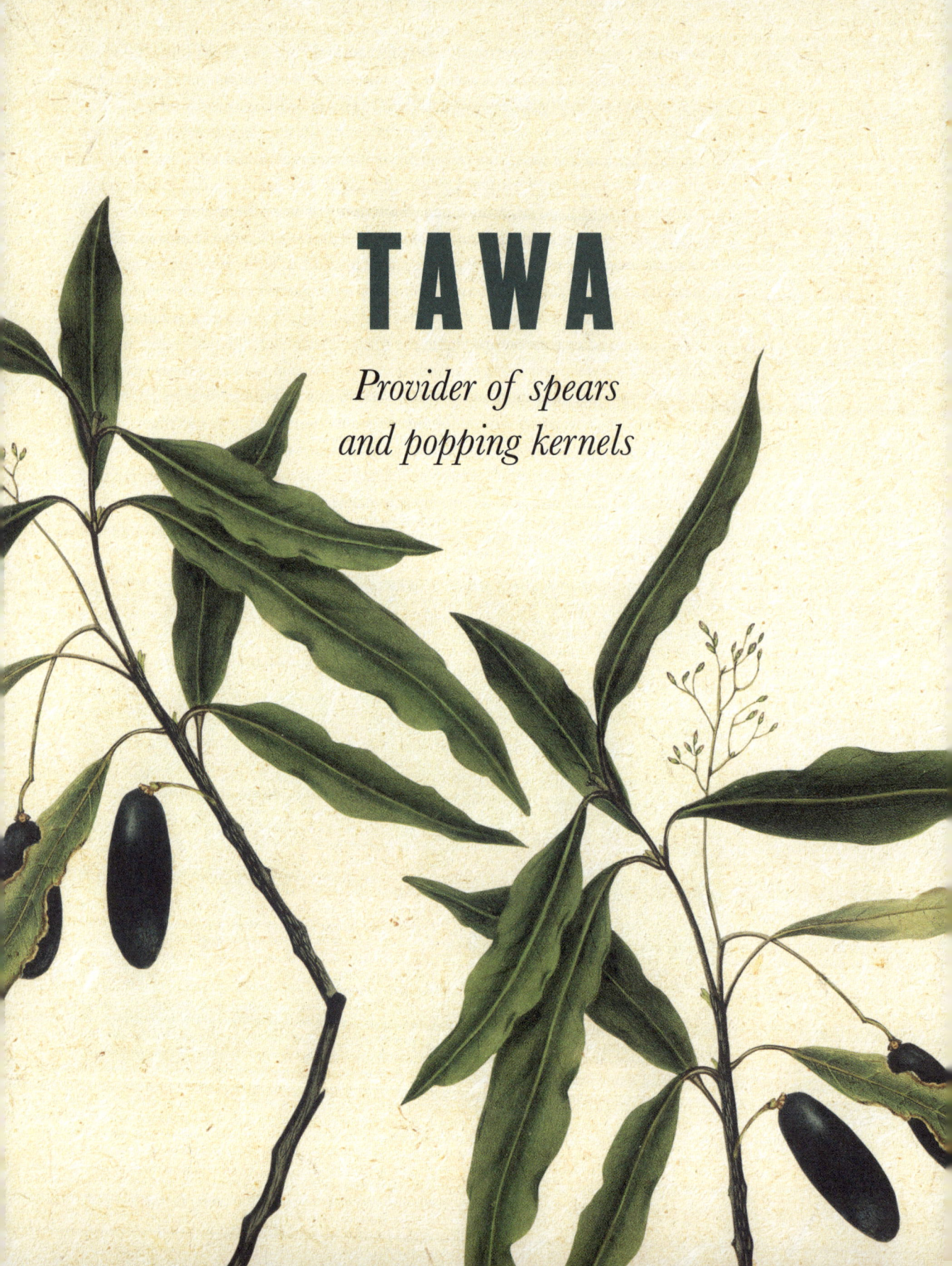

TAWA

*Provider of spears
and popping kernels*

Tawa has stolen the lives of many kererū in its time. Māori would construct immense lances out of tawa wood — sometimes greater than 10 metres long — to spear the birds while they sat digesting their meals. Sometimes platforms would be built in the trees where a hunter could sit in ambush. Other times, hunters would climb great trees, with their torso covered in flax mats to avoid scratching their chests on the climb. Perching among the branches, they would inch the giant tawa lance closer and closer to their prey, until at the final moment they would the thrust the lance through the heart of the bird.

These spears were prized possessions, crafted over many years and handed down through the generations. Great care and ritual was associated with their use, and if a hunter was foolish enough to touch the blood of one of 'Tāne's flapping children', then their spear would instantly lose its mana and never catch a kererū again. The spear-points were often made with the sharpened thigh bone of slain enemies, or — for the privileged few — delicately carved out of pounamu.

Tawa (Beilschmiedia tawa) by Martha King *(Alexander Turnbull Library, PUBL-0011-13-2)*

COOKING THE KERNELS

As well as providing kererū, tawa was an important source of food in its own right. The large, purple drupe resembles a stretched-out plum, and when the skin is peeled away it reveals a striking green flesh like an avocado. While this soft flesh can be eaten, it does have a distinct turpentine taste common in many New Zealand fruit. While not very appetising at first, it can be a refreshing snack once the taste is acquired, leaving the mouth feeling cool and clean.

But it was the kernel inside the fruit that provided the most valuable food source. It was boiled, roasted or steamed in a hāngī. It tastes rather like a potato. The cooked kernels kept remarkably well and could store for years, making them an incredibly valuable standby food in case of difficult times. In later times the mashed kernels were mixed with honey and made into a type of cake.

When tawa kernels were cooked on a fire or hot coals, the seeds burst with a loud popping noise, like the sound of popcorn. The phrase *ahi tawa* — tawa fire — came to mean anything noisy, and was used to describe loud noises, loud people and even musket fire on the battlefield. Noisy children were often compared to a crackling tawa fire, where it was remarked:

Ko te ahi tawa hai whakarite.
They are as noisy as a tawa fire.[18]

Māori admired the strength of tawa kernels and great warriors were often compared with the tough little nuts:

> *Ka mahi te tawa uho ki te riri!*
> Well done tawa-kernel fighting away! [19]

In contrast, the name of the soft flesh of the berry was used as an insult — *he tawa para!* (tawa pulp!) — and referred to cowards who were easily crushed and fled in battle.

The thin leaves of tawa cast dappled light on the forest understorey. *(Edin Whitehead)*

THE GOD IN THE TREE

The importance of tawa in Māori culture is shown by a number of legendary specimens that were thought to be infused with spiritual power. One such tree named Pari-kori-tawa stood on Whirinaki hill on the upper Whanganui River. It is told that one day a woman named Matakaha went to get tawa berries from the tree when a demigod named Mata-o-te-rangi emerged from the tree and made love to her. Later she fell pregnant and began to go into labour, but, instead of emerging the normal way, the child burst out of her back between her shoulders, like a cicada emerging from its skin. The horrific birth killed the mother, but the boy was unharmed, and would eventually grow up to become a powerful tohunga. These events made the tree very sacred, and it is said a number of people have died from breaching this tapu. Occasionally its leaves were used for medicine, but only by the very skilled or the very brave.

EASILY SHAPED

Other than for spear-making, tawa timber was used by Māori to make tools such as paddles, spears, clubs and adze handles. It was harvested by European settlers as well, and it proved to be a useful timber tree, with a soft wood that was easy to shape. It was used to make fences and houses, and was even shipped to Australia for a time.

Tawa was often used medicinally as well. A brew from the bark was drunk to treat stomach aches, coughs and colds, and to ease a gassy stomach. Pākehā found this infusion made an enjoyable beverage when travelling the country, and Bishop George Selwyn regarded it as 'a wholesome as well as a grateful beverage, which does not require the addition of sugar'.[20]

Right: Tawa is excellent for crafting tools and tasty brews. *(Edin Whitehead)*

Far right: Tawa by Sydney Parkinson. *(Te Papa 1992-0035-2353)*

TUTU

*Scourge of farmers, cattle
and elephants*

Tutu is one of New Zealand's deadliest plants. While the luscious dark berries are sweet and delicious, the plant contains high concentrations of the neurotoxin tutin. Consuming even a small amount of this deadly compound is enough to send someone into a foaming neuromuscular spasm, with enough force to throw limbs out of joints. Those who overdose on tutin have been known to become giddy and delirious, filled with restless excitement, before being racked with violent convulsions and entering a comatose state. Many never wake up, and those who do survive have been plagued with ill health and memory loss.

The greatest number of human deaths have been the result of the seductive purple fruit, which dangle like clusters of purple grapes along walking tracks and waterways. Perhaps the deadliest thing about them is that they really are quite delicious, and after an initial taste test, people decide that they must be safe. But it is the black seeds within the fruit that contain the deadly neurotoxin.

People have died after making tutu remedies, wines, beer and pies that accidentally contained the seeds. Old newspaper reports record the deaths of a shocking number of young children who fell victim to the plant in the early days of European settlement. The same tragic story played out again and again across the colony, and was particularly common among recent immigrants not yet acquainted with the land.

Remedies for treating tutu poisoning were by no means pleasant either. One Māori treatment involved hanging the victim upside down over a fire and forcing them to consume repulsive liquids until they vomited up the seeds. There are also accounts of victims being buried in sand to prevent them convulsing, or being held in freezing water till their blood circulation stopped.

Poisonings still occasionally occur in modern times, although deaths are almost unheard of. An interesting recent case of poisoning, however, occurred in the Waitākere Ranges when a tramper mistook a tutu shoot for the edible supplejack vine. He took the shoot home and boiled it with carrots and broccoli for dinner, but found it tasted revolting and quickly spat it out. Later that night he turned blue, began foaming at the mouth and was racked by seizures that were so violent they threw his arm out of its socket. He was rushed to hospital and very fortunately made a full recovery.[21]

TAXONOMY

The most common and widespread tutu is the tree tutu (*Coriaria arborea*), which is found along stream banks and in regenerating bush. There are six other species of tutu in the *Coriaria* genus, which are much smaller, low-growing shrubs but are no less poisonous. *Coriaria* plants occur overseas as well, and *C. ruscifolia* is used in Chile to make a rat poison. *Coriaria* are the only members of the Coriariaceae family.

TUTU HONEY

If that wasn't enough, tutu is also responsible for outbreaks of toxic honey, and beekeepers need to be especially wary of it. The honey becomes poisoned when the passion-vine hopper insect feeds on tutu sap and excretes poisonous honeydew, which is then collected by bees. Since 1889, there have been 141 cases of people becoming ill from toxic honey and four cases of death.

There was even a case where 30 schoolchildren in England became ill after being sent a gift of New Zealand honey. In 2008, 20 people were poisoned from an outbreak in the Coromandel, leading to stricter regulations of the industry and a minimum allowable amount of tutin in honey for beekeepers.

A DANGER TO ANIMALS

While human deaths are now uncommon, farm animals continue to be plagued by the plant, and have been ever since their very first introduction to New Zealand. The first sheep released in Queen Charlotte Sound by Captain Cook survived only a few days. They ate a poisonous plant — almost certainly tutu — and promptly died. The dreaded 'toot' has remained a curse of farmers, with huge numbers of stock dying after grazing on the plant, and it is often a major source of mortality. One farmer reported that three-quarters of his stock were killed off by tutu.

Tutu has even claimed the lives of the largest animals on land. Not one but two circus elephants have been killed by grazing on tutu in separate incidents. The first was during an exhibition in Otago in the 1860s, when an elephant was marched inland and allowed to graze on tutu shoots and was found dead shortly after. In 1957, Mollie, a Buller's Circus elephant well known for her ability to stand on her head, met the same grisly fate. She was able to get out and feed on tutu plants, and was later found dead in a river. Remarkably, two more circus elephants nearly joined this depressing club in the 1960s, when they were let out and fed on tutu and began having seizures. However, they were injected with barbiturates and made a full recovery.

ETYMOLOGY

The name of the genus *Coriaria* comes from the Latin *corium* meaning 'hide', and some of the species in the genus have been used for tanning leather. The species name *arborea* means 'tree-like', an uncommon trait among members of this group. The name 'tutu' is given in Rarotonga to the Asian snakewood plant (*Colubrina asiatica*) to which tutu bears a passing resemblance, with the leaves arranged in opposite pairs with clear veins. Tutu is also colloquially known as 'toot' and the word is sometimes used as a verb: when stock is 'tutu'd', it has been poisoned with tutu.

JUICE AND WINE

Despite the potential danger, tutu was an important source of food and medicine for many Māori iwi in former times. The poisonous seeds were carefully removed by filtering them out using the fluffy flower heads of toetoe, and then the berries were squeezed to extract the juice. The resulting beverage, known as waitutu, was consumed in massive quantities and was one of the few beverages drunk by Māori other than plain water.

The juice had a laxative effect and was used to relieve the constipating effects of tōtara, rimu and karaka berries. It could also be boiled with seaweed to make jelly, known as rehia. When fermented, tutu juice makes a potent fruit wine. While there is some suggestion that Māori were aware that fermented tutu berries could have an intoxicating effect, it was only after the arrival of Europeans that drinking this wine became popular. The missionaries in particular were fond of the beverage, and it is said to resemble a claret in colour and flavour, and taste similar to elderberry wine.

SHOOTS, FLUTES AND SOOT

The leaves and shoots were used to dress wounds, and could be made into lotions for the treatment of cuts, sores, bruises and boils. They are an important rongoā plant in many areas, and an infusion of the leaves is still made into an ointment for the treatment of sprains, strains and broken bones.

The stems of larger species of tutu could be hollowed out and made into kōauau flutes. Care had to be taken, though, as some people experienced mild poisoning symptoms after playing the flutes. One researcher has suggested that this may even have been done on purpose, and that it could have provided shamanic, out-of-body experiences while playing.

Red and black dyes were extracted from the bark and fruit, and soot from burning tutu wood was mixed with oils to make ink for tattooing. The juice from the berries stains skin brown, and young Māori warriors who had not yet been tattooed would paint their faces with tutu juice before battle.

An unfinished kōauau made from a hollowed-out tutu stem. (Auckland War Memorial Museum, 1957.5, 35792.1)

RAUPŌ

*A water plant used for boats,
cakes and poi*

When harakeke, kiekie and raupō were young, kiekie went to ride the shoulders of
Tāne, whereas harakeke and raupō went to live with their ancestor Wainui, the mother
of waters, to be nurtured on the banks of her rivers. Raupō is still found here, in
wetlands and rivers. Its thin, strap-like leaves wave gently in the breeze, while the end of
its tall flower stalk is crowned with an iconic fluffy bulrush.

MŌKIHI

Raupō provided Māori with the most convenient source of boat-building equipment
when travelling inland. When a river became too wide, or too unruly to cross, a
temporary waka made of raupō could be constructed. These craft were known as
mōkihi, and were ideally made of dry raupō leaves, but could be made from wet leaves
when in a hurry. The dry kōrari of harakeke forms the internal structure, with masses
of raupō leaves bound around them in tight bundles. The finished result resembles the
rafts of papyrus the ancient Egyptians used to sail down the Nile. These rafts could be
quickly made and used, then left for the next traveller who might cross the area. Pākehā
adventurers exploring the country for the first time also used these light temporary craft
when charting the forest interior.

Raupō was a useful plant to have around for making sturdier ocean-going waka
as well. The fluffy material of the seed heads could be stuffed into the cracks in waka,
helping to keep them watertight. The leaves were strapped around the wooden joining,
woven into sails or rolled up and used as fishing floats.

ESCAPE RAFT

One legendary tale shows how useful these raupō mōkihi could be. Kōpūwai was a
giant with a dog's head and a man's body that was covered in scales. He lived in a cave
in the upper part of the Matau River, and hunted human beings with a pack of two-
headed dogs. When local people went further inland following
food resources, many were captured by Kōpūwai and his dogs,
and disappeared without a trace. One time Kōpūwai captured
a woman, Kaiamio, as a slave, and had her tied to him with a
long rope. Kaiamio lived there for years until she devised a plan
to escape and gathered some raupō stalks to construct a mōkihi.
Once Kōpūwai was asleep, she untied the rope and tied it to
raupō root, then rode her mōkihi to safety. Kōpūwai would pull
on the rope from time to time, and, feeling the plant give and
take, was not aware she had escaped until much later. When
Kaiamo made it back to her people they planned their revenge.
They returned to Kōpūwai's cave, placed bundles of raupō stalks
around the exits and burned him alive.

TAXONOMY

Raupō (*Typha orientalis*) is a
widespread plant, native to Australia,
and much of Asia and eastern
Russia. *Tyhpa* is found worldwide
in marsh and wetland habitats, and
has a long history with humans.
The baby Moses, for example, was
said to have been found among
bulrushes on the river Nile. The
genus belongs to the bulrush family,
the Typhaceae.

RAUPŌ STRUCTURES

It wasn't just for watercraft that raupō came in handy. It was one of those plants in New Zealand with a thousand uses — in travelling, play and domestic life. For example, the lightness of the leaves made them particularly suitable for making kites, which were woven to resemble birds, and were enjoyed by children and adults alike.

Perhaps the most valuable use of this plant was for making simple but sturdy shelters, either for temporary whare when travelling or to create comfortable, permanent settlements. When used to build storehouses, the leaves and stalks were woven closely to make them as airtight as possible, to protect food and precious taonga.

European pioneers often used raupō whare as their first shelters. Later, they too would use raupō to build more permanent buildings, crafting European-style homes and mission houses out of the leaves. Gradually the building of raupō whare declined in favour of wooden houses. But according to some, raupō huts were far warmer and more comfortable than their wooden counterparts.

ETYMOLOGY

The name *Typha* comes from the Greek name for 'bulrush'. The species name *orientalis* means 'from the Orient', and refers to its distribution across Asia. The word 'raupō' is an old Polynesian term for bulrushes, and similar words are used across Polynesia to describe a variety of aquatic sedges. The Maori word 'hune' is used to describe the fluffy seed heads, and is derived from the Polynesian word 'fune', which refers to the downy core of the breadfruit. *Typha orientalis* was also known to Aboriginal Australians as 'cumbungi'. Europeans have called it bulrush, reedmace and cattail, and *Typha* species are known in America as corn dog grass and water sausage.

The iconic fluffy flower stalks of raupō. The male flowers form at the top and the female flowers form the brown sausage-like structure beneath. *(Jacqui Geux)*

The iconic bulrush flowers had their domestic uses as well. The fluffy pith inside the stalks and the downy pappus of the seed heads were used as stuffing in bedding, mattresses and pillows, and could be used on wounds and old sores to keep out dust.

MAKING POI

Raupō was the traditional material for making poi, which have become one of the most iconic and visible symbols of Māori culture. The pith from the central stem and the fluffy flower down were used to create a sphere that was then wrapped in leaves, and suspended on a length of woven flax rope.

Swinging and beating poi was initially a pastime, which over time evolved into a major performance art. Some say that the poi evolved as a way for men to keep coordinated and flexible for fighting; others say that women used the poi as exercise to keep limber for weaving. During the 1900s local Māori created a small industry making raupō poi to sell to tourists around Rotorua, and even included mini raupō poi for earrings. Poi has now gone global, and raupō has given way to synthetic materials, and the ever-increasing array of techniques and styles include fire poi, glow-in-the-dark poi, light poi and meteor poi. Recent research has shown that swinging poi can be a particularly good activity for the elderly, improving arm strength, grip and dexterity.

A pair of poi made from raupō leaves. (Auckland War Memorial Museum, 782)

CHILDREN'S TREAT

The raupō root also provided a valuable starchy food source. The outer part was peeled off, and the soft inside was eaten raw or cooked. Raupō root was said to be a favourite of children, especially in summer, when it provided a mild, cool, refreshing snack. Travellers were also fond of it, as it could be relied on when out exploring new lands.

The roots were kept in a storehouse until needed, and then pounded and mixed with water to make a type of porridge, rerepe. Occasionally the mānuka beetle, tūtae ruru, was collected and pounded with the root, to add an interesting taste and texture before cooking.

The yellow pollen from the flowers resembles mustard, and was gathered by beating the flower stalk. Large quantities of pollen could be collected during flowering in the summer months, filling up plenty of gourds and baskets. When mixed with water this pollen could be baked into a sweet, light cake, pungapunga. The botanist William Colenso was able to try the delicacy, which reminded him of gingerbread.

JURASSIC GIANTS

Kauri and the podocarps

KAURI

The whale of the forest

The first encounter between the first human settlers and kauri must have been a remarkable experience. In their homeland of eastern Polynesia, there was nothing that could have prepared the travellers for these immense cathedrals of timber.

In some northern traditions, kauri trees are thought to be the legs of Tāne Mahuta holding apart the sky and the earth and allowing light into the world. In another traditional whakapapa, this giant rangatira of the forest had a connection with a giant of the ocean, the sperm whale or parāoa. Kauri and sperm whales were seen as brothers, children of Tāne Mahuta born at the beginning of the forest. At the time of their conception, the sperm whale had four legs and walked about on the land, feeding in swamps and wetlands. However, he longed to enter the realm of Tangaroa and explore the vast oceans, and asked Tāne to place him there. After sailing around the sea for many years he returned to the coast and called out to his brother Kauri, asking him to join him swimming the ocean. But Kauri refused to leave his home in the forest. The whale realised he could not change Kauri's mind, so he told him, 'If you will not join me, let us swap skins. For a day will come when humans will cut you down and make you into waka, and with my skin you will be able to withstand the salty seas.' For Māori, this connection between the two brothers explains why the bark of kauri is thin and full of resin like the oil of a whale, and why it oozes gum like the ambergris of sperm whales.

Kauri belongs to an incredibly ancient plant lineage that stretches back hundreds of millions of years. The plant world has changed a lot since the first kauri trees evolved. Slow-growing conifers have been replaced as the masters of the planet by faster-growing flowering plants — angiosperms — which make up 80 per cent of all plants on earth.

However, kauri has an ingenious strategy that helps to level the playing field with these young upstarts. It drops a layer of acidic leaf litter, which strips the soil of the

These slow-growing giants of the forest are able to hold their own against their faster-growing competitors. (Robert Vennell)

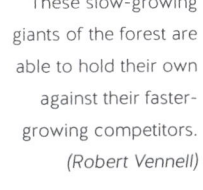

Kauri (*Agathis australis*) by Matilda Smith, 1914. (*Biodiversity Heritage Library*)

nutrients that many angiosperms need to fuel their rapid growth. Kauri can cope in these awful conditions, as it has formed an alliance with mycorrhizal fungi in the soil that are more efficient at extracting the remaining nutrients. The changes kauri makes to the soil are so dramatic that it has led scientists to describe the tree as an ecosystem engineer. It radically reshapes the environment around it to suit its needs, and in doing so changes the structure of the forest. Plants such as māhoe, supplejack and nīkau are driven out, while others such as māpou, kauri grass and mingimingi, which can tolerate poorer soil conditions, thrive.

TIMBER TITAN

Māori valued kauri timber highly, and kauri was typically harvested to make prestige items such as grand waka capable of carrying hundreds of people.

Particularly useful was the resinous gum that oozes from the trunk. It could be used as a fire-starter, and was placed into torches when night-fishing. When the gum is burned, the smoke has a pleasant aromatic odour, which has been compared to frankincense and myrrh. It has the added benefit of keeping away insects, and was burned in between crops to protect the harvest. After it was burned, the soot produced was ground into a fine powder and mixed with fats and oils to make a black ink for tattooing. The resin was also used as chewing gum; it had a strong piney flavour and would be chewed and passed among good friends and preserved for a long time.

For Europeans, kauri became the most important tree in building the new settler colony of the north, and was used to construct houses, boats and furniture. It is the material that forms many of New Zealand's oldest and most historic buildings, including churches and the first Government House. The geologist Ferdinand von Hochstetter estimated that in 1859 'nearly the whole of Auckland with the exception of a few stone buildings consisted of houses built of Kauri timber, and it is especially to the Kauri pine that the province is indebted for its first rise'.[22]

The tall, unbranching trunks were long, strong and light, making them perfect to form masts for the British navy's battleships. It is even claimed that when Lord Nelson defeated Napoleon at the Battle of Trafalgar, his ship was fitted with kauri masts. Kauri was often shipped overseas and used to build houses, and was one of the timbers used to rebuild San Francisco after the 1906 earthquake.

Felling these giants was no easy feat, however, and the men involved in cutting them down were incredibly hardy. They hacked at trees all day long with axes and pit saws, hauled great timber jacks through the forest, and worked long hours with no breaks except Sundays. It was a hard life, and it was common

Kauri was perhaps the most important resource shaping the destiny of pioneer towns in northern New Zealand.
(Edin Whitehead)

TAXONOMY

Kauri (*Agathis australis*) is the only member of the *Agathis* genus in New Zealand, although there are a number of other species in Australia and the Pacific. It belongs to the ancient Araucariaceae family, which includes exotic trees familiar in the New Zealand landscape, such as monkey puzzle (*Araucaria araucana*) and Norfolk pine (*Araucaria heterophylla*).

for men to be crushed and killed by falling kauri, or injured in accidents in the mills. Kauri were hand-sawn and felled in the direction of nearby rivers, hauled by teams of bullocks, and floated downstream to the sea. In some places, great dams of kauri were piled up, then, when enough had been harvested, they were released in an almighty torrent of water, the kauri scouring the landscape in a mad rush to return to the ocean and its brother, the sperm whale.

THE GUMDIGGERS

Timber wasn't the only resource kauri had to offer the new settlers. Beneath the burnt and blackened forests left from kauri logging they discovered a precious treasure — kauri gum. When kauri branches fall off or trunks are damaged, large amounts of gum flow out of the wounds. Beneath the swamps and bogs of Auckland and Northland, this fossilised gum could be found in huge quantities, the legacies of millions of years of bleeding kauri forests. Pākehā recognised the value of the gum as a varnish, and both Pākehā and Māori joined in the search for it. Prices for the gum soared, sparking something of a gum rush, with small towns booming as diggers swarmed there to make their fortunes. Between 1850 and 1900, kauri gum became New Zealand's biggest export, more valuable than timber, wool or gold.

SWAMP KAURI

In the past decade, the price of swamp kauri timber — fossilised trees preserved in wetlands and bogs — has sky-rocketed to become one of the most expensive timbers in the world. This has led to the latest rush on kauri, as wealthy prospectors buy up land in Northland looking to strike big.

These old kauri stumps have an unparalleled scientific value as well, and scientists have been able to work with swamp millers to obtain 'biscuits' — cross-sections of the trees — to use for research. These biscuits provide a fantastic historical library, as each year the trees produce another layer of growth, thus recording information about the climate at that particular time. By matching up the kauri growth rings from different plants, scientists can reconstruct an unbroken climatic history stretching back thousands of years into the past. In some cases, they can tell exactly which year a ring occurred, and even analyse the humidity, vapour pressure and carbon in the atmosphere. Once the wood is cut up for timber and sold, however, these precious records are forever lost to science.

ETYMOLOGY

The name *Agathis* comes from a Greek term meaning 'ball of thread', and refers to the shape of the female cones. The species name *australis* means 'southern', and refers to its status as a New Zealand native, in contrast with the tropical members of the genus. The name 'kauri' is thought to derive from the ancient Polynesian term 'kauli', which was originally used to describe black-coloured trees such as the Samoan ebony (*Diospyros samoensis*). Related names have since been applied to a range of different trees across Polynesia but are no longer necessarily associated with black colouring.

The tree rings of fossilised kauri trees contain precious data about the history of the earth's climate. (*Jacqui Geux*)

A doomed tree, infected by the dreaded kauri dieback disease. (*Jacqui Geux*)

KAURI DIEBACK

Since European arrival, the story of kauri has been one of exploitation. Today, however, kauri has become a cultural icon, protected by New Zealand law. Tāne Mahuta and Te Matua Ngahere — the largest trees in New Zealand — drive tourism to the north, and thousands of international and domestic tourists make the pilgrimage to Waipoua Forest every year to pay their respects.

But a new menace threatens to destroy kauri for good. Kauri dieback (*Phytophthora agathidicida*) is a water-mould that infects the tree's roots, and it is devastating kauri forests. The mould destroys the tree's conductive tissue, preventing it from absorbing water and nutrients and leaving it to slowly starve to death. The root and base of the tree begin to rot; the plant bleeds gum profusely, drops its leaves and collapses. Once infected, kauri are doomed, and there is currently no cure. The disease is spread by soil movement, and shoes are a common vehicle for moving it around the forest. The future of kauri remains uncertain, and care is needed from everyone to ensure their boots and gear are clear of soil where kauri dieback can live.

KAHIKATEA

*A tower of timber with
a long way to fall*

On the end of its branches, kahikatea holds bundles of delicious red-orange berries. Although tiny, they are super-abundant and were a valued food source for Māori. The only trouble is collecting them. While some berries fall and carpet the forest floor, most remain high above in the treetops.

To gather them, Māori scaled these gigantic skyscrapers, the tallest trees in the New Zealand forest. There were several approaches to the task. All were incredibly dangerous. If a vine was wrapped around the trunk, then this could be used, grabbing a hold of it and hauling oneself up. More often than not, however, the trees needed to be scaled directly. Using hand cords and foot loops bound with flax, the climber would slowly ascend the trees, adjusting their ropes as they went. Sometimes they repeated simple mantras and charms to themselves to keep their focus on the task ahead and away from the deadly drop below. On their chests they sometimes wore a woven flax pad to avoid scratching themselves on the rough bark as they clung on for dear life. On the largest trees it became impossible to manipulate the hand ropes and cords, and so a ladder was built using vines and poles.

Once they arrived in the treetops, the climbers carefully navigated their way through the branches, collecting bundles of fruit into woven flax baskets, and lowering them to the ground using a pulley system. For trickier fruit that were hard to reach, a whole branch might be snapped off and tossed to the ground below. In this way thousands of fruits could be collected, and many mouths could be fed. In one giant feast at Matamata, it was reported that there were 60 flax baskets full of the tiny kahikatea fruit.

TAXONOMY

Kahikatea (*Dacrycarpus dacrydioides*) is the only member of this genus in New Zealand. It belongs to the ancient podocarp family Podocarpaceae, of which tōtara (*Podocarpus totara*), miro (*Prumnopitys ferruginea*), mataī (*P. taxifolia*) and rimu (*Dacrydium cupressinum*) are also members.

Kahikatea fruit is a tasty and bountiful food, if you can brave the climb required to gather it. (*Jacqui Geux*)

Although the rewards were great, many who sought the kahikatea fruit were killed in the attempt. So much so that it was said: *He toa piki rakau, he kai na te pakiaka* (A tree-climbing expert is food for the roots).[23] It wasn't only the danger of the fall, however; the top of a kahikatea was a very vulnerable position to find yourself in when there was an attack from an enemy. Several accounts have been passed down of chiefs who were engaged in snaring kererū or collecting berries in the high branches of a kahikatea tree when they were raided by their rivals.

One legendary story recounts the cunning Te Noni. His enemies raided his village while he was stuck up a kahikatea tree, and began hacking the tree down with adzes. However, Te Noni convinced them to cut the tree in the direction of a nearby shallow river, claiming that the fall would surely kill him. Taking the bait, they felled the tree directly into the river, which turned out to be a deep pool of water. Te Noni survived the fall and swam to safety, cursing his pursuers as he went.

In a more recent tale from history, besieged Māori warriors holding off the British forces at Ōrākau pā made a desperate attempt to secure kahikatea berries to supplement their dwindling food resources, but were spotted by the British and forced to retreat.

AN UNDERWATER TREE

Like many of the most important plants in Māori culture, kahikatea was thought to have some special connection with the Polynesian homeland of Hawaiki. In one tale of the origin of kahikatea, the chief Pourangahua was carried out to sea in his waka, and wrecked on Hawaiki. Stranded without hope of return, he persuaded a large bird,

Kahikatea and podocarps hug the shore of a wetland. Forests like these would have once covered much of New Zealand. *(Edin Whitehead)*

Tawhaitari, to fly him back to Aotearoa. Upon sighting New Zealand, Pourangahua pulled out some of the finest, downiest feathers from under the wings of the great bird and cast them into the ocean. From these feathers grew a giant tree able to survive underwater. It was a branch of this tree that washed ashore in New Zealand and became kahikatea.

This tale helps to explain a number of kahikatea's curious characteristics, such as its feathery leaves and its ability to live in waterlogged soil. This is where kahikatea is commonly found, in wet and swampy ground, often growing large buttress roots that twine around its neighbours to prop itself up. In days gone past, kahikatea would have dominated the swampy lowland of New Zealand, forming pure stands that covered much of the Waikato and central North Island.

KAHIKATEA AND COOK

When the first Europeans arrived in New Zealand, they were amazed by these towering giants of wood, huddled together along the shoreline. Lieutenant James Cook and his crew first encountered kahikatea emerging out of the reeds and rushes as they paddled up the Waihou River, near Thames. Cook eagerly noted in his journal that kahikatea would make a supreme building material for ship masts, and named it white pine. He wrote in his diary that Thames would make the finest location he had seen for a future colony, with this ready supply of timber for houses, defences and ships. Joseph Banks, the ship's botanist, was similarly excited by the tree:

> The banks were completely clothed with the finest timber my eyes ever beheld ... every tree as streight [*sic*] as a pine and of immense size ... [it] would make the finest plank in the world.[24]

As naval wars with revolutionary America and France drew on, there was a growing demand for timber, and this spurred entrepreneurs to investigate Cook's white pine trees. A number of European vessels travelled to Thames to collect white pine logs and trade with local Māori. In this way kahikatea became the focal point for one of the earliest sustained interactions between Europeans and a large population of Māori. For the most part, these encounters were positive, and Māori would help cut and load timber in exchange for iron tools. However, conflicts and miscommunications occasionally arose when Europeans took kahikatea without permission or ceremony — a breach of tapu and a serious insult to the mana of the rangatira. In any case, the kahikatea industry was short-lived, as when the logs were delivered overseas it was found that they rotted easily in water, and for a while this gave New Zealand timber a poor reputation in the world market.

Had the Europeans consulted with local Māori, they might have saved themselves the bother. Māori knew that kahikatea was an inferior wood for building waka, but had many other ingenious uses for it. Once the sapwood of a decayed kahikatea tree had rotted away, it left the durable resinous heartwood. This made a great fire torch when tied in bundles, and was burned outside marae, or used when night-fishing or travelling across country.

Blue and black dyes could be extracted from the heartwood and mixed with oils to be used in tattooing. The timber was hard and difficult to crack, and carried a point well, so was prized for making long eel spears. It was also used to make all manner of implements, from fine-toothed combs to gardening tools, weapons, musical instruments and toys.

Europeans found other uses for it as well, in fencing, bridges, furniture and flooring, although it never managed to shake off its poor reputation of being unable to resist rot.

The bark of kahikatea served a number of medicinal uses for both Māori and Pākehā. Wood was infused in water and this brew was drunk as a tonic for stomach complaints and bladder problems, or boiled as a vapour bath. When chewed, the bark causes a numb, tingling sensation; its resin has a bitter-sweet taste and was used as a form of chewing gum.

ETYMOLOGY

The generic name *Dacrycarpus* means 'tear-drop fruit', and refers to the shape of the fruit and seeds. The species name *dacrydioides* means 'resembling a *Dacrydium*', the genus to which rimu belongs. 'Kahika' is an ancient Polynesian name deriving from the name for the Malay apple (*Syzygium malaccense*). It is not entirely clear why the name should be applied to kahikatea, as the Malay apple is physically different and belongs to the unrelated myrtle family. Perhaps the namers of the tree saw a similarity between the red flowers of the kahika and the red fruit of kahikatea, which can make the whole tree appear scarlet in heavy fruiting years. The European name 'white pine' was given by Captain Cook on account of the colour of its wood, but the name is rarely used nowadays.

The bright orange fruit of kahikatea is actually a type of cone, with a fleshy orange aril sitting on top of a single seed. (*Jacqui Geux*)

The immature blue seeds and unripe green fruit. (*Jacqui Geux*)

FARMING AND BUTTER

Unfortunately, kahikatea's preferred home in flat, low-lying areas put it squarely in the path of European farming and settlement, and it was extensively burned and milled. This widespread destruction of kahikatea increased rapidly with the advent of refrigeration. The growing overseas demand for New Zealand dairy meant that butter boxes and cheese boxes were needed. Kahikatea, with its pale, odourless wood, was perfect for the task, as it did not taint the products on their long journey to the United Kingdom.

Kahikatea was practically eradicated from many parts of the country, and the pure kahikatea forests that Cook marvelled at along the Waihou River were all but obliterated. Some strongholds, however, still remain, like the majestic kahikatea forests of South Westland and a few scattered fragments dotted among farmland.

MATAĪ

A tree of beer and music

The mighty mataī tree was considered to be among the rākau rangatira, the chiefly trees. Its worn and weathered bark flakes off in great chunks as if beaten with a hammer, like the survivor of many battles. As this hard, outer surface flakes away, it exposes a startling blood-red colour. In some traditions this was said to represent the blood of the eel god Tunaroa, when he was slain by Māui.

Mataī bark often appears as if it has been bruised and battered with a hammer. (*Edin Whitehead*)

For such a noble old tree, it is surprising to learn that it begins life as a tangled shrub of wiry leaves and twigs. These young plants look so different from the forest giant that mataī becomes that the first botanists to visit New Zealand assumed they were different species. It is only when mataī gains a few metres in height that a trunk begins to form and the tangle of little branches dies away. It is not entirely clear why mataī has this unusual growth form, which is not seen in its close relative miro, but it does fit a common pattern in the New Zealand flora. There is a much higher proportion of divaricating shrubs — those with tangled, interlaced branches — in New Zealand than anywhere else in the world, and the same growth pattern has evolved multiple times in unrelated plants. One theory for the abundance of this growth form is that the plants create warmer temperatures inside their tangled mass of branches, allowing them to inhabit cooler, more exposed sites. Another is that the structure is a relic from a time when moa were the dominant herbivore in New Zealand. The tangled mass of leaves may have served as a defence against moa, protecting vulnerable leaves from prying beaks.

TAXONOMY

Mataī (*Prumnopitys taxifolia*) is found in lowland forest across the North and South Islands. The only other species of *Prumnopitys* in New Zealand is miro (*P. ferruginea*). Mataī can be distinguished from miro by a distinct divaricating juvenile stage, non-curved leaves and spherical purple fruit. Both belong in the podocarp family Podocarpaceae, along with their relatives rimu, kahikatea and tōtara.

MATAĪ BEER

The edible berries were gathered in large baskets by Māori and eaten. Their taste is sweet, fragrant and slimy, but like many native fruits the strange turpentine taste takes some getting used to. The more important food item, however, was beneath the surface of the bark: a sap that produces a beverage known as 'mataī beer'. At the end of a hard day, bushmen would drill into the bark with an auger and tap the tree like a barrel. The sap produces a rich light-brown coloured brew, which was said to be very refreshing at first, though it became stale when left exposed to the air. The taste is reminiscent of the berries: sweet and bitter at the same time.

The sap was also claimed to have medicinal benefits: it was said to help stop the advance of tuberculosis, soothe stomach ache and ease neck swellings, and was applied to wounds as an antiseptic. It is still drunk in some parts of the country, and while the sap is alcohol-free it can be brewed to make an alcoholic beverage. The sap contains a plant lignan known as matairesinol, which was first identified in mataī trees but occurs in a number of plants around the world. Matairesinol has been shown to reduce cell division in mice, and so may have potential applications in cancer research.

The juvenile mataī (top) is a tangled shrub, while the adult (bottom) grows into a tall tree. *(Jacqui Geux)*

VERSATILE TIMBER

As one of the rākau rangatira, mataī timber was highly prized and used for a variety of different requirements. The dark, hard, durable wood was crafted into containers, vessels, fine-toothed combs, trays, troughs, spades, weapons, bowls and beaters. It was a popular choice for crafting waka huia — beautiful ornately carved containers for storing precious taonga such as huia feathers or pounamu.

It was also an important waka tree, used for building the ships themselves, as well as paddles, bailers and the inner crossbeams. The thin, flexible stems of the younger mataī trees were used for making eel pots (hīnaki), or fences to guide eels into the hīnaki. On the east coast mataī was even used to build toboggans to ride down grassy slopes, and was crafted into

ETYMOLOGY

The name *Prumnopitys* is thought to mean 'plum-fruited pine', and derives from the Greek *prunum* (plum) and *pitys* (conifer). The species name *taxifolia* means 'leaves like the yew tree [*Taxus baccata*]'. One suggestion on the meaning of the word 'mataī' is that it may derive from a combination of the words 'mata', meaning 'unripe', and 'ī', meaning 'fermented' or 'sour'. This could be a reference, perhaps, to the bitter taste of the 'beer' that exudes from the trunk. Mataī was called 'black pine' by European settlers, on account of the colour of the timber.

spinning tops for children. Pākehā valued the tree highly as well, and it was used to produce floors, furniture and cabinets.

TRUMPETS AND INSTRUMENTS

Mataī was often the preferred wood of choice for making Māori musical instruments, and it was carved into bull roarers, flutes, jaw harps and war gongs. Mataī was also used to construct pūkāea — long trumpets that produced a clear, round sound that could carry for many miles. To make the hollow trumpet, sections of wood were gummed together and wound with supplejack vines to cover the joins. Pūkāea were often used as a war trumpet to raise the alarm and assemble everyone when an attack was imminent.

It was perhaps a mataī pūkāea that was first sounded in response to Abel Tasman's arrival in Golden Bay, in 1642. There he encountered the local iwi Ngāti Tumatakokiri, who sent two groups in waka to paddle alongside his vessel, recite karakia and blow blasts on a pūkāea. The Dutch response was to blow their own trumpets as a sign of peace. However, more likely this was interpreted as accepting a challenge of war. The next day a host of waka launched from the shore and rammed into a small Dutch boat, killing four sailors. Tasman named the area 'Murderers Bay' and never set foot on the coast of New Zealand.

An illustration by Isaac Gilsemans from 1642, showing the first encounter between Māori and Dutch mariners. *(Dutch National Archives)*

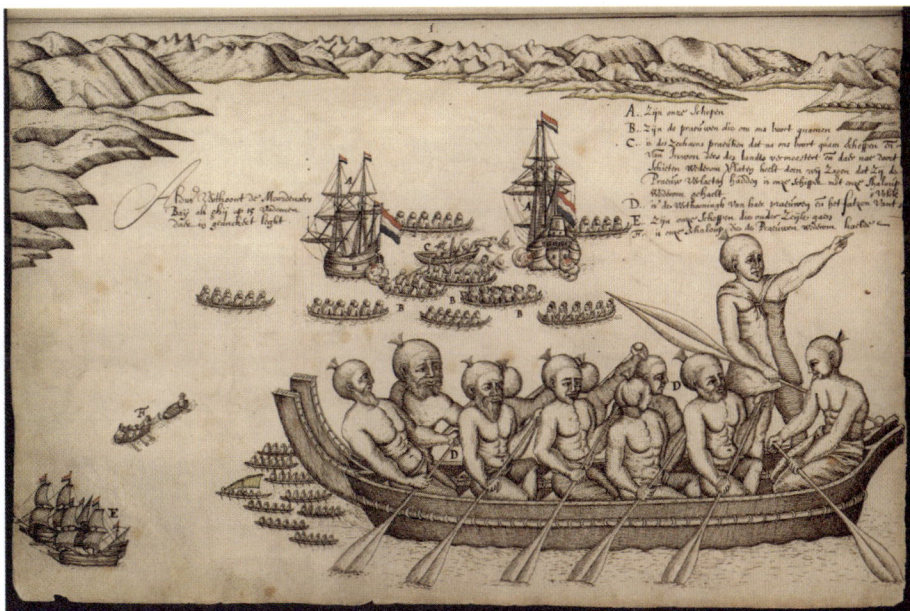

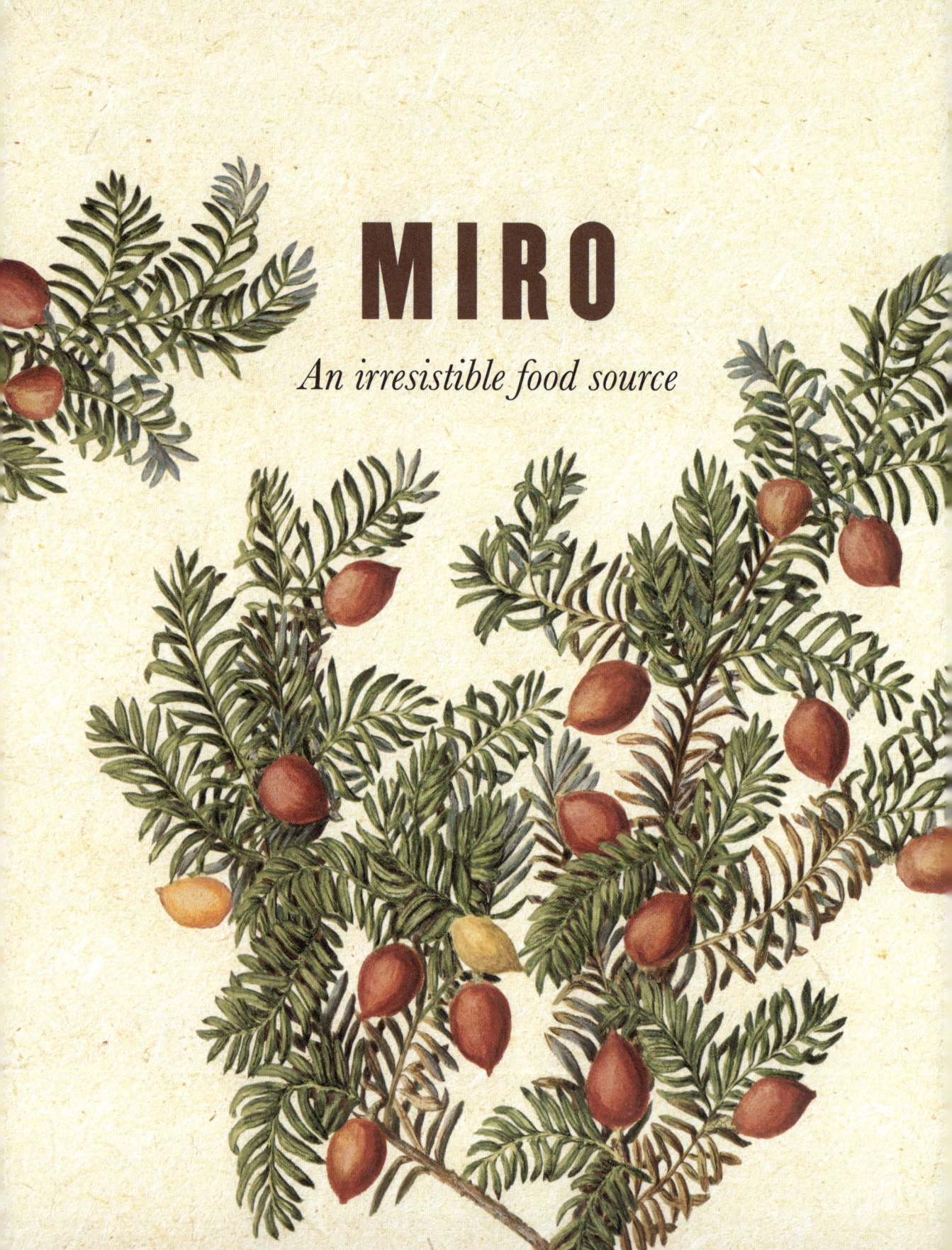

MIRO

An irresistible food source

Perhaps the most stiking aspect of the miro tree is its bright pink berries, which stand out against a canopy of feathery green leaves. This pink fruit is edible, and was eaten by both Pākehā and Māori. It is aromatic, bitter, sweet and nutty; some even say it resembles nutmeg. It carries a strong turpentine taste, which can be too overwhelming for some, although this taste can be acquired with persistence, and it makes a refreshing palate cleanser.

TAXONOMY

Miro (*Prumnopitys ferruginea*) is found throughout the mainland of New Zealand from lowland to montane habitats, and is generally considered the most shade-tolerant podocarp, with juveniles growing up in the forest understorey. The other member of the *Prumnopitys* genus is matai, which can be tricky to tell apart at first glance, but miro has longer feathery leaves and bright red-pink fruit. Both are members of the Podocarpaceae family, and have a long history in New Zealand.

But the true value of miro was not as food for humans, but in its irresistible lure to kererū. During fruiting season, the birds gorge themselves all morning on the berries, and then spend the rest of the day perched lazily in thc branches digesting their meals. One study looking at kererū diets found the birds could eat up to 100 berries per day, and one individual kererū was responsible for eating over 10,000 miro fruit from a single tree across a fruiting season.[25]

Eating this many miro berries makes kererū incredibly thirsty, an observation that Māori exploited to great effect. In fact, some legends say it was Tāne Mahuta himself who first noticed how the fruit of miro trees would drive kererū to seek water, and realised this knowledge could be used to trap and kill the birds. Fashioning snares from the leaves of harakeke and the cabbage tree, he placed them over nearby streams and waited for the birds to take a drink.

SETTING A TRAP

Following in these prestigious footsteps, Māori used the same methods to trap kererū, concealing the traps in streams by placing fern fronds over them. Where streams were not available, Māori constructed waka kererū — drinking troughs up to 1.5 metres long which were filled with water and placed in or around miro trees. After gorging themselves on the berries, the birds would become thirsty and move to the troughs for a drink. The overlapping snares covered the trough so that the birds could not take a drink without slipping their head through a noose. When they tried to pull away, the noose pulled tight. Bird hunters tended to check these traps every day during a heavy miro-fruiting season, and would sometimes have to come back several times a day to clear out birds when there was a particularly successful haul.

Pākehā hunters also discovered the same trick, and would camp out near miro trees with muskets and rifles in hand. In this way huge hauls of kererū could be captured. Sometimes hunters did not even have to go to this much effort, as the birds would do the work for them. When kererū eat too many overripe berries, the fruit can ferment in their crop, turning to alcohol. In years with bumper crops, drunk kererū are often observed falling out of trees, and the birds are frequently handed into bird rescue centres to sober up in safety.

Miro (*Prumnopitys ferruginea*) by Sarah Featon, c. 1885. (*Te Papa, 1992-0035-2277/64*)

MIRO MARINADE

Kererū caught while feeding on miro were regarded as a delicacy, the strong turpentine flavour of the fruit infusing the flesh of the birds, and this was a prized food to offer up at feasts on the marae. Now that kererū are a protected species, those wanting to partake in this age-old custom have opted for an alternative — stuffing chicken with miro fruit to re-create the effect. According to those in the know, the resulting taste is not as good as the real thing, but pretty close.

Another tasty miro-marinated meat was the flesh of the Polynesian rat, kiore. It was sometimes hunted after it had feasted on miro berries and become infused with their flavour, and miro berries were often used as bait. The berries were placed in pit traps — dug-outs in the ground — to lure the rats to fall in; or several miro fruit might be placed in portable rat traps, such as the tāwhiti makamaka, made of split supplejack. Miro berries are beginning to make in-roads into modern cuisine as well, with a few experimenters starting to trial the berries in their dishes to add a unique and distinctive flavour.

VALUED COMMODITY

Miro often occurs scattered throughout a landscape, and only female trees produce fruit. Forests with a steady supply of fruiting miro were therefore valued very highly and known as whenuapua, fruitful land, providing food for humans, kererū and kiore. Important trees and stands were well known and marked out, and sometimes given individual names.

The name *Prumnopitys* is thought to mean 'plum-fruited pine'. The species name *ferruginea* means 'rust-coloured', from the appearance of the dried herbarium specimens. The name 'brown pine' was used in the early days of European settlement to refer to the colour of the timber. In the Pacific, the words 'milo' and 'miro' are used to describe the rosewood *Thespesia populnea*, which is quite unlike miro in appearance and from an entirely different family, Malvaceae. The other name for the plant, 'toromiro', is also used in Easter Island to refer to a tree rather like our kōwhai, *Sophora toromiro*. While neither of these trees look very much like the New Zealand miro, there may have been other qualities that led to the shared name, perhaps their attractive fruit and leaves or the beautiful timber.

Miropiko pā in Hamilton city was named after a single twisted miro tree at its centre. The tree was a rākau tapu, a sacred and important landmark. So many kererū, huia and bellbirds were caught at this prestigious tree that they could not be eaten at once, and were stored in their own boiled fat for later consumption. Unfortunately, the tree was burned and chopped down to make way for the development of Hamilton city in the late 1860s.

Miro had its uses in timber and is a fine wood, although it is not regarded as highly as mataī or tōtara. In the past, miro was used mainly for building houses, house beams, flooring, weatherboards and furniture. The timber looks like rimu, and has similar properties.

MEDICAL BENEFITS

When the fruit is squeezed, it releases an oil that was used in a similar way to tītoki oil. It was flavoured with various herbs, smeared over the body and used as a massage oil in front of the fire. It was also used to stop wounds bleeding, and is claimed to be a sure-fire cure for warts.

Miro leaves often have a feathery appearance. *(Edin Whitehead)*

The gum that exudes from the trunk and branches has medicinal value as well, and was used as an insecticide and antiseptic. It was applied to tubercular lesions and ulcers, and used by bushmen on chapped hands and feet. The bark was also infused with water; this brew was drunk to treat gonorrhoea and stomach ache, and the steam could be inhaled to treat bronchitis.

TŌTARA

*A wooden warrior that swims
through the ocean*

Tōtara is a giant of the forest, with a massive woody trunk covered in thick, stringy bark. At the end of its branches it holds aloft thousands of sharp needle-like leaves. When the first settlers arrived in Aotearoa, they must have been struck by these spiky leaves, for they called it 'tōtara', the name for the porcupine fish in Polynesia.

For Māori, it was a rākau rangatira — a chiefly tree — and its timber was prized above all others. Tōtara was used to construct houses, tools, weapons, musical instruments and toys. It was the primary wood for carving, as it can be shaped easily using simple stone tools, and carved tōtara are used to adorn marae, houses and waka. The bark flakes off in large sheets, which was useful for constructing containers or wrapping inflated bags of bull kelp (pōhā) to take muttonbirding.

The prestige of tōtara was so great that when an important rangatira passed away it was said that a mighty tōtara had fallen in the forest of Tāne.

WAKA TŌTARA

One way in which tōtara stands supreme among all of the other trees in the forest is in the craft of building waka. Other trees were openly mocked for being inferior to tōtara in this respect:

> *Na wai te puia hinahina i ki hei tu i tuatea moana; tena ra*
> *te wao tōtara mana e tu tuatea moana.*
> Who said that the hinahina [māhoe] should provide vessels
> to brave the ocean surge; when there is the tōtara forest to
> ride the angry billows.[26]

TAXONOMY

Tōtara (*Podocarpus totara*) is common throughout the North and South Islands, occurring from lowland to montane habitats, and sometimes forming pure stands. There are a number of other species in the *Podocarpus* genus in New Zealand, including the needle-leaved tōtara (*P. acutifolius*), the Hall's tōtara (*P. laetum*) and the shrubby snow tōtara (*P. nivalis*). They are all members of the Podocarp family, which includes the other emergent trees of the forest: rimu, kahikatea, matai and miro.

Tōtara makes such excellent waka because it is incredibly durable and long-lasting, but also because it is easy to work and carve. A single tree could be made into a mighty war canoe capable of bearing 100 warriors into battle across the waves. Because of this important role in battle, tōtara was sometimes connected with the war god Tūmatauenga, with tōtara trees referred to as Tū-kau-Moana — Tū that swims through the ocean.

TŌTARA TANIWHA

Tōtara is remarkably resistant to rot, and fallen logs can last for incredible lengths of time. This ability to resist decay means tōtara trunks that are washed downstream often float around in harbours and rivers for a long time. To some Māori, these floating tōtara logs became associated with the legendary taniwha.

In Lake Rotoiti, locals believed that a taniwha had inhabited the trunk of a tōtara log that floated around the lake. It was known as Te Upoko o Huraki Tai — the head of Huraki Tai — and when it appeared near settlements people would go out and recite karakia, and adorn it with feathers, in the hope that they could persuade it not to cause harm.

Another famous tōtara taniwha was called Rangiriri, and lived in the Northern Wairoa River, below Dargaville. It was considered a demon tree, and was often tossed up and down the river in an erratic fashion, appearing to swim against the flow of the river. Its appearance was looked upon by local Ngāti Whātua as a terrible omen. If a kererū or shag were spotted perching on Rangiriri as he floated solemnly down the river, this was interpreted as an evil omen that someone would soon die.

AN ANTIMICROBIAL COMPOUND

The tree's exceptional resistance to decay prompted researchers to investigate the chemistry of tōtara trees. From the strong heartwood of the tree they extracted a chemical compound they named totarol, which has since been found in a number of other species in the podocarp and cypress families. Totarol is an antimicrobial, and has been shown to be effective against nematodes, protozoans, insect larvae, crustaceous marine foulers and a range of different bacteria, including globally significant pathogens such as *Mycobacterium tuberculosis*. Totarol is currently being investigated for its potential as a type of natural food additive, and to find out whether it is effective against antibiotic-resistant bacteria such as methicillin-resistant *Staphylococcus aureus* (MRSA). Currently the main commercial use of totarol is in cosmetics, where it is incorporated in anti-ageing creams and ointments treating dental plaque and acne.

ETYMOLOGY

The name *Podocarpus* literally means 'foot fruit' from the Greek *podos* (foot) and *karpos* (fruit), referring to the fleshy fruit that sits underneath the seed. The specific name *totara* refers to the Māori name tōtara. The word 'tōtara' is likely a reference to the spiky leaves. The word 'tara' in Māori and throughout Polynesia refers to spikes and thorns and spiny things, and 'totara' is a word used across the Pacific to refer to the porcupine fish. The word 'totara' is also found in other spiky things in New Zealand – the puffer fish kōpūtōtara, and the prickly shrub pātōtara (*Leucopogon fraseri*).

A WINDY TREE

Not all of the traditions surrounding tōtara are so noble and prestigious. One amusing tale regarding tōtara serves to explain the curious popping noise it makes when it burns. The story goes that the trees of the forest — tōtara, miro, matāi, rimu and maire — met together and argued about who was the tallest tree. They debated back and forth, each saying that if they stood on their heads and reached skywards they and not the others would win the contest and reach the heavens. Tōtara was the first to try, and while stretching and straining with all his might there was a popping noise as he broke wind. The other trees erupted into laughter, and tōtara left for the depths of the forest to hide his shame. This embarrassing noise can still be heard when the wood is burned, as the timber gives off small crackling and popping noises. Other trees, however, are not immune to similar accidents, and can be heard creaking and groaning when the wind blows.

A HARDY SURVIVOR

Tōtara timber is highly prized by Pākehā as well, and was used for tasks requiring strength and durability, such as in fence posts, floor pilings and railway sleepers. It provided excellent timber for wharf piles, as it resists boring by ship worm.

Tōtara was used medicinally by both Māori and European settlers for a range of ailments. The wood was burned to produce a smoke that could be used in the treatment of haemorrhoids, venereal disease and skin complaints. Bushmen would make an infusion of the bitter leaves for upset stomachs, and the inner bark could be boiled to produce a sweet liquid to treat fevers.

The red flesh of tōtara berries is sweet and edible, and ranks among the best-tasting native fruits.

Today, it is common to see tōtara dotted across farms and paddocks, as the prickly leaves protect it from grazing by stock. Birds such as tūī and kererū assist with its dispersal, allowing it to colonise open pasture. In Northland, the spread of tōtara into farmland is so vigorous that many farmers treat it as a weed. It commonly pops up along fence lines, strangled by wire and fence posts but continuing to fight for survival.

A gnarled old tōtara, reaching out of the canopy towards the sunlight. *(Edin Whitehead)*

RIMU

*A life-saving beer
and a kākāpō aphrodisiac*

The mature rimu tree towers over the canopy with its weeping leaves and shedding bark. If not uprooted by strong winds or felled for timber, it can live to over 1000 years old and grow up to 50 metres tall.

When Pākehā laid eyes on these immense towers of timber, they immediately saw their value as a superior building wood. Rimu quickly became one of the most important materials in the new settler colony of New Zealand, and was often the main wood used for houses and furniture south of the Waikato, where kauri did not grow. Because of extensive logging, however, its range was greatly reduced, and government policies now prevent it from being logged on public land. Speciality items are still made from wood scavenged from stumps and roots of trees felled many years ago, or sourced from sustainably managed forests on private land.

Dacrydium cupressinum by Sydney Parkinson (Te Papa, 1992-0035-2353/1900)

RED PINE DANCERS

The old European name for rimu, 'red pine', has since fallen out of favour, but describes the wood, gum and sap of the tree, which all have a deep red colour. Māori attributed this to the blood of Tunaroa, a giant eel god slain by Māui.

For European sawmill workers this red colouring had very important consequences. It fell to the lowest-paid workers to handle the rimu logs, and these men would have their hands stained red by the end of the week. When it came time for the local Saturday night dance, they were marked out as poorer workers and had trouble impressing the local girls. Some mills found a work-around for this problem by switching to kahikatea logs on the night before a dance, so that the local girls could not tell the difference between the lower- and higher-paid workers.

FIRE TREES

Māori have long valued the wood of the rimu tree, and found a variety of uses for it as tools, waka and weapons. Rimu provided the material to create spears up to 6 metres long, which were thrust through the walls of palisades and into the legs and torsos of invading warriors.

When burned, rimu makes a great firewood. It gives off a peculiar aroma with very little smoke, and was said to drive away evil spirits. On several occasions, the missionary William Colenso observed large living rimu trees being turned into 'fire trees'. A large tree with a hollow was found and it was set alight inside. The fire slowly burned its way up the tree, eating it from the inside out, as smoke poured from the branches. Such trees provided a constant source of fire, so that sticks could be lit from the burning centre at any time.

FRUIT AND BEER

Māori used rimu fruit as a food source, particularly in mast years — when the tree produces a bumper crop. The fruit forms only at the very end of branches, which made harvesting a dangerous task, and serious injuries were common. The fruit has a constipating effect when eaten in large quantities, and a tutu juice was drunk to counteract it.

On his second voyage to New Zealand, Captain Cook noticed the similarity of rimu to the American spruce tree. While anchored in Queen Charlotte Sound, Cook experimented with brewing rimu beer to help prevent scurvy among his crew, and presumably to keep morale high as well. The beverage he created using the bark and leaves of rimu and mānuka was the first beer in New Zealand, and was a great success, well appreciated by all on board. Cook wrote down the recipe, and made another batch when he arrived in New Zealand again years later. A number of other early explorers copied Cook's recipe when they made their travels around the country. Several craft breweries in New Zealand now market genuine 'Captain Cook' spruce beers based on Cook's original recipe.

The now critically endangered kākāpō, as depicted by John Keulemans in 1888. A good crop of rimu fruit is vital for their breeding success. (Alexander Turnbull Library, PUBL-0012-19)

AN APHRODISIAC

Rimu plays an integral role in the mating cycle of the kākāpō — an unusual flightless, nocturnal parrot, and one of the rarest birds in the world. Kākāpō have an intriguing mating system, whereby males dig out small burrows in the ground and use this artificial bowl to help project the sound of their booming calls to as many females as possible. Females, attracted by the noise, can then decide whether it's time to mate.

For most birds, this is almost entirely dictated by the rimu fruit crop. Unripe rimu fruit has been described as kākāpō aphrodisiac, stimulating birds of both sexes into breeding, whereas the ripe fruit contains the perfect combination of nutrients and energy for growing chicks. However, as noted, rimu trees are mast seeders, reserving their fruit resources for long periods before releasing a massive bumper crop of fruit all at once. So kākāpō usually only get one shot at mating every few years. For a species perilously close to the edge of extinction, that means their survival is intimately tied to the fate of the rimu fruit. If temperatures are not suitably warm, the crop will fail, with devastating consequences for the tiny kākāpō breeding population.

ETYMOLOGY

The name *Dacrydium* means 'tears', and may be a reference to the resinous gum that exudes from the tree. The species name *cupressinum* refers to its similarity to cypress trees (*Cupressus* spp.). The word 'rimu' or 'limu' is a generic term in Māori and Polynesian languages for seaweeds, lycopods and mosses. Its use for a tree is rather unusual, therefore, and suggests the name must have been given for the similarity between its leaves and seaweed. It certainly bears a remarkable resemblance to the green seaweed rimurimu (*Caulerpa brownii* and *Caulerpa flexilis*). European settlers gave it the name 'red pine' on account of the red colour of the timber.

THE KAKAPO OR OWL PARROT.
STRINGOPS HABROPTILUS.
(ONE-HALF NATURAL SIZE)

Close-ups of rimu
bark and foliage.
(Edin Whitehead)

Before each season conservation workers scale rimu trees and count the percentage of green fruits on the tips to work out the likelihood of breeding. In the past, conservationists have attempted to boost rimu fruiting frequency by spraying the trees with plant hormones, but the results have been inconclusive. Today, work is focused on developing supplementary diets and pills that mimic the benefits of rimu fruit.

BALMS AND DYES

A decoction of the bark was used to treat wounds, and was also bruised into a pulp and applied to burns, cuts and ulcers. The gum is bitter but edible, and was applied to wounds to stop bleeding, and rubbed on horses' sores to help them heal. It could also be brewed into tea and drunk to stop internal bleeding, stomach aches and headaches.

The bark has been used to make brown, black and blue dyes, and Ngāpuhi would mix soot from burning rimu wood with shark oil to make a black paint for their canoes.

Dacrydium cupressinum
by Sydney Parkinson
(Te Papa, 1992-0035-
2353/1900)

TREES OF THE GODS

The spiritual and symbolic

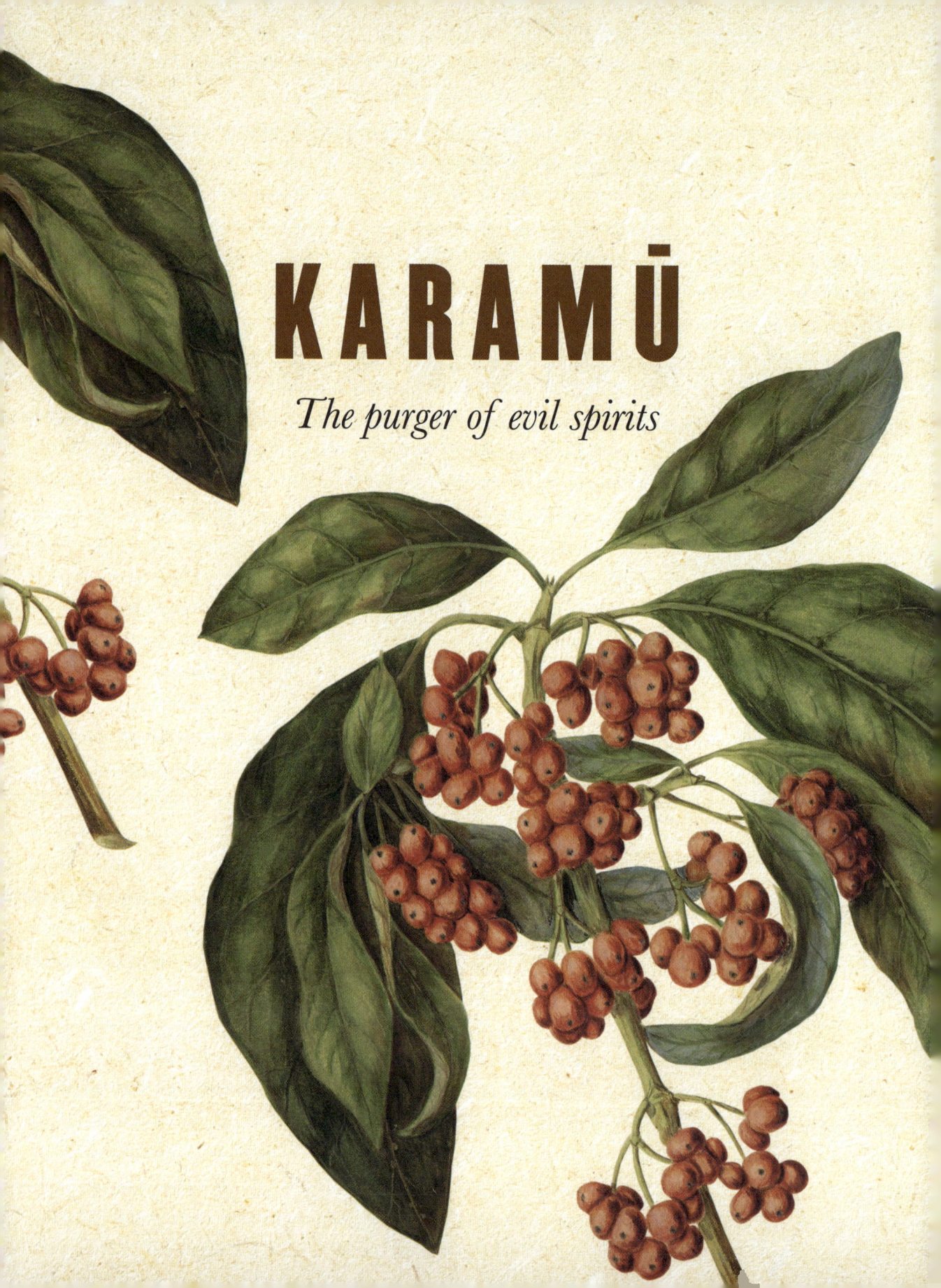

KARAMŪ

The purger of evil spirits

The humble karamū is a rather unassuming plant, with simple green leaves and tiny white flowers. It is only in the summertime that it commands more attention, when it produces bundles of tiny bright orange berries that are eagerly sought after by birds. It is at this time you realise karamū is everywhere, self-seeding in the garden, sprouting up along forest margins, waterways and rivers, and planted in restoration projects and alongside the motorway.

This little tree was highly valued in Māori culture, and was revered as a spiritual tool, used in communication with the gods. Some tohunga were considered so intensely tapu during their work that they could not wear any clothing, except for the leaves of karamū worn as a garland around their head or as an apron around their waist.

The branches were a central feature in many birthing ceremonies, too, helping to cleanse and purify the child for their life ahead. A berry-laden branch of karamū might be laid around a baby boy's head to increase the chances that he would one day become a great warrior; or during the naming of a child, the umbilical cord might be attached to a karamū branch and allowed to drift away in a river. Later in life, when a war party was heading off on an expedition, karamū branches would be dipped in water and sprinkled over the warriors' heads to help combat evil spirits and witchcraft.

Karamū served as a form of medical diagnosis as well. When a sick patient was touched with a karamū branch, it was thought to absorb the essence of the spirit causing the illness. The branch was then carefully taken to a tohunga to diagnose the problem, and to work out which form of tapu had been broken. If it was determined that the illness had been brought about by some malevolent spirit, then the branch was sent downriver carrying the evil force with it, where it was said to travel to *te waha o te parata*, a portal to the underworld. The use of the karamū leaf was symbolic, as some traditions described the figure of death Aituā travelling to Aotearoa and back to the underworld on a waka named *Karamū rauriki* — the little-leaved coprosma.

TAXONOMY

Karamū (*Coprosma robusta*) is found in the North and South islands, and naturalised on the Chatham Islands. It has even become established in Victoria and Tasmania in Australia, and may become a weed there. There are around 45 endemic species of *Coprosma* in New Zealand. Some of the most common large-leaved and easily recognised species are the shining karamū (*C. lucida*), taupata (*C. repens*) and kanono (*C. grandifolia*). Many of the other species in the genus are divaricating shrubs, with tangled, wiry branches. They all belong to the coffee family Rubiaceae, which includes the coffee plants (*Coffea* spp.).

BURIAL TREES

Moriori had a tradition of using karamū in their funeral rites — most probably the Chatham Island karamū *Coprosma chathamica*. The bodies of loved ones would be bound tightly with vines to a grove of small karamū trees, standing upright so they faced the sea. Over time, as the trees grew, the bones became embedded in the wood. When Europeans settled the island, these remains were sometimes discovered as the settlers wandered through the bush or chopped down trees for firewood. Frederick Hunt, an early Pākehā settler on the Chatham Islands, recalled an accidental encounter with one of these funeral groves when cutting down timber:

> A few years since, in sawing across a karamu tree, something offered
> unusual resistance to my saw; to my great astonishment I had sawn
> through the hip bones of a man; he had been lashed against the tree; it
> had grown and enfolded him in its embrace.[27]

The plant was used in medicinal treatments as well. Young shoots and leaves could be boiled and the water drunk for problems with the bladder and kidneys. A vapour bath of the leaves could be used for treating all manner of ailments, from broken bones to cuts, ulcers, wounds and eczema. It also formed a rather unusual treatment for tuberculosis, whereby an infusion of the bark, taken only from the sunny side of the tree, was poured into the ears, nostrils and anus. This boiled bark water was also drunk to ease stomach ache.

THE DUNG PLANT

The Latin name *Coprosma* means 'smells like dung'. The name was given in 1778 by the botanist Johann Forster and his son Georg, the naturalists on Captain Cook's second journey to New Zealand. While travelling through the bush they encountered a plant that 'stank very violently'. This was the stinkwood plant (*Coprosma foetedissima*), the foul odour being the result of methanethiol in the leaves. In modern times it has been known affectionately as the 'fart plant'. The large majority of *Coprosma*, including karamū, do not smell like dung, but this bad egg has given the rest of the genus a bad name.

A large number of plants in the *Coprosma* genus have a divaricating growth form, meaning their branches grow at wide angles, resulting in an interlaced, tangled shrub. New Zealand has a higher proportion of these plants than anywhere else, and it has been suggested that this could be an adaptation against moa browsing. However, divaricating *Coprosma* species are common in coprolites (fossilised dung) of forest moa species, so if this was an adaptation to stop moa browsing it may not have been particularly effective. Intriguingly, in the herbivore gap — the time after moa became extinct but before the widespread introduction of mammalian herbivores — there was a spike in the numbers of divaricating *Coprosma* species at various sites in the country, suggesting that these species were released from browsing pressure after the extinction of the moa.

ETYMOLOGY

The name *Coprosma* means 'dung-smelling', from the Greek *kopros* (dung) and *osme* (smell), and refers to the smell produced by certain species when the leaves are crushed. The species name *robusta* means 'strong' or 'sturdy'. The origin of the Māori name 'karamū' is difficult to piece together; there could perhaps be some connection with the word 'kakara' (scent), but it is not at all clear.

TEA AND COFFEE

Karamū leaves were used to line hāngī and impart flavour to food such as cooked karaka kernels. The leaves sometimes dyed the food yellow, a property that was also employed in dyeing harakeke leaves for weaving.

Karamū was one of the plant leaves used by settlers as a substitute for tea, although getting a decent-tasting brew must have been a fine art, as even with extensive boiling it still tastes rather bland and uninteresting.

The berries of karamū and a number of other *Coprosma* were eaten by Māori, especially children. They have an interesting bitter-sweet taste, and are quite variable from plant to plant. Modern experimentalists have boiled them with sugar and citrus to make sauces.

Karamū berries have also attracted interest for their potential to make coffee, as they belong to the same family as the coffee plant. In 1877, James Crawford believed the seeds of shining karamū and taupata could be the basis for a coffee industry in New Zealand. He grew them in his garden and made ground coffee, which he served to the Wellington Philosophical Society in order to encourage interest. A number of people have attempted to produce karamū coffee over the years, with generally poor results. While the resulting brew has a familiar coffee smell, and the taste is in the general coffee ballpark, it hardly seems worth the trouble of extracting the tiny seeds from the small, sticky fruit.

Karamū leaves have been used for tea, while the edible berries have been added to sauces and used to make a kind of coffee. (Matthew Cattin)

PŪRIRI

*The ironwood tree that
laughs at death*

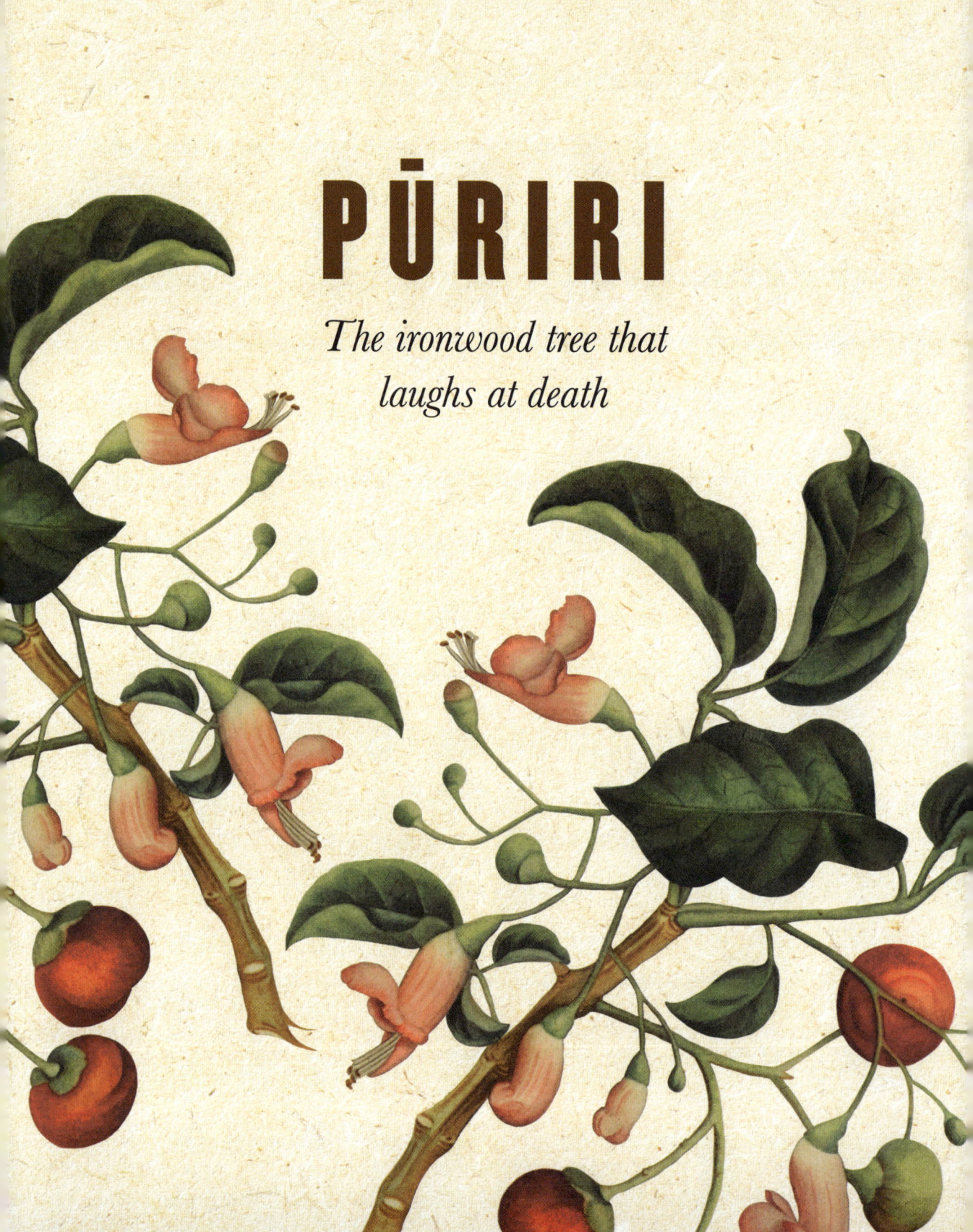

There are pūriri alive today that were already ancient when the first humans set foot on New Zealand. Some may even be older than the oldest kauri trees, as they have a remarkable stubbornness when it comes to death. Pūriri can be found uprooted, grazed by stock, cut in half, rotten to the core and yet still producing new shoots.

It is not surprising that for such a stubborn old tree, the wood of pūriri is one of the strongest in New Zealand, and is incredibly heavy and dense. Although it can be difficult to work with, it was a useful and durable timber, described as the New Zealand equivalent of teak or mahogany. It was used by early colonists for buildings, framings, bridges, ships, railway sleepers, firewood, foundation blocks, poles, fence posts, gears and engine bearings. The wood was so tough that staples to attach fencing wire struggled to penetrate it, and a special 'pūriri staple' had to be developed. Some referred to it as the 'ironwood', as it was so strong that it would blunt any axe that tried to hack it down. There are still pūriri fence posts today that are nearly 100 years old, and in Northland there are water pumps that still run on pūriri bearings.

Pūriri (*Vitex lucens*) by Fanny Osborne. (*Auckland War Memorial Museum, CCBY*)

ROBUST PROTECTION

Māori used pūriri timber to make garden tools and weapons. The strength of the wood made it useful for splitting other softer timbers, and it was a good material for constructing fish and eel traps, as it was one of the only native timbers that would sink.

The rich pūriri groves of Northland provided much of the material for building the famous pā of the northern wars. It has been said that when these palisade walls were fired upon, shotgun shells would ricochet off the dense wood rather than lodge within it. At the battle of Ōhaeawai, Kawiti and Hōne Heke built a flimsy outer wall covered in matted flax as a decoy to hide the true strength of the inner walls of the pā. This was constructed out of great trunks of pūriri, and known as *kiri-tangata*, the warrior's skin. For over a week the largest British force amassed in New Zealand at that time bombarded the pā with cannons and musket fire. Thinking that the Māori forces must be broken, the British led a frontal assault on the pā, and were mowed down by bullets as the mostly unharmed Māori warriors unleashed a volley of musket fire.

Pūriri is generally associated with fertile or volcanic soil, which was highly sought after by Europeans for pasture and cropland. As a result, it was extensively milled, cleared and burned. Today, the image of a lonely, gnarled pūriri in the middle of a paddock has become iconic of the species. However, this may be something of an artefact of selective logging. Because only the best and straightest trees were logged, many of the ones that remain today are those that were passed over for being particularly twisted and distorted.

Pūriri is one of the few New Zealand trees with colourful flowers, which provide a year-round food source for birds. *(Jacqui Geux)*

CEREMONIAL TREE

To many tribes the tree was deeply sacred and associated with mourning and the burial of the dead, a connection that still lives on in some places today. After the death of a chief or a person of high mana, the body would be adorned with a coronet of pūriri leaves, and washed with an infusion of the leaves and water. The body was left to decompose, after which a ritual scraping ceremony was performed and the bones were entombed in the hollow of a pūriri.

ETYMOLOGY

The name *Vitex* means 'to weave or bind', and was said to have been given to the genus on account of the twigs of some plants being used for basket-making, although pūriri does not share this characteristic. The species name *lucens* means 'shining', a reference to how the wavy green leaves shine in the light. The name 'pūriri' appears to be endemic to Aotearoa. It does have an alternate name 'kauere', which possibly contains a tenuous link to 'auere' (*Grewia crenata*) in Rarotonga. Europeans called it the New Zealand oak, teak and mahogany on account of its strong, beautiful timber.

Taketakerau — a giant burial tree in Ōpōtiki — is estimated to be around 2000 years old, and served as an important burial site for local Upokorehe hapū. The tree was considered highly sacred, and interference with it was a religious offence punishable by death. During the early phase of European settlement, a storm damaged the tree and exhumed the bones, forcing the local hapū to remove them for reburial.

Occasionally hunters, farmers and trampers have stumbled across these old remains in pūriri hollows while out in the bush, and pūriri are still sometimes used as a burial place for kōiwi — human remains — today.

A SYMBOL OF JOY

Despite this deep association with death, the pūriri is also considered a symbol of joy at being alive. *Ka kata ngā pūriri ō Taiamai* is a Ngāpuhi proverb that was used as a greeting, congratulation or when honouring a guest. Translated, its meaning is 'the pūriri trees of Taiamai are laughing', Taiamai being a region in the Bay of Islands in the north of the country with fertile soils and abundant food. It represented a delight and happiness that Nature was content and all was well with the world. Another interpretation, however, says that it was actually a lament by the defeated Ngāti Pou, after they had been evicted from their lands around Taiamai by Ngāpuhi. As they made their bitter exodus, they saw Ngāpuhi fires on their homeland and heard the sound of burning pūriri timber sputtering and laughing in the wind.

Infusions made with pūriri leaves were used by Māori to treat backache, joint pain, ulcers, sore throats and sprains. *(Robert Vennell)*

A male pūriri moth, *Aenetus virescens.* *(Landcare Research, CCBY)*

PŪRIRI MOTH

Pūriri is an important source of food for birds, and is commonly used in restoration planting, as it produces striking purple-pink flowers and squishy pink fruit year-round. The fruit was not known to be a food source for Māori or Europeans, and is very bitter and unappetising. Pūriri also serves as the main home for New Zealand's largest moth, the pūriri moth (*Aenetus virescens*). The young caterpillar burrows into the trunk and lives off the tree's sap. After around seven years it pupates into a moth, and flies off to find a mate.

At this stage it was regarded by Māori as a type of ghost, and thought to serve as a spiritual messenger. The moth leaves marks in the wood, which could be a problem for timber workers, but sometimes these markings are somewhat decorative and can add to the piece. A commonly heard whakataukī refers to how the little larvae (mokoroa) burrow into wood and can cause even the great pūriri trees to fall, suggesting that even the smallest enemy is deserving of fear and respect.

PONGA

*An enduring symbol
that points the way home*

Cyathea fern by Walter Hood Fitch, 1853. (Biodiversity Heritage Library)

Ponga, or silver fern, is perhaps the most ubiquitous symbol in New Zealand. No other icon is more commonly used to identify New Zealand here and to the world. Ponga fronds are found on the country's coat of arms, notes and coins, on dairy products, airplanes, company logos, tattoos and tobacco. The silver fern is the dominant symbol of almost all of our major sports teams: men's and women's rugby, netball, basketball, hockey, sailing and the Olympics. Government departments and political parties use the fern in their logos, and Tourism New Zealand uses it to market the country's brand overseas. In a recent referendum, it very nearly became the national flag of New Zealand, but was narrowly rejected.

The unfurling koru of the fern frond is a similarly powerful symbol, which could almost rival the outstretched fern for its dominance in daily life. The unfurling frond embodies new life and growth, and its spiralling motif symbolises perpetual movement and a return to the point of origin. It is a particularly important symbol in Te Ao Māori, and is used in the design of carvings, marae, tā moko and artwork. It forms the central pattern of the Tino Rangatiratanga flag, which was chosen as the symbol of Māori protest and self-government in New Zealand.

A DISTINCTIVE PATTERN

Exactly why the silver fern has become so deeply embedded in the national psyche is hard to pinpoint. New Zealand has an unusually high number of fern species, with a wide variety occurring nowhere else in the world. And the silver fern symbol does seem to capture something of New Zealand's unique, wild and natural quality. But perhaps

Ponga belong to the scaly tree fern family and the unfurling fronds are covered in brown scales. *(Jacqui Geux)*

The pale underside of the fern – one of the most famous symbols of New Zealand identity. *(Brian Gratwicke, CCBY)*

more important is simply its long history. The fronds were first used as a national symbol by New Zealand rugby teams playing overseas in the late 1880s, and soon were being placed on dairy and butter products sold to Britain. During the South African War, New Zealand troops serving overseas for the very first time wore silver fern badges to identify themselves. By the First World War, the silver fern was the dominant badge of the New Zealand army and was carved on the gravestones of fallen soldiers.

Perhaps another reason why ponga was seized on as such an identifiable symbol is that it is immediately distinctive in the New Zealand forest. When the fronds are turned over, a white underside is exposed, which marks it out from any other species in New Zealand. Although called a 'silver' fern, it is actually very rarely silver, but fronds can occasionally be found with a silver hue.

These pale white fronds glow brightly in the moonlight, and have been an invaluable tool to help those travelling in the bush find their way home. When out catching birds at night, Māori hunters would lay out fern fronds on the track that they could follow on their return. Today, bush guides recommend the same trick as a survival tool if you have lost your way in the forest.

ETYMOLOGY

Cyathea means 'little cup', and comes from the Greek word *kyathos*, meaning 'wine ladle'. It refers to the shape of the indusium, the covering that contains the spores. The species name *dealbata* means 'whitish', referring to the distinct white undersides of the fronds. The word 'ponga' is used widely across the Pacific as a general term for tree ferns and large ferns. The name 'punga' is a European corruption of the word 'ponga', and the name 'silver fern' refers to the white and occasionally silver underside of the unfurled fronds.

THE PUNGA LOG

The log of the punga — a corruption of the Māori name 'ponga' — has also become something of a symbol of New Zealand, and is commonly associated with hard work and a do-it-yourself mentality. Punga logs are frequently used in landscaping for fence posts, retaining walls and edging for gardens. Some gardeners use the logs to create living green walls, with other plants growing out of them.

Māori also found many uses for these logs in building walls, forts and whare. The trunk of ponga was used for carving into a variety of shapes, and the rough, fibrous material provided a form of simple sandpaper for polishing tools. This black woody fibre of the log is actually poisonous, and Māori used this knowledge in the art of war.

Throwing spears — kōtaha — were constructed using lengths of wood tipped with sharp ponga fibres about the length of a man's thumb. A cut was made around the ponga tip, so that once it pierced an enemy's body it would break off at the cut, leaving the poisonous tip embedded in the flesh and causing a foul and festering wound.

Unlike the closely related mamaku, the pith inside the ponga trunk cannot be eaten. Johann Forster, the naturalist on board Captain Cook's second voyage, found out the hard way. The crew had observed local Māori boil mamaku trunks and eat the white inner pulp, so Forster eagerly acquired some fern trunks for himself, but collected ponga by mistake, and found it was completely inedible. This white pith did, however, have its uses, as Māori used it medicinally as a soothing lotion for preventing infection. The pith was bruised, steeped in water and applied to running sores, ulcers, tired eyes and even sweaty feet.

There are a number of edible ferns in the New Zealand bush, but ponga is certainly not one of them. *(Edin Whitehead)*

RANGIORA

*A bushman's friend when
nature calls*

Rangiora is a daisy that has grown into a tree. It sprouts giant papery leaves covered in smooth white hairs, and its newly growing shoots are covered in brown felt like the velvet on the antlers of a deer. In early spring it produces bunches of creamy-white fragrant flowers, which can often be smelled while walking along a forest path.

It is an incredibly useful plant to know about, as the soft paper-like leaves make a reliable emergency toilet paper. However, it is far better to collect leaves in advance, as rangiora is always mysteriously absent when it is needed most. Early bushmen relied on rangiora leaves for this purpose when travelling the countryside, and consequently gave it the endearing name 'bushman's friend'.

The white underside of the leaves makes it a good track marker, and it was used by Māori in a similar way to ponga: they laid the underside of the leaves face-up on a track to help them find their way home in the forest.

These leaves may have an antiseptic quality, as they were wrapped around wounds and sores to keep dust and flies away. They also make a surprisingly good substitute for notepaper, and children have been known to draw on them. A number of *Brachyglottis* species were used as letter paper, and there was even a trend of posting rangiora leaves through the mail until the postal service threatened to dispose of them.

Warangi (Rangiora)
by Martha King, 1842.
(*Alexander Turnbull
Library, A-005-017*)

THE LIVING SKY

The name 'rangiora' translates as 'rangi' (sky) and 'ora' (health or alive). For Māori, rangiora was a symbol of health and the living, and contrasted with kawakawa, which was often a symbol of death. This is demonstrated by a traditional dance song that was occasionally performed at tangi to contrast the two plants. The first group would emerge wearing crowns of kawakawa, the symbol of death, then those wearing rangiora would walk forward with its leaves, singing:

> *He aha te tohu mo te ora?*
> *He Rangiora!*
> *E tuku ki runga kia ora,*
> *E, kia arahia!*

What is the emblem of the living?
It is Rangiora!
Lift it up, so all is well,
Oh, lift it up![28]

It featured in haka as well. During the New Zealand Wars of the 1860s, a group of Māori warriors composed a haka targeted at Governor George Grey, comparing him to a cow that eats up rangiora leaves. The metaphor becomes more significant when it is considered that rangiora was a symbol of life and wellness in the world, and that the greedy governor was gobbling up this life force of the Māori people.

Rangiora was a symbol of life and health, and was sometimes worn during tangi to symbolise the living. *(Jacqui Geux)*

A POISONOUS CHEWING GUM

Although rangiora was a symbol of life, it may have the power to take it as well. The entire plant is poisonous, and stock have become poisoned from browsing its leaves. Interestingly, the gum that exudes from the bark was a favoured source of chewing gum for Māori, useful in freshening the breath after a pungent meal of shark or eels. It was stored with water to keep it fresh and soft, and was kept for a long time and shared between friends. It is possible Māori knew of some way to treat the gum and make it safe to eat, or just that they ate very carefully, aware of the consequences if the gum was accidentally swallowed. In the 1940s two schoolchildren became sick after eating the gum.

The gum could also be heated to make a fragrant oil, and was collected in pāua shells and then rubbed over fish hooks to preserve them and keep them from rusting. Despite their poisonous content, the leaves were also commonly used in cooking, to wrap hīnau cakes, aruhe, eels, kiore and mushrooms.

Rangiora was once used as chewing gum, but it is poisonous if swallowed.
(Jacqui Geux)

RANGIORA PLANES

The broad, flat leaves were used to make a type of 'paper' aeroplane, known as a 'topa', with a long piece of grass or reed inserted at the end to act as a counterbalance. The craft was then launched forwards, and, if done right, it could fly for a long distance with a slow, gradual descent. Māori children would attempt to fly the craft to the opposite bank of a river, and the games could become quite competitive.

But rangiora aeroplanes were not only for children. They could be used in the art of love, serving as a type of charm. The thrower called on the leaf to fly to the person they would fall in love with, and then sent it among a crowd of hopefuls. It was also used as a way of divining the future. Before the onset of war, a rangiora leaf might be sent into the air while karakia were recited. If it sailed well, it was a good omen, but if it turned and fell short, it spelled certain defeat.

ETYMOLOGY

Brachyglottis means 'short tongue' and describes the relatively small size of the ray florets. The species name *repanda* means 'undulating margins', a reference to the edges of the leaves. The name 'rangiora' is a unique plant name that appears to have evolved in Aotearoa. It is composed from the Māori words 'rangi' (sky) and 'ora' (living or health). The other name for rangiora is 'pukapuka', the same word used for paper and books. It is not clear whether books were deliberately named after rangiora, or whether this was a happy coincidence. The other name for rangiora is 'whārangi', which means 'spread out', and relates to the broad leaves. Whārangi is also the word for a page of a book.

TĪTOKI

Prized for its chiefly oil

Tītoki is a familiar plant to many of us, as it is one of the most popular choices for street planting, with its glossy leaves, twisting trunk, smooth, dark bark and attractive spreading canopy. But certainly the show-stopper has to be the fruit, which bursts forth from the hairy brown capsules to reveal a dazzling raspberry-red berry and shiny jet-black seed.

Unfortunately, the tantalising berries are far more appealing to the eye than the tongue, and are rather tart, dry and uninteresting. They were not an important food supply for Māori, although they were eaten by children, and occasionally adults when better food was unavailable. If a woman suddenly began eating tūtoki berries out of the blue, then it was interpreted as a sure sign that she was looking for a lover. Today, the berries are used to develop a liqueur that has been used for desserts and cocktails and is sold in New Zealand and overseas.

The titoki. A forest-tree by Martha King, 1842. (Alexander Turnbull Library, PUBL-0011-13-1)

THE BEAUTY OIL

Far more important than the berry was the attractive black seed. The fruit would be collected in baskets, softened with water, and trampled underfoot to separate out the flesh. The prized seeds were washed to remove any remaining flesh, and crushed and beaten. They were then placed in a plaited bag of flax filled with hot stones. At each end, long rods were twisted around and around, as when wringing out a wet towel. Slowly, due to the immense heat and pressure, a rich dark-green oil was squeezed out of the seeds and began to trickle down into a bowl or bag waiting below.

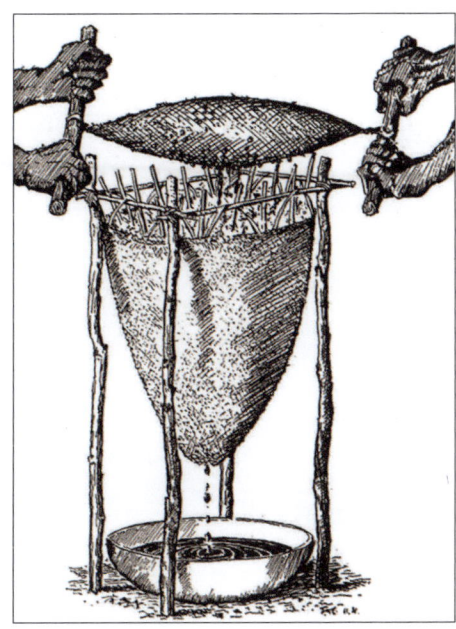

The process of extracting titoki oil could be long and tedious. The seeds were heated and wrung out in flax bags like this one. *(New Zealand Electronic Text Collection, CCBY)*

This green liquid — hinu tītoki — was perhaps the finest oil product available to Māori prior to the arrival of Europeans, and was a traditional cosmetic used for beautifying the body. It could be used as a luxurious hair oil, or mixed with red ochre and smeared over the body. This had a dual benefit: the colour red was venerated as a sign of mana and royalty, and the oil also helped ward off sandflies. Hinu tītoki took the scent of fragrant plants well, which made it a great base for making perfumes. It could be steeped in the leaves, flowers or gum of sweet-smelling plants such as tarata, raukawa and mairehau. It was then placed in a small wooden vessel or soaked in a ball of bird skin and suspended around the neck.

STATUS SYMBOL

This beauty oil was held in very high regard and seen as a major status symbol, in part due to its scarcity. As well as the laborious process required to prepare it, huge numbers of seeds were needed to produce a small amount of oil. Tītoki often occurs sparsely throughout the forest, so there was often not enough oil to go around, and it was generally reserved for rangatira and their immediate family. However, every few years tītoki produces a bumper crop, allowing large amounts of oil to be made. In these years, commoners could share in the bounty, which led to the expression 'a chief of the tītoki season'. This was a chance for the lowest members of society to adorn themselves in red ochre and tītoki oil and feel like they were rangatira, at least for as long as the season lasted.

ETYMOLOGY

In Greek mythology, Alectryon was the name of a young soldier who was tasked with guarding the door while Ares carried out a love affair with Aphrodite. The soldier fell asleep on the job, and the enraged Ares turned him into a rooster. *Alectryon* was chosen as the name of the genus because the aril – the fleshy red part of the fruit – resembles the cockscomb of a rooster. The species name *excelsus* means 'tall', 'elevated' or 'lofty'. The name 'tītoki' is thought to be a relative of the Polynesian word 'taputoki'. This name is given to trees in the genera *Cupaniopsis* and *Alectryon*, which belong to the same family as tītoki and have very hard wood. The word 'toki' in both Māori and Polynesian languages means 'adze', and all of these trees have been used for making adze handles for stone or pounamu blades.

Tītoki oil was a major status symbol in traditional Māori society, as finding enough berries to make it was difficult. *(Jacqui Geux)*

The ripe red fruit of tītoki is eaten by many birds. Here it is depicted with a pair of extinct huia (*Heteralocha acutirostris*) in a painting by John Keulemans, 1888. (*Alexander Turnbull Library, PUBL-0012-02*)

THE MEDICINE OIL

The oil was also used medicinally, and applied to wounds, sores, skin diseases, sore breasts, bruises and painful joints. If someone had a strain in their back, they might lie down beside the fire to have a standing massage, where someone would stand on their back, digging their feet in and using tītoki as a massage oil to rub into sore muscles.

As well as warding away sandflies, the oil was said to help reduce the sting associated with insect bites. For babies who developed sores under their arms and legs when in the crib, the silky down of kahakaha could be soaked in tītoki oil and gently dabbed on the affected area.

The oil was also used on inflamed eyes and placed in the ear to cure earache, and small amounts were drunk to help move the bowels after eating too much fern root or constipating fruit.

THE LUBRICATING OIL

The oil was used by Pākehā settlers as well, especially in the early days of settlement when other oils were not commonly available. It was used in machinery work such as watch-making, and even sent back to England for this purpose. However, once the whaling trade became firmly established in New Zealand, there was ample supply of whale oil, hair oils and fats, which were much easier to procure than tītoki oil.

Pākehā settlers also prized the excellent timber tītoki produces, calling it the New Zealand ash or New Zealand oak. The wood takes a polish well, and was used for tasks requiring strength and elasticity, such as building coaches and cabinets.

WHAU

*An unsinkable floater
with floppy leaves*

Whau is a distinctive sight in the New Zealand forest, with its large, floppy, heart-shaped leaves and spiky bommy-knocker seeds. It would have looked immediately familiar to the Polynesians who first settled in New Zealand, as its tropical leaves resemble aute, which they brought with them and used to make tapa cloth.

In one tradition from Tainui, whau was believed to be a mutant form of aute. The captain's wife, Marama, had an affair with a slave on the voyage, and, because of this terrible deed, the seed plants she brought to New Zealand were cursed: her kūmara became *Convolvulus*, her gourd plants became the native cucumber māwhai, and her aute plants all turned into whau.

There are even some traditions which point to a friendly rivalry between the two plants. In this dialogue recorded by the Reverend Richard Taylor, whau and aute bicker about their roles, mocking each other for the ways in which they are used by humans:

> *Whau: Hei kona koe, tu ai hei parepare.*
> Whau: Here you are decking a woman's head.
> *Aute: Haere koe ki te moana hei whau kupenga, ka mutu hei pouto kupenga.*
> Aute: Go you to sea to make the net float, and when the fishing is over remain attached to it.[29]

TAXONOMY

Whau (*Entelea arborescens*) is the only species of *Entelea* in the world. It belongs to the mallow family, Malvaceae, which includes mallow, hibiscus and some plants of world economic importance, such as cacao, cotton and durian. In New Zealand it includes natives such as hibiscus (*Hibiscus diversifolius*), houhere (*Hoheria* spp.) and ribbonwood (*Plagianthus* spp.).

STAYING AFLOAT

Whau, however, excelled in its role as a net float. It produces one of the lightest woods in the world, and is even less dense than cork. Its most common use was as floats for fishing nets and marker buoys. Some accounts from early European explorers describe nets that are nearly 2 kilometres long. All along the top edge of the net were sections of whau wood, to keep the net floating above the water, while the bottom half was weighted with large rocks, and could be around 10 metres deep. These vast nets were carried out with waka and used to catch shoals of fish and pull them to shore. Then all of the fish would be distributed among the families who had helped construct the net. European explorers used similar nets with cork floats as they travelled around New Zealand, and frequently commented that the Māori design was far superior. Whau trunks could also be lashed together with supplejack to construct small rafts for hunting crayfish.

The plant was of such value to Māori that it was actively cultivated in some places. The Māori name of Auckland's iconic Mt Eden is Maungawhau, 'the mountain of the whau tree', and in the past its slopes must have been covered in whau, providing a constant supply of float material. The islands of the Hauraki Gulf were known as Ngā Pōito ō te Kupenga ō Toi te Huatahi, the floats in the fishing net of Toi te Huatahi, an early explorer in the region. Māori must have visualised these islands as great whau tree floats in a vast net across the gulf.

Whau also found its way into symbolism and oratory. The following quote is attributed to Mohi Tāwhai, one of the Ngāpuhi signatories to the Treaty of Waitangi. Tāwhai uses the poetic imagery of the light whau wood in a remarkably prescient statement about the nature of the proposed treaty:

> Let the tongue of every one be free to speak; but what of it? What will be the end? Our sayings will sink to the bottom like a stone, but your sayings will float light, like the wood of the Whau-tree, and always remain to be seen.[30]

ETYMOLOGY

The generic name *Entelea* means 'perfect', which in botanical language means that both male and female reproductive organs can be found on the same flower. The species name *arborescens* means 'becoming a tree'. The common name, New Zealand mulberry, recognises its similarity to aute, the paper mulberry. Whau was also known as 'corkwood' on account of its light wood. The name 'whau' most likely derives from the word 'fau', which throughout Polynesia is the name for the beach hibiscus (*Hibiscus tiliaceus*). Fau also possesses very light wood, and was used in the construction of boats and floats.

Whau's large floppy leaves, bright white flowers and spiky seeds make it instantly recognisable in the forest. (*Edin Whitehead*)

RAPID GROWER

Whau is a true pioneer species. When a gap opens in the forest, it pops up instantaneously, thriving in the high, light environment. It races through its life cycle before succumbing to old age after around 10 years of age, or once the trees around it shade it out. It does this by flooding the environment with long-lived seeds. These lie dormant in the soil, waiting for the opportune moment to breach the surface and begin the next mad dash to reproduction. As with many of New Zealand's plants, the large, floppy leaves are eagerly consumed by browsing mammals, and this may be why whau is less common than it once was.

Whau sprints through life, rapidly reaching reproductive age and spreading seed though the environment. *(Jacqui Geux)*

TRAVELLER
BEWARE

Climbers, stickers and stingers

BUSH LAWYER

A prickly pest that
won't let go

Bush lawyer is New Zealand's answer to blackberry, a scrambling, thorny climber studded with sharp, backwards-curving hooks. Unlike blackberry, however, bush lawyer can be found in the middle of the forest, where it snares unsuspecting trampers in dense, spiky tangles. Once it grabs hold of you, it is difficult to get free — presumably the rationale behind its quirky English name. Due to the shape of the hooks, pushing through a tangle of bush lawyer only makes things worse, and often the only way forward is to stop and patiently unpick the thorns from clothing and skin.

Māori were very familiar with the trials and tribulations of running through a mass of bush lawyer, tātarāmoa. It was one of the plants said to have been laid down by Kupe as an obstacle to prevent the husbands whose wives he had stolen from catching up with him.

The white flowers of bush lawyer bear a strong resemblance to their close cousin the introduced blackberry. (Jacqui Geux)

A PRACTICAL PLANT

The hooks of bush lawyer did not originally evolve for the purpose of snaring unsuspecting hikers or slowing down angry husbands. Their actual purpose is to hook onto trees and allow bush lawyer to climb into the canopy to reach the light. The young plants are quite robust and can grow straight up for about 60 centimetres, but if they are unable to find a tree to latch on to they bend back down to the forest floor. They then spread out, hunting for trees and shrubs that they can climb to reach the light. Older bush lawyers that have become established in the treetops grow thick, woody vines that can easily be mistaken for tree trunks.

Despite the anguish it causes, bush lawyer has proved itself a useful and practical plant. The berries can be eaten raw, and were a favourite of Māori children. It played a useful role in rongoā as well, with the bark and leaves being used in a number of herbal remedies. Infusions of the leaves were drunk to combat sore throats, chest complaints, stomach aches, diarrhoea and painful menstruation. A vapour bath of the leaves and roots was used as a cleansing remedy after childbirth to assist with removal of the placenta.

Pākehā were quick to spot the resemblance of bush lawyer to its cousin the wild blackberry, and they used the fruit in similar ways, making it into stews, preserves and jams. Sometimes the tartness is a little too much for some, especially when compared with the sweet fruit of its cousin. But it can still make a pleasant dish, especially when plenty of sugar is added. The large, thick vines of older plants can be cut and drained to produce a juice-like beverage, a valuable source of liquid in a survival situation.

TAXONOMY

The name 'bush lawyer' can refer to a number of native 'lawyers' in the genus *Rubus*. Perhaps most common is *R. cissoides*, which is found in scrub, forest and bush margins throughout the country. There are also the swamp lawyer (*R. australis*), the creeping lawyer (*R. parvus*) and the white-leaved lawyer (*R. schmidelioides*). Overseas *Rubus* species include blackberry (*R. fruticosus*) and raspberry (*R. idaeus*). Bush lawyer belongs to the rose family, Rosaceae, which includes the roses, as well as many important food plants, such as apples, pears, peaches, apricots, plums and strawberries.

The spiky leaves are studded with sharp hooks used for ascending into the forest canopy to reach the light. *(Josie Galbraith)*

Bush lawyer fruit was added to stews and jams and infusions of the leaves were used to treat a variety of health complaints. *(Josie Galbraith)*

ETYMOLOGY

The name *Rubus* is the Latin word for 'blackberry'. The species name *cissoides* means 'resembling *Cissus*', a genus of woody vines in the grape family. The word 'tātarāmoa' is used in some form or another across the Pacific to describe plants from the *Caesalpinia* genus. This is a different plant altogether, but it has a very spiky fruit, which is probably the connection. The Polynesian meaning of the name is said to refer to the spurs on the foot of roosters – *tara* (spike) and *moa* (chicken). The name 'moa' was later transferred onto the giant flightless birds of New Zealand. Other native spiky plants include 'tara' in their name, notably tōtara and taramea.

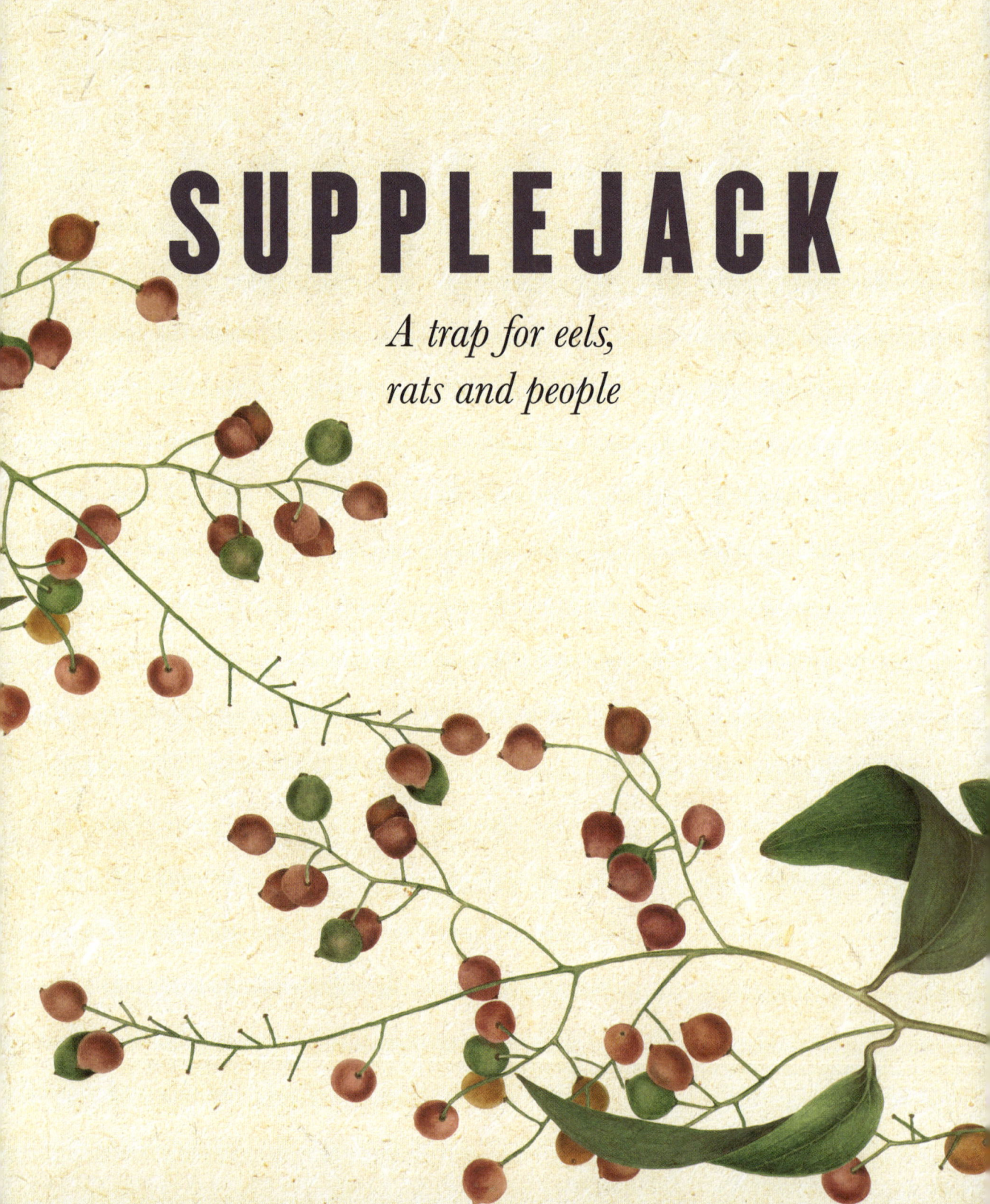

SUPPLEJACK

A trap for eels,
rats and people

The thick, black, scrambling vines of supplejack are a distinctive feature of the New Zealand forest. In Māori tradition, the vines were known as 'pirita' or 'kareao', and grew from the tail of the monstrous eel god, Tunaroa. When Māui's wife, Raukura, was gathering water from a stream, Tunaroa knocked her over with his giant tail and insulted her. In revenge, Māui ambushed Tunaroa, digging a trench for him to follow and then catching him and hacking him to pieces with his axe. The blood of Tunaroa was spattered across birds such as pūkeko and kākāriki, and plants such as rimu, tōtara and matai, giving them their distinctive red colouring. Tunaroa's dismembered head was thrown into the sea to give rise to marine eels, while the tail gave rise to the freshwater eels. The very tip of the tail took root in the forest to become the supplejack vine, which from then on was used to construct eel traps, to catch the children of Tunaroa. Māui's example is a good guide to catching eels: dig trenches, steer them into shallow water then construct traps for them with supplejack vines.

TAXONOMY

Supplejack (*Ripogonum scandens*) is found in all types of forest throughout New Zealand, from the coast to the mountains. It has no other relatives in New Zealand, but several *Ripogonum* species exist in Australia and New Guinea. Until recently they were thought to belong to the Smilacaceae family, but they were recently reclassified as the only genus of the Ripogonaceae family.

Fruit of the supplejack, *Ripogonum scandens*, by Martha King, 1842. (Alexander Turnbull Library, A-005-034)

A WALL OF VINES

Ever since these legendary times, supplejack has proven something of a trap for people as well. Dense thickets of supplejack provide an almost impenetrable barrier to moving about in the bush. Anyone who is familiar with tramping off-track in New Zealand forest is likely to be familiar with the peculiar form of bush yoga that is required to navigate through the tangled vines. Some Māori believed that these dense walls of supplejack were created by the magical patupaiarehe, or fairy folk, who weaved fortifications to keep people out of their misty forest homes.

The trials of contending with supplejack were recounted by the first Europeans to explore New Zealand on foot. While anchored in Dusky Sound, Captain James Cook wrote in his journal:

> In many parts the woods are so over-run with supplejacks, that it is scarcely possible to force one's way amongst them. I have seen several which were fifty or sixty fathoms long.[31]

Ever since, the plant has provided a barrier to all kinds of explorers, settlers and soldiers. One early Nelson settler surveying land for the New Zealand Company compared weaving through a supplejack forest to a blowfly trying to move through a tangled hairbrush.

The long vines were also the cause of a number of accidents and deaths in the early days of settlement. There are tales from the timber industry of men attempting to flee from falling trunks and rolling logs, only to be tripped up by a length of supplejack and crushed. Wayward supplejack vines have sent people plummeting to their deaths off the edges of cliffs, and one missing goldminer was eventually found strangled by supplejack in a gully.

Despite the anguish it causes, supplejack can occasionally be of assistance when clambering about in the forest. The famous Pākehā explorers Thomas Brunner and Charles Heaphy used the vines to abseil down perilous cliff faces and precipices when making their famous trip around the north-west of the South Island. More recently, the survival expert Bear Grylls used supplejack to descend a cascading 37-metre waterfall while demonstrating survival techniques in the New Zealand forest.[32]

A TERROR OF THE BUSH

Supplejack was to play a decisive role in the New Zealand Wars of the 19th century. For Māori, supplejack was an advantage, as it allowed them to bind together palisade walls and rescue wounded warriors from the battlefield by looping vines around their ankles and dragging them to safety. The broken stems were applied to cuts and grazes, and are said to have astringent properties that stop bleeding. For larger wounds, a piece of dry supplejack was ignited and burned near the cut to cauterise the wound.

In contrast, the colonial forces had to fight a double war against Māori and supplejack. Heavily clad infantry were frequently held up by the plant catching their bulky packs and bayonets, and strategic manoeuvres were often critically delayed by this slow progress. This led many British soldiers to develop an intense fear of the bush. One soldier recounted during the Taranaki wars that his platoon would retreat in the face of even the smallest bush fragment:

> I can only suppose that we were scared by the terrors of the bush in front of us, to the extent of losing our reasoning faculties. It is the trees which fight the battles for the natives, and the very sight of a supplejack insures us a whipping …[33]

It was in large part as a result of supplejack, as well as the tough terrain of the New Zealand bush, that the British army created an elite corps of 'Forest Rangers' — the forerunners of today's Special Operations Forces. These lightly trained bushmen were equipped with short knives, small packs and revolvers, and were trained in tramping off-track, weaving through supplejack vines, and firing off rounds as they ducked behind trees.

STRONG AND PLIABLE

Even though it can be a nuisance, supplejack has proved itself an incredibly useful and practical plant as well. It was a valued

A tangle of supplejack vines was a terrifying sight for colonial soldiers fighting battles in the bush.
(Edin Whitehead)

medicinal plant for Māori, with an infusion of the root being used to treat blood disorders, skin diseases, rheumatism, fever, bowel complaints, sexually transmitted diseases and heavy menstrual flow. There are even some reports that the decoction was drunk by pregnant women in order to cause an abortion.

Perhaps its greatest value was in construction, where it was used extensively by both Māori and Pākehā. The tough, pliable, woody stem provided an excellent material for making baskets and sheep hurdles, and was useful in binding together fences, houses, canoes and platforms. The sturdy vines also made excellent pots, traps and nets for catching crayfish, eels and fish such as kōkopu. A length of the vine could be fashioned into a walking stick or hollowed out and made into a musical instrument, such as a trumpet or bullroarer.

Supplejack vines were commonly employed by Māori when hunting kiore, the Polynesian rat. Little sections of vines could be cut to make small trapdoor cages that swung shut. They were also made into spring snare traps, such as the tāwhiti makamaka. One end was split, propped open with twine, and baited with forest berries such as miro. In order for the rat to access the bait, it had to gnaw through the twine holding the split stem apart. This released the supplejack, which sprung back with great force, catching the poor kiore in a noose and killing it instantly.

BUSH ASPARAGUS

The bright red flesh of the berry was eaten, although the seed accounts for most of the fruit, with only a thin layer of relatively tasteless flesh on the outer surface. The seeds, too, can be eaten once they have been cooked and softened, but again are rather tasteless. The roots have been used to flavour beer; the result is described as sweet-tasting, similar to sarsaparilla, and soothing to the throat.

A more important food source was the soft growing shoots. Affectionately known as 'bush asparagus', these shoots taste like green beans and provide an excellent thirst-quenching snack. Māori ate them as a treatment for scabies and itchiness. A large amount of moisture can be extracted from the vine, too, by blowing it out of a short-cut section.

Supplejack is even beginning to find its way into modern cuisine, where it can be used anywhere you would use beans or asparagus.

MANGEMANGE

A vine that never wears out

At first glance the thin, wiry stems of mangemange look easy to break, but they are much stronger than they appear. Māori used a single narrow stem of mangemange to saw pounamu in half, grinding down bare rock with water and sand. Mere humans stand no chance, and trampers often find themselves strung up by the plant, snagged around the body, arms and ankles struggling to break free. British soldiers roaming in the bush would frequently catch their bayonets on the vines, leading many to adopt knives and revolvers instead. And yet when it comes to annoying plants in the bush, it is generally supplejack that gets all the attention. As annoying as supplejack is, there is a knack to getting through it, and it can be slowly navigated with skill. Mangemange, however, forms impenetrable curtains that resist all attempts to master them.

WOVEN TRAPS

Māori believed these tough wiry stems were so durable they could last a hundred years, and it was said:

> *Kia pēnei te mārōrō o tō kākahu me te mangemange.*
> Let your clothes be made strong as the mangemange,
> which never wears out.[34]

Mangemange stems were used for anything that needed to be tied or bound, and came in particularly handy when binding the thatching of raupō whare and meeting houses. They could also form hooks, when made to grow into the right shape and hardened with fire.

This woven hīnaki is made almost entirely of split mangemange stems. *(Auckland War Memorial Museum, 1984.111, 50850)*

Perhaps mangemange's most valuable use was for constructing hīnaki — traps for eel or fish such as whitebait or kahawai. These wicker-basket-style traps could be crafted entirely from mangemange. The stems were painstakingly split in half, and expertly woven together to create a fine mesh. Many are works of art, gradually tapering to a small hole, just big enough for fish to swim in. Once inside the pot, a circle or pointed sticks kept the prey from escaping, this ingenious trick being the bright idea of the demigod Māui.

Depending on the river and the type of fish, mangemange could be woven into a wide array of different shapes and structures, with little mangemange pouches placed inside filled with bait. In some cases, great eel weirs might be constructed, with a V-shaped fence of mānuka stakes being used to block the passage of the eels and guide them into the hīnaki pot at the centre. If well looked after, these mangemange hīnaki could last a lifetime. Once they had served their purpose, they were soaked with water, and packed away pressed flat and lashed together. When they were needed again, they were untied and would spring back to their original shape.

THE SLAYING OF TAKERE-PIRIPIRI

A number of tales grew up around the use of mangemange as a trap for taniwha and other fantastic beasts. One such story features the great lizard known as Takere-piripiri, who resembled a giant tuatara. He was kept as the pet of a rangatira of Otau pā and fed with steamed eels every day. In return he fought against the chief's enemies and kept the people safe. One day the rangatira sent his grandchildren to feed the lizard, but the children became hungry and decided to eat the delicious eel tails and feed Takere-piripiri only the heads. Furious at this betrayal, Takere-piripiri ate the children instead and went on a rampage. Eventually a group of Waikato warriors determined to put an end to him. They built a wire cage of mangemange, and placed a lone soldier in the middle as bait. As Takere-piripiri tried to access the cage he became stuck, and the warriors rushed out from their hiding place and slew him.

THE BUSHMAN'S MATTRESS

It is somewhat surprising to learn that this strong, wiry plant, with its regular branching leaves, is in fact a fern. Botanically speaking, the entire vine, from the ground to the tips of the leaves, is one large fern frond, making it one of the longest leaves in the world.

Mangemange was transplanted to England and grown there, and when the Māori King Tāwhiao visited in 1870 he was delighted to spot it growing in an English greenhouse. To Pākehā settlers, mangemange was known as 'bushman's mattress' or

TAXONOMY

Mangemange (*Lygodium articulatum*) is found in the north of the country, and is the only species of *Lygodium* in New Zealand. It has around 40 relatives overseas, especially in tropical areas, all of which share the ability to climb by twining. This group also includes a number of invasive species, such as the Old-World climbing fern (*L. microphyllum*). They give their name to the family of plants, the Lygodiaceae.

'bushman's bunk'. Early Pākehā travellers observed how Māori would make beds out of the corkscrew coils of the mangemange vine, and emulated them, stuffing the coils into a sack to make a rough bed for the night. The springy coils make a surprisingly effective mattress, helping to keep the sleeper away from the floor and insulating them from the cold, as one colonial traveller noted:

> I have slept very comfortably in a whare on a sack filled with the very elastic and twisting brown stems of the monga [mangemange]; one could hardly wish to have a better spring mattress than they make.[35]

ETYMOLOGY

The name *Lygodium* means 'supple', 'wiry' or 'flexible', and comes from the twisting, twining habit of the stems. The species name *articulatum* means 'jointed', another reference to the stems. Europeans called the plant 'bushman's mattress' or 'bushman's bunk', as the coiled vines were often used by travellers as a makeshift bed. The origin of the word 'mangemange' is difficult to untangle. It may have some relationship with the Tongan word 'maamange', for yam, which also climbs up trees toward the light, but this is not certain. Other names for the plant include 'tarikupenga', which means 'snare net', and 'makamaka', which comes from the word 'maka' (fish hook).

Mangemange was also used by northern Māori to string up dead bodies in trees as part of burial customs. The bodies were allowed to decompose in the tree, bound in a canoe or a burial chest, and then the kōiwi (human remains) would be interred in a cave.

The leaves of mangemange were useful as well. When dried out, they produce a pleasant aroma, and they were used as a type of diaper. The fronds were also infused in water and this brew was drunk to soothe stomach ache.

The leaves of mangemange give off a pleasant smell when dried. (Robert Vennell)

ONGAONGA

A deadly stinger
with pain-killing properties

Unlike its neighbour, Australia, New Zealand has very few dangerous animals. But plants are a different story. Lurking in the New Zealand forest is one of the largest stinging nettles in the world, packed with enough poison to kill a fully grown human, and regarded by some as the world's most dangerous stinging plant.[36]

In 1961 two young hunters in the Ruahine Ranges stumbled into a patch of the New Zealand tree nettle ongaonga. They were lightly clad, and were badly stung on their arms and legs. An hour later one of the men had difficulty walking and breathing, and soon lost his sight. He died five hours later in hospital. While this remains the only confirmed human death on record, there is an unconfirmed report of a man who went skinny-dipping in a river, was stung all over by ongaonga before he could get his clothes on, and died soon after.[37] Most who are stung lightly by ongaonga survive, but a number have been bedridden for several days in a serious condition.

The source of ongaonga's toxicity is an array of poisonous syringe-like spines. When an unfortunate victim disturbs the plant, the spines are released — the sharp tip breaks off and the toxic substances are released into the skin. This injects a potent cocktail of compounds — histamine, serotonin and acetylcholine — which enter into the bloodstream and manipulate the nervous system. The skin becomes strongly inflamed and intensely painful, and in severe cases the victim begins drooling and losing their sight. With higher doses, the victim loses motor coordination and begins to convulse violently.

Research on the toxic compound has found that just five of these stinging spines are enough to kill a guinea pig, and ongaonga has killed dogs, cattle and horses in the past. The historian James Cowan recalled one such event when two men accidentally rode a pair of horses through a patch of ongaonga. The horses were stung ferociously. Driven wild, they threw their riders and bolted. One horse rushed into a river and drowned; the other was found dead in the forest sometime later. Interestingly, however, possums, goat and deer appear to eat ongaonga with no apparent effects.

TAXONOMY

Ongaonga refers to the tree nettle (*Urtica ferox*), which typically occurs on the margins of lowland and coastal forest from the North Island through to Otago in the South. There are a number of other *Urtica* species in New Zealand, including the southern nettle (*U. australis*) and the swamp nettle (*U. perconfusa*). The *Urtica* genus also includes the common stinging nettle of the northern hemisphere (*U. dioica*), and belongs to the wider nettle family, Urticaceae, many of whose members possess stinging hairs.

A HUSBAND TRAP

Māori believed ongaonga had been placed in the bush to prevent people moving around freely. One version of the tale is that Kupe had stolen the wives of his brother-in-law Hoturapa. As Kupe fled the angry husband, he left obstacles on the path behind him — tātarāmoa, matagouri and the stinging ongaonga — as a way of slowing down his pursuer. The same story is told in a variety of different ways, and the names of the characters and plants differ depending on where you are in the country. The overall idea, however, remains the same: that from the very earliest days ongaonga was a plant used to slow people down and annoy and irritate them.

There are even anecdotes that Māori intentionally planted ongaonga as a protective barrier against intruders, and used the plant in defensive palisades, growing it between burnt stakes of mānuka. Ongaonga was often invoked for anything in Māori life that was irritating or annoying. A frustrating person was called *he tangata ongaonga* — a prickly person. And when performing a rite of divorce, a tohunga might call upon ongaonga to cause the unhappy couple's skin to prickle any time they were together.

PAIN RELIEF

Traditionally, Māori boiled the bark of ongaonga with kawakawa leaves as a treatment for eczema and venereal disease. It was either drunk or applied to the skin. Overseas, dock is a traditional remedy for nettle stings, and the leaves of introduced dock have been used to treat ongaonga stings by Pākehā and Māori.

Somewhat counterintuitively, the stinging leaves of ongaonga may one day provide a medical treatment for chronic pain. When a victim is stung, there is an initial rush of intense pain, but this is then followed by a period of prolonged numbness and insensitivity. While scientists have a fairly good handle on what causes the strong stinging reaction, the compounds responsible for the numbing

ETYMOLOGY

Urtica is the Latin word for stinging nettles, from the Latin verb *urere*, which means 'to burn'. The word *ferox* means 'fierce', 'wild' or 'savage', and is used to describe spiny or dangerous plants. The name 'ongaonga' is used for anything spiky, irritating or annoying. In New Zealand it is also used for biting sandflies and stinging sea nettles. The name seems to have had a long association with prickly, annoying things. The words 'ongaonga', 'hongohongo' and 'okaoka' are used across Polynesia to describe stinging, biting insects.

after-effects are poorly understood. Currently an international research team has begun preliminary work to isolate these numbing compounds.[38] If successful, the work could result in new therapeutics for chronic pain from conditions such as diabetes, leprosy and autoimmune diseases.

Despite the danger, ongaonga was occasionally eaten by Māori as food. The large stems were peeled, and the pith inside, which somewhat resembles the inner threads of lacebark, was eaten raw; it is said to taste rather sweet. The flowers can also be used as the basis for a delicately flavoured honey, similar to that produced by thistle.

RED ADMIRAL

One animal, however, has become immune to the toxic effects of ongaonga. The red admiral butterfly lays its eggs on the new growth of ongaonga leaves. Here, its caterpillar larvae hatch and spend up to six weeks feeding on the leaves. In this vulnerable stage the caterpillars use the leaves for protection, wrapping them around themselves like a blanket or constructing a small tent in which to hide from would-be predators, such as birds, spiders and other insects. Red admiral populations appear to have been declining in recent years, and it is speculated that this may be partly the result of people treating ongaonga as a weed and removing it from bush, lawns and parks.

The New Zealand red admiral (*Vanessa gonerilla*) lays its eggs on ongaonga leaves so that they are protected from predators. (*Biodiversity Heritage Library*)

PIRIPIRI

The hair of the
goddess of death

Piripiri is a curse to sheep, farmers and those with hairy legs. The seed heads are covered in hooked barbs that latch on to passers-by to disperse their seeds. This means they stick to stockings, trousers and leg hairs in the thousands, and can be a right pain to remove. Sometimes it is far easier to abandon socks covered in piripiri seeds than laboriously unpick them.

Poor bedraggled sheep can become so covered in the spiny seeds that their wool is matted together and they are made practically blind. The seeds can make it impossible for shearers to remove wool, and they will often spoil an entire fleece.

Māori were well acquainted with the spiny burrs of piripiri and had many fascinating names for them. The plant was called *huruhuru o Hine nui te po*, 'hair of the great woman of night and death', the ruler of the underworld responsible for luring humans to their death. One of the other names for the plant is pirikahu — 'attach to clothing' — which suggests the plant has had a long history of sticking to clothing and ruining garments. Imagine a painstakingly woven kahu, made with precious kurī fur or thousands of kiwi feathers, becoming covered in the spiny seeds and ruined forever. Another name, hutiwai, alludes to pulling or plucking out, which is surely a reference to the tedious process of removing the seeds from hair and clothing.

TAXONOMY

Piripiri refers to a number of different species in the *Acaena* genus. The most common is *A. anserinifolia*, which is found throughout the mainland of New Zealand and has become naturalised on the Subantarctic Islands. New Zealand is a hotspot of diversity for *Acaena*, which also occurs in South America, Australia and Hawaii. *Acaena* are members of the rose family, Rosaceae, which also includes many edible fruits, such as apples, plums, strawberries and the native bush lawyers (*Rubus* spp.).

Piripiri has a long history of sticking to clothing and being a general nuisance.
(Jacqui Geux)

STICKY SEEDS

This strategy of latching seeds onto animals with hooks and barbs is known as epizoochory. In other countries, such seeds often disperse by latching on to the fur of mammals, but throughout its history New Zealand had almost no native land mammals, and today has only two living species of bat. Despite this, New Zealand has an incredibly high proportion of plants that use epizoochory, and plant groups such as hook grasses (*Carex* spp.) and piripiri (*Acaena* spp.) are remarkably diverse, with more species found here than in other countries. This suggests that despite the lack of mammals, the sticky seed strategy of piripiri and other plants has been very successful in New Zealand.

Most likely, piripiri and other hooked- and spiny-seeded plants evolved to take advantage of flightless bird species, particularly those, such as kiwi, moa and weka, whose loose plumage would have acted like velcro.[39] Many of these species have become extinct or had their ranges dramatically reduced, which may explain why a number of species in the *Acaena* genus are now threatened.

However, one native piripiri, *Acaena novae-zelandiae*, seems to be doing fine in the modern era. It arrived in England on exported wool, and has since become invasive. The pirri-pirri burr, as it is known there, invades the coastal shore, forming dense mats of vegetation, outcompeting native species and covering birds with so many seeds that they struggle to feed themselves.

ETYMOLOGY

Acaena comes from the Greek word *akanthos*, meaning 'thorn' or 'spike', and refers to the spiky seed heads. The species name *anserinifolia* suggests a similarity to the leaves of silverweed (*Potentilla anserina*). A wide diversity of names has arisen for this plant. The word 'piri' means 'sticky' or 'to attach', and is used in New Zealand and Polynesia for a range of sticky plants. Some other names are based around the words 'kaiā' and 'rure' (kaiā, kaikaiārure, kaiārurerure, kaikaiā), where 'kaiā' means 'stealing' or 'thief', and 'rure' means 'to toss or scatter about'. The connection with theft may preserve knowledge of an ancient Polynesian association between sticky plants and theft. For example, in ancient Tahiti, thieves were marked out by placing a sticky plant of taupuri on their door. Pākehā commonly misheard the Māori 'r' sound as a 'd' sound, and 'piripiri' became 'biddy-bid'. The word 'biddy' even became a verb in some places: 'to biddy oneself' meant to remove the seeds from clothing.

MEDICINAL TEA

Piripiri is not without its uses. Māori discovered that by boiling the leaves they could make an excellent healing tonic. The resulting broth was drunk cold, and used as a remedy for headaches, kidney and bladder problems, and sexually transmitted diseases. This beverage was so highly thought of that it was fed to babies whose mothers could not produce milk. The infusion was also used as a lotion, and applied to sores, wounds, bruises and infections. Rather ironically, the lotion produced from this itchy, irritating plant could be used to treat itchy skin. The smoke of burning piripiri has been used to revive patients who have been poisoned with the dreaded tutu.

The leaves of *Acaena anserinifolia* have a silvery underside and are covered with silky hair. *(Jacqui Geux)*

British settlers were quick to make use of the plant's leaves for tea, as was done with similar plants in Australia. Bidibid tea, as they called it, was drunk in times of scarcity when supplies of China tea ran low. William Colenso, the botanist missionary, experimented with native teas, and found that his favourite was a mix of piripiri, toatoa and kāretu. When fresh, the tea is rather uninteresting, but when it is tied up in small bundles and left to dry for several days to a week, the taste becomes reminiscent of weak green tea. Despite its poor reputation overseas, piripiri has been grown as an indoor and outdoor garden plant in Britain, America and Germany.

Piripiri tea was a healing tonic popular with British settlers and tastes somewhat like green tea. *(Jacqui Geux)*

FRINGE DWELLERS

Plants of the coast

BULL KELP

Guardian of the underworld

Bull kelp is an otherworldly creature, with its long tentacle-like blades stretching up to 10 metres in length, swirling back and forth in mesmerising patterns in the surf. The hypnotic twisting and turning is sometimes enough to tie itself into knots. The more violent and exposed the waves, the longer and narrower bull kelp grows, and it thrives in the rough, exposed waves of the west coast.

It seems fitting that in some Māori traditions the eerie tendrils of bull kelp guard the entrance to the underworld. After the spirits of the dead leap off the headland at Te Rerenga Wairua, some believe they descend the long strands of bull kelp down into the passage to the underworld to return to Hawaiki.

Long tendrils of bull kelp swirl in a strong tide. (*Edin Whitehead*)

RUBBER BALLS

In order to withstand the pounding surf, bull kelp has developed some incredible adaptations. It resists being yanked off the rocks by virtue of a solid disc known as the holdfast — a root-like structure that is stubbornly fused onto the surface of the rock. If the waves do manage to pry it free, more often than not it will take a chunk of rock along with it. The stalk or stipe that connects the holdfast to the kelp blade is incredibly elastic, in order to withstand the force of the waves pulling it back and forth. It is thought that the chemical alginate in the stipes is responsible for its extraordinary springiness; this same compound is used to make bouncy balls. Residents of the South Island recognised the elastic, rubbery quality of the stipe, and have a tradition of fashioning it into rubber balls. When paired with a driftwood bat, they make for an excellent homemade game of beach cricket. South Island iwi Ngāi Tahu also noticed the strange texture of the stipes, and were known to fashion them into flutes.

Durvillaea antarctica by Walter Hood Fitch, 1853. (*Biodiversity Heritage Library*)

PŌHA BAGS

Another adaptation to help bull kelp survive in the surf is an internal honeycomb-like structure filled with air pockets, which helps it float in water. It is this quality that made bull kelp of supreme importance to Māori, for using as a carry-bag and cooking vessel. The kelp was split open along the honeycomb struts and inflated to produce a balloon-like sack that was hung up to dry. The bags, known as 'pōhā', were incredibly useful containers, and were used to transport fresh water and to store food such as eels, weka, pork, and even human flesh. They were great vessels to cook food in as well, and when the pōhā became charred and started to split it was a good sign that the contents were ready to eat.

Pōhā were also used to transplant and propagate seafood species, a practice known as *whakawhiti kaimoana*. Shellfish, such as pāua, were kept alive in a pōhā filled with seawater while being taken to a new area, where they were released and allowed to breed and, hopefully, provide an ongoing source of food. When it came time to collect seafood, bull kelp could be made into a makeshift wetsuit worn over the torso and limbs to prevent being scratched on rocks, or fashioned into shoes to avoid cutting feet on barnacles.

> ## TAXONOMY
> There are four species of bull kelp in New Zealand. *Durvillaea antarctica* is the most common and found from the Three Kings to the Subantarctic Islands. *D. poha* is a Far South variety, with broader, flatter blades, *D. willana* has a thicker trunk and side branches, and *D. chathamensis* is endemic to the Chatham Islands. Despite the common name 'kelp', *Durvillaea* are not a true kelp but a fucoid, and belong to the Durvillaeaceae family

Bull kelp is an ideal material for coastal living: a wetsuit and a food container rolled into one. *(Edin Whitehead)*

But perhaps the best-known use for bull kelp is for muttonbirding. The sooty shearwater was a highly prized food source, said to taste like mutton, and was especially valued by southern iwi. The annual harvest of the young chicks was a huge event and remains so today, requiring months of preparation and planning to make the voyage out to the Tītī Islands near Stewart Island/Rakiura.

ETYMOLOGY

The generic name *Durvillaea* honours the French explorer Jules Dumont d'Urville, who collected plants on his travels around New Zealand and the Pacific. The species name *antarctica* refers to its distribution throughout the Southern Ocean, New Zealand, Chile and the Subantarctic Islands. The common name 'bull kelp' may be related to its whip-like shape, as similar-looking seaweeds overseas are called 'bullwhip kelp', or perhaps it refers to the leathery texture of the blades that can appear like the hide of a bull. The Māori name, 'rimurapa', is derived from the word 'rimu', which is a generic name for seaweed in Polynesian languages. It is also given to a range of things that look like seaweed – mosses, clubmosses and the rimu tree. The noodle-like shape of rimurapa may have been the basis for the modern Māori word for pasta: parāoa rimurapa, which combines 'parāoa' (bread) and 'rimurapa' (bull kelp).

To make the most of this bountiful harvest, a receptacle for storing and preserving the chicks was essential. In traditional times, bull-kelp pōhā were the only plant up to the task, as the hue or gourd did not grow in the south. Ngāi Tahu would mass-produce pōhā in the months leading up to the harvest. As there are no dry landings on the Tītī Islands, it was important that the container could be thrown and caught like a rugby ball, and so the pōhā were designed with that in mind. Still used today, they resemble little wooden backpacks, wrapped in tōtara bark and bound tightly with flax. When the birds have been collected, they are

Perhaps the most unusual use of bull kelp was to make inflatable dinghies that could ride the ocean waves. (Edin Whitehead)

cooked then stuffed into pōhā, and sealed with boiling fat. Some pōhā could carry over 100 birds, with an average bag holding around 50 birds and lasting several years.

The bull kelp most commonly used by Ngāi Tahu has recently been recognised as a unique species, and in honour of this use given the scientific name *Durvillaea poha*. It has broader, flatter blades than *D. antarctica*, making it perfect for pōhā bags.

KELP FLOATIES

Inflated pōhā pouches make surprisingly effective floats, and Moriori on the Chatham Islands used them to make a type of inflatable dinghy. Known as *waka kōrari*, these vessels were made with the flower stalks of harakeke and blades of inflated bull kelp. Water would soak through and the vessel became waterlogged, but it remained remarkably buoyant. Because it was partially submerged, it was very difficult to capsize in rough surf. It is said these waka kōrari could travel up to 50 kilometres in rough seas, and carried large numbers of people to the offshore islands to collect albatross chicks.

There are also stories that Ngāi Tahu used the inflated pōhā for surfing in ancient times — a practice known as 'kauai' or 'kaukau'. Two inflated pōhā were tied together and placed under each arm. The surfer would then swim out past the breakers and ride the waves back into the shore. A number of legendary tales recount people swimming Cook Strait with nothing but an inflated bull kelp for support.

KELP AS FOOD

Bull kelp has a long food history both in New Zealand and overseas. It can be eaten raw, but was most commonly cooked. The blades and tips were tossed in the fire, and once cooked the charred ash would be scraped off, leaving a chewy meal reminiscent of liquorice. It was believed that eating these roasted kelp tips was a cure for itchiness and intestinal worms. Bull kelp was also made into a type of jelly. The kelp was cut into small pieces, washed and dried, and then boiled with the juice of tutu berries until it disintegrated. When chilled, this liquid took on a jelly-like consistency, and was a popular dish in traditional times.

More recently, foragers like Johanna Knox have oven-baked thin straps of bull kelp to make healthy, nutritious kelp chips. *Durvillaea antarctica* also occurs along the coast of Chile. There, the holdfast and stem are known as *cochayuyo* and used in local cuisine, normally being cut up and incorporated in a range of salads and stews.

Bull kelp can be eaten raw or cooked, and is a popular ingredient in Chilean cuisine. *(Matthew Cattin)*

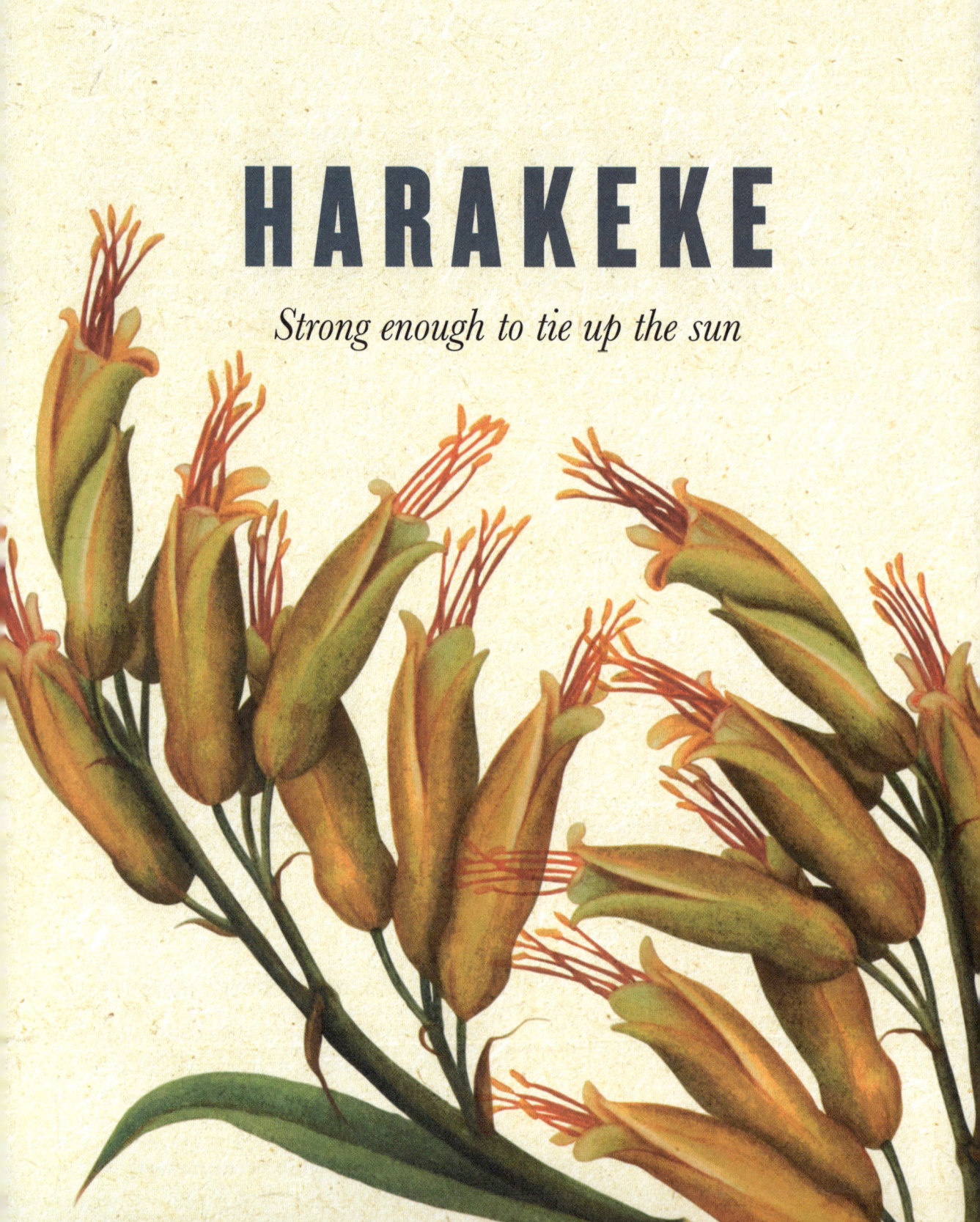

HARAKEKE

Strong enough to tie up the sun

When the botanist and missionary William Colenso told Māori chiefs in the Bay of Islands there was no harakeke in England, they simply could not believe it, asking: 'How is it possible to live there without it? I would not dwell in such a land as that.'[40]

Their surprise is easy to understand, as harakeke — New Zealand flax — is one of the most essential and revered plants in all of Aotearoa. The sword-like leaves are incredibly robust and able to withstand considerable force, but can also be easily manipulated and woven. The outer leaves provide a tough and durable material, and the outer flesh can be scraped away with a shell to reveal the more delicate and refined fibres beneath.

Harakeke leaves were put to use by Māori for just about everything that was required for day-to-day life — clothing, cloaks, sandals, fishing lines, nets, mats, kete (baskets), fans, fly swats, belts, house panels, sails and rope. Nearly every marae or settlement cultivated a flax plantation — pū harakeke — and Māori horticulturists developed a range of different cultivars specially bred for desired qualities: some for softness or strength; some for their colour; some for making clothing, baskets, rope or dyes. Writing in the 1850s, the geologist Ferdinand von Hochstetter was amazed by the omnipresence of harakeke:

What the bamboo is to the inhabitants of eastern and southern Asia, this plant is to the natives of New Zealand. The various uses it is put to are innumerable. Near every hut, every hamlet, on every way-side its bushes, whether wild or cultivated, are at hand for use.[41]

Wharariki (*Phormium cookianum*) by Fanny Osborne. (Auckland War Memorial Museum, CCBY)

ROPES IN THE SKY

With such an important plant, it is no surprise that harakeke is commonly found throughout Māori mythology. The great demigod Māui is said to have hauled up the North Island of New Zealand, Te Ika a Māui, using only a rope of harakeke and his grandmother's magic jawbone.

In perhaps his most famous feat, Māui used ropes of harakeke to slow down the sun. It is told that in the far distant past, the sun sped across the sky so fast that the people had no time to work or get anything done. So, Māui decided to slow down the sun, and to achieve this he plaited strong ropes from the muka (fibre) of harakeke and infused it with the power of karakia. Māui and his brothers then bound the sun, tying it to the earth with the ropes. Weakened by the ordeal, the sun struggled slowly across the sky. The harakeke ropes can still be seen as rays of sunlight reaching down to earth.

Not only do these stories show the Māori reverence for the strength of harakeke, but they also serve as a powerful metaphor: if there was one plant in New Zealand that made life possible and allowed all of the tasks to be completed in the day, it was harakeke.

PĀKEHĀ AND HARAKEKE MEET

Harakeke was perhaps the first resource in New Zealand to really capture the imagination of European explorers. The crew onboard Lieutenant James Cook's ship, the *Endeavour*, were stunned by its versatility, and traded iron tools and clothing with Māori in order to acquire woven kete and cloaks. Cook himself was fascinated by the plant, and called it 'flax' after the linen flax (*Linum usitatissimum*) of Europe. Joseph Banks, the botanist on board the ship, believed it was the best plant New Zealand had to offer:

> But of all the plants we have seen among these people that which is the most excellent in its kind … is the plant which serves them instead of Hemp and flax … So useful a plant would doubtless be a great acquisition to England.[42]

Strong, versatile leaves make harakeke one of the most useful plants in the country. *(Edin Whitehead)*

These glowing reports were of great interest to the British navy, which was always in need of strong rope fibres for its ships. Eager entrepreneurs began making plans to develop a flax industry in New Zealand, but few could match the skilled work of Māori weavers. Flax-processing became a huge Māori enterprise, with flax stations all across the country, producing thousands of pounds per year, which was sent to Australia and Britain.

FLAX FOR GUNS

However, harakeke soon became drawn into a vicious cycle of trade and warfare that ravaged the country. The introduction of muskets radically rescaled tribal conflicts, converting what would have been minor skirmishes into major wars with devastating consequences. It became essential for iwi to arm with muskets, or face extermination, and trading harakeke was one way of doing this. Harakeke was so important to this new musket economy that iwi often moved away from homelands to be closer to harakeke swamps, and worked other food crops less so they could focus on cultivating harakeke.

The Ngāpuhi leader Hongi Hika was the first to acquire a large arsenal of muskets through trade, and led a series of assaults across the North Island, leaving a massive trail of destruction as far as Tolaga Bay. He captured somewhere in the region of 2000 slaves, who were put to work harvesting and preparing harakeke to trade for more muskets.

A VERITABLE MEDICINE CHEST

But if harakeke has helped to fuel war and conflict, it has also helped to soothe the injured and heal the sick. It is one of the most significant medicinal plants of New Zealand, and was favoured by Pākehā as well as Māori, with the leaves, roots and gum all providing useful remedies.

The leaves supplied everything required to deal with injuries and wounds. The soft scraped muka was used to sponge wounds and mop up blood, and was a vital tool when performing bush surgeries. Lengths of muka could be used to stitch wounds together; scalp wounds were treated by binding the hair either side of the wound and pulling tight. The thicker leaves provided a protective bandage, and the base of the leaves formed a natural splint to demobilise a broken limb.

The roots were a significant medicinal remedy, made into infusions and ointments used to treat everything from sexually transmitted diseases, skin diseases and ringworm to smallpox. The root itself could be held on wounds to stop bleeding, and treat boils, abscesses, swelling, rashes, chilblains and tumours. Dr Monckton, a Pākehā doctor from the west coast of the South Island, experimented extensively with native plants in his treatments, and swore by harakeke above all else:

ETYMOLOGY

The name *Phormium* comes from the Greek *phormos*, meaning 'basket' or 'basketwork', referencing the use of the plant by Māori. The specific name *tenax* is a Latin word meaning 'hold fast', which refers to the strong fibres. The name 'flax' was used by Cook's crew and later explorers, who noted the plant's similarity to the unrelated linen flax (*Linum usitatissimum*). The words 'hara' and 'whara' are related to the ancient Polynesian word 'fara', and similar words are used widely throughout the Pacific to refer to *Pandanus* plants. By itself the word 'whara' in te reo Māori refers to any plant that has sword-shaped leaves similar to *Pandanus*, such as those of the genus *Astelia*, which includes plants such as kōwharawhara and pūwharawhara. The word 'keke' has roots in Polynesia, meaning 'hard' or 'strong', giving harakeke the meaning 'strong *Pandanus* plant'. The word 'riki' is used to signal something is little, thus the smaller alpine wharariki becomes 'little *Pandanus* plant'. The name of the flower stalks, kōrari, appears unique to Aotearoa, and in the Far North refers to the whole plant.

I have used it [harakeke] in a hundred cases, including lacerations and amputations of every description, and I have no hesitation in saying that there is nothing known in the Old country that can equal it in producing healthy granulations.[43]

An infusion of the roots in water is highly purgative, and was used by Māori and Pākehā to treat syphilis, intestinal worms, problems with menstruation and problems with the bladder. One of its best-known uses was to clear up constipation. The effect was said to be rather violent, and caution was advised, as the bowels were rapidly and completely evacuated, often accompanied by blood and mucous membrane.

At the base of the leaves is a thick, gelatinous edible goo that provides yet another medical treatment. This gum is soothing, and was used on burns, wounds, sores, cuts, cracked skin, chafed lips and sore teeth. It can also be rubbed inside socks to soothe sore, blistered heels when hiking. Pākehā doctors were known to use the gum as a substitute sticking plaster, by smearing it onto a piece of paper. It also worked for sealing envelopes. Today, the gum has found its way into a range of cosmetics using natural ingredients, including moisturisers, soaps and shampoos.

Harakeke's nectar-filled tubular flowers are greedily sought out by birds in summer. *(Edin Whitehead)*

BENEFICIAL SEEDS

The long flower stalks, known as 'kōrari', carry hundreds of crimson red flowers, which become little goblets full of sweet nectar. The flowers were gathered up and their contents emptied into a gourd, sometimes mixed with water. This drink was greatly relished by Māori and, prior to the arrival of Europeans, was one of the only beverages consumed by Māori other than plain water. It was mixed with hīnau cakes and fern root to sweeten the taste.

Māori also ate the gum at the base of the leaves, which is clear and rather tasteless. The seeds are also edible. At first they are white and meaty, but with time they become dry and black and lodge in your throat like popcorn kernels. The seeds are a great source of essential fatty acids, and are currently being prepared and sold as flaxseed oil and used in skin ointments. A few keen experimentalists have even attempted to make coffee from the flax seeds, and while the result bears a vague resemblance to coffee, those accustomed to modern café culture are unlikely to be very impressed.

The sweet nectar from the flowers is edible, and the seeds have been made into coffee. (Edin Whitehead)

PŌHUTUKAWA

The New Zealand Christmas Tree

Today, New Zealand's plant life is widely admired and individual species are readily adopted as symbols of our identity and culture. But for many of the early European settlers first setting foot on New Zealand, the forest was a hostile, fearful environment. They had been sold on a promise that New Zealand was an agricultural paradise of manicured fields and rolling pastures. What they found instead was a land covered in dense, rugged, unfamiliar forest; it is not surprising that many were intimidated.

One tree, however, quickly managed to charm itself into early settler society: the pōhutukawa. Its showy blooms of crimson flowers coincided with Christmas preparations each year, and soon became firmly entrenched in Christmas tradition. Branches of 'Antipodean holly' were used to decorate churches and houses, and its status as 'the New Zealand Christmas tree' has been celebrated ever since. Today, the pōhutukawa remains the quintessential symbol of the northern New Zealand summer Christmas, and is celebrated in artwork, postcards and calendars. Families hauling their cricket sets and boogie boards to the beach will battle for shade under their favourite pōhutukawa, staking out territory with beach towels and jandals.

A quintessential symbol of a Kiwi summer – bright red pōhutukawa flowers at the beach. (*Matthew Cattin*)

Pōhutukawa must have made a monumental impact on the early Polynesian explorers, and would have been one of the first trees they saw in this new land, gripping to the coastline as it does with tentacle-like roots. One Māori tradition holds that when the captains of the *Tainui* waka arrived in New Zealand and saw the red blossoms of pōhutukawa, they believed them to be flocks of red-feathered birds. In their excitement, they cast their prized red-feathered headdresses into the ocean.

Other traditions link the flowers with Tāwhaki, a demigod associated with lightning and thunder. It is told that Tāwhaki's father was killed by the ponaturi, strange goblin creatures that only came out at night. Tāwhaki was filled with rage and planned a

Pōhutukawa (*Metrosideros excelsa*) by Fanny Osborne. (*Auckland War Memorial Museum, CCBY*)

journey of revenge. He would ascend to the Tenth Heaven and steal Tama's herd of heavenly dogs to help lay siege to the ponaturi. However, when Tama got wind of Tāwhaki's plans to steal the dogs, he sent a bird to attack him. As Tāwhaki was climbing to the heavens, he was attacked by the bird and fell to his death. The next morning the blossoms of the rātā and pōhutukawa were stained red with his blood.

TE RERENGA WAIRUA

One pōhutukawa in particular holds great significance for Māori, and is perhaps one of the most important individual trees in all of New Zealand. Located at Cape Reinga, this gnarled and twisted pōhutukawa grips onto a rocky outcrop that juts out into the boundary between the Tasman Sea and the Pacific Ocean. The tree is supposedly around 800 years old, which would place its origin among the early years of Māori settlement in New Zealand. In fact, tradition states that the great navigator Kupe, who is believed to have discovered New Zealand, established this point as the site where his descendants would travel in spirit form back to Hawaiki.

Spirits of the dead are said to travel Te Ara Wairua, the spirits' pathway across the country, until they arrive at Cape Reinga. The tree marks Te Rerenga Wairua, the leaping place of the spirits, where the spirits of the dead leap off the headland and descend down the roots of the tree on their journey back to the ancestral homeland of Hawaiki.

Iwi in other places around the country also have traditions of using a root, most commonly pōhutukawa, to descend to the underworld, and the phrase 'to slide down the pōhutukawa root' is a polite way of saying someone has passed away and their spirit has returned to Hawaiki.

Pōhutukawa was the perfect tree to serve this role, due to its distribution along the boundary between land and sea, and in some whakapapa pōhutukawa was seen as a descendant of Tangaroa rather than Tāne. It is supremely adapted for this pioneering lifestyle, able to tolerate harsh environmental conditions and salty spray that would kill most plants.

The genus to which pōhutukawa belongs is *Metrosideros*. It includes species that can spread across great distances by producing thousands upon thousands of tiny seeds that can be held aloft on the slightest breeze. Not only that, the seeds are incredibly hardy and can survive up to a month of immersion in salt water and temperatures well below freezing.

While most New Zealand plants are thought to have made their way here and then adapted to the islands' unique environments, New Zealand may have been the original source of *Metrosideros* trees. Over millions of years, sporadic waves of dispersal have

TAXONOMY

Pōhutukawa (*Metrosideros excelsa*) is found along the coasts of northern New Zealand, although its natural distribution is hard to pin down, as it is thought to have been cultivated by Māori. It belongs to the *Metrosideros* genus, which includes the northern and southern rātā (*M. robusta* and *M. umbellata*, respectively), as well as a number of climbing rātā vines. It belongs to the myrtle family, Myrtaceae, which also includes feijoa and eucalyptus, which have similar red flowers with bundles of protruding stamens.

spread the group out of New Zealand and across the Pacific. Today, *Metrosideros* has an extensive range, including the Subantarctic Islands, the Bonin Islands near Japan, and the Hawaiian Islands — one of the most remote island groups in the world. The official flower of the island of Hawaii, the ohia, is a close relative of pōhutukawa, and is remarkably similar to it.

A TROUBLESOME WEED

While pōhutukawa's hardy pioneering nature has often endeared itself to those in the upper part of the North Island, it is these very characteristics that cause it to be a source of frustration and anguish elsewhere. Prior to the arrival of Māori, pōhutukawa would have formed an almost continuous forest around the coastline of northern New Zealand. However, it was never found south of New Plymouth until the arrival of Māori, who, it is thought, planted it further south. Now it has firmly established itself there and is something of a menace. On the west coast of the South Island, the Department of Conservation lists pōhutukawa as a medium-priority weed due to its invasive nature and ability to displace other natives.

It has also caused problems further afield. In California, widespread planting of pōhutukawa in suburban lawns and gardens has caused extensive infrastructure damage, with its root systems destroying sewer lines and pavements. In South Africa, Japan, Spain, England and Ireland, it is listed as a high-priority invasive species. However, one Spanish city, La Coruña, has developed a fondness for pōhutukawa. It has a 200-year-old specimen and has adopted it as the city's floral emblem.

ETYMOLOGY

Metrosideros means 'iron-heart wood', referring to the strength of the timber, and *excelsa* means 'tall' or 'supreme'. Various meanings have been given for the name 'pōhutukawa'. It is said to mean 'splashed by the spray', a reference to its coastal habitat on the seashore. It may also refer to hutukawa, a headdress of red flowers, as stories of the arrival of the *Tainui* waka recount the captains throwing away their hutukawa when they saw the plant's brilliant red flowers. It may also reference its whakapapa: in some traditions it is a descendant of Hutu, a child of Tangaroa, god of the ocean, perhaps reflecting its proximity to the ocean realm. Linguistically it is related to the word 'futu', which is used across Polynesia to describe the fish poison tree (*Barringtonia asiatica*), which is also common along the coast and has colourful pink flowers with lots of stamens.

MEDICINE, HONEY AND TIMBER

Both Māori and Europeans used a decoction from the inner bark in the treatment of dysentery. Modern chemical analysis has provided some validation for this use, as the bark is shown to contain ellagic acid, which is used in diarrhoea and dysentery treatments for its astringent properties.

The nectar from the flowers was collected by Māori and used in the treatment of sore throats, although it can be rather difficult to extract without getting a mouth full of the long red stamens. The honey made from this nectar is pale and sweet, and honey produced from the pollen is white with a distinctive flavour. It has apparently caught the attention of Queen Elizabeth II, who is rumoured to regularly order a batch of pōhutukawa honey from Rangitoto Island.

Pōhutukawa produces a swirly-grained, dark-red wood that is particularly strong and dense. It was used by Māori to make paddles, fern-root beaters, digging sticks, hammers, mauls, clubs, containers, spinning tops and weapons. It also served as a timber tree for European colonists, and was used extensively by boat-builders for its natural bends and its immunity to sea worms. It also has a high proportion of tannins, which made it useful for tanning leather and producing dyes.

The leathery leaves are able to resist sea salt, allowing pōhutukawa to thrive between land and sea. (Edin Whitehead)

Pohutukawa by Sydney Parkinson. (Te Papa, 1992-0035-2353/1566)

Metrosideros tomentosa, A. Rich.

NGAIO

The tree you can see on the moon

Ngaio (*Myoporum laetum*) by Fanny Osborne. *(Auckland War Memorial Museum, CCBY)*

Hold the leaves of ngaio up to the light and you will see it is studded with oil glands. These glands are packed full of the toxin ngaione, which kills its victims by shutting down the liver. Most often these victims are sheep and pigs, which after grazing on the leaves become constipated and anorexic. This strong defence makes ngaio resistant to browsing by introduced mammals, and there are places where ngaio is one of few remaining species.

The ripe berries were sometimes eaten, especially by children, but are now known to contain ngaione and should be avoided. They are rather bitter and unpleasant, so there is nothing to be missed. However, the oil is not without its uses. Māori discovered that rubbing the leaves on their skin helped repel mosquitoes and sandflies. Early European farmers even used the oil as a sheep-dip, covering their sheep in it to help ward off parasites.

Ngaio had a number of medicinal uses as well. The leaf buds were chewed to help soothe the stomach after eating bad mussels. The inner bark was scraped and rubbed on sore gums and teeth, as it was said to be effective in easing the pain. It was also infused with water and used to treat cuts, bruises and ulcers. One curious remedy to treat leprosy involved mixing the leaves of ngaio and kawakawa with human or dog faeces. It is not clear how this was meant to be applied, but apparently it was important not to touch a dog after the treatment or it would fail.

The leaves of ngaio are studded with glands that release an oil that is toxic to insects. *(Edin Whitehead)*

CARRIED AWAY

The importance of ngaio in Māori culture is underscored by its adoption into the Man on the Moon myth. Cultures all around the world have interpreted the craters on the moon differently, seeing them as everything from biblical figures to banyan trees and even a giant rabbit mixing the elixir of life. In one Māori tale, the craters resemble a female figure holding a ngaio tree. The story goes that a woman — Rona — went down to the river to gather water, but tripped and fell when the moon passed behind a cloud. Furious, she hurled insults at the moon until at last the moon became so enraged that he grabbed Rona and pulled her up to the sky. She grabbed the nearest thing — a ngaio tree — and held on for dear life, but the moon tore the tree out by the roots and carried them both into the night sky forever. The story is often told as a cautionary tale against cursing and using swear words, and when someone was using foul language they might be told:

> *Kia mahara ki te he o Rona.*
> Remember what happened to Rona.[44]

THE NGAIO WEEVIL

Ngaio hosts a special type of insect: the large, flightless ngaio weevil (*Anagotus stephenensis*). This weevil is able to process the toxic compounds in the leaves, and can feed almost exclusively on ngaio. It was once widespread across the country, as indicated by its retrieval from many of the nests of the extinct laughing owl (*Sceloglaux albifacies*). Unfortunately, it is now considered critically endangered and found only on Stephens Island in the Marlborough Sounds.

A ngaio weevil
(*Anagotus stephenensis*)
on Stephens Island.
(Mark Anderson, CCBY)

ETYMOLOGY

The name *Myoporum* means 'closed pore', and refers to the glands on the leaves. The species name *laetum* means 'bright' or 'attractive'. The word 'ngaio' or 'naio' is also used in a number of Polynesian languages, all for closely related species in the genus *Myoporum*. The word 'ngaio' in Māori has an array of different meanings. It can refer to an expert or professional, or a grub or parasitic worm, or it can describe a deliberate, thorough action. The exact relationship between these meanings and the ngaio tree is unclear, but an old ngaio tree can have an aura of wisdom about it, and there may be some link between the use of the tree as an insecticide and the use of the word 'ngaio' to mean 'grub'.

TASMANIAN NGAIO

The Tasmanian ngaio (*Myoporum insulare*) is listed in the national pest plant accord as an unwanted species in New Zealand. It was planted around the coast in New Zealand, presumably as a result of being confused with native ngaio. Unfortunately, it competes with the native species and hybridises with it. Our own ngaio is itself considered a pest plant in parts of the world where it has been introduced. For example, it is regarded as an alien pest plant in California, where it spreads rapidly, creates dense monocultures outcompeting native species and presents a serious wildfire risk.

NĪKAU

The coldest palm in the world

Around 20 million years ago, in the early Miocene, New Zealand forests would have been almost unrecognisable. Aotearoa had a much warmer climate at the time, and contained distinctive tropical elements in its flora. Australian plants, such as eucalypts, acacia and bottlebrush, were common, as were tropical plants — palms, cinnamon and even species of coconut, such as the small-fruited *Cocos zeylanica*. With the advent of the ice ages, massive glacial walls of ice scoured the landscape and temperatures plummeted, purging this tropical flora from the landscape. Only one representative of the palm family survived, the nīkau, which was able to adapt to the colder climate in Aotearoa despite its tropical origins. This is a remarkable feat, considering no other palm in the world grows as far south as the nīkau.

NO NUTS

It has been said that when the Polynesian ancestors of Māori arrived in New Zealand they first attempted to find a coconut tree, which in the Pacific is a vitally important food plant and serves a great number of practical uses. Upon discovering the nīkau, they were dismayed to find it lacked the all-important feature of coconuts. Indeed, one somewhat dubious translation of the word 'nīkau' is 'niu-kau': without nuts. While this makes an enjoyable story, and it is quite possible those early explorers were disappointed, it is most probably apocryphal. Either way, the Polynesians surely recognised the likeness, and would have immediately begun using nīkau in similar ways.

FROND CRAFTS

Nīkau fronds are incredibly versatile, and have been used by Māori to weave into hats, mats and baskets, with the outer portion of the trunk being made into containers and pots. For protection in scrubby undergrowth, leggings could be made by weaving fronds together, and the stiff leaves could also be used as makeshift splints for broken or dislocated bones.

Sometimes the fronds were used to make a cooking vessel. Kiore were skinned and put in the cylinder formed by the lower part of the frond. Red-hot rocks were placed inside the curled frond, and the heat melted the kiore's fat and baked it.

The fronds were also used extensively for thatching roofs and provided an excellent source of waterproofing. A common whare design was a mānuka-stick framework thatched with nīkau fronds, and it has been said that this design could be as strong and watertight as if made of iron.

Although the green immature berries are edible, the red mature berries, despite looking appetising, are actually incredibly dense. They were made into necklaces and, later, even used to shoot birds when ammunition was unavailable.

Rhopalostylis sapida by Sarah Featon, c. 1885. (Te Papa, 1992-0035-2277/5)

The rito — the heart of the palm — is a white, fleshy cylinder where the new growth forms. It has a slightly laxative effect, and so was used as a medical treatment for pregnant women, relaxing the pelvic ligaments before childbirth. This rongoā was highly revered in some parts of New Zealand, and Māori would think nothing of traversing many miles in search of the rito when required.

While nīkau lack an edible coconut, the root, immature flowers and the immature green berries have all been used for food. Best of all, however, is the rito. This nutty, refreshing meal was an important survival food, but its removal kills the plant, and because it is painstakingly slow-growing the nīkau's harvest was carefully managed. Rito was regarded as something of a delicacy, cooked as a kīnaki (relish) along with eel and other meats.

A SPECIAL SALAD

The first recorded encounter between Europeans and the plant is noted in the journals of the crew of the *Endeavour*. They ate the heart from the centre of the palm and thought it a delicious meal, as Cook later recounted:

> This vegetable is not only wholesome but exceedingly palatable and proved the most agreeable repast we had had for some time.[45]

The generic name *Rhopalostylis* means 'a club-shaped style', and refers to the shape of the female flower organ. The species name *sapida* means 'savoury' and refers its use as food. The Māori name 'nīkau' is derived from similar words in the Pacific, such as 'nikau', 'nī'au' and 'niau', which are all used to refer to the frond of the coconut palm. The original name for nīkau in the journals of James Cook and Joseph Banks was 'cabbage palm' – a common name given to palms at that time due to their edible heart.

Various other accounts from European settlers describe the heart as excellent eating. Young plants were said to taste more like lettuce leaves; older rito were described as being like a nutty cabbage or like a cross between celery and coconut. Rito was sometimes cooked and eaten and at other times pickled.

Because harvesting the heart kills the palm, nīkau came to be known among Europeans as 'millionaire's salad', and it was only taken when necessary. It has served as an important survival food for those lost in the bush, as it is often readily available and easily recognisable. The missionary and botanist William Colenso remarked:

> [It] is excellent eating, even in a raw state, juicy, succulent, and nutty, with an agreeable taste, and is very wholesome. It proved of very great service to me once when I had both lost my way and my companions too, in travelling in a new country, and was starving.[46]

Nīkau became an important staple food for the Bohemian settlers in Pūhoi, whose first years there were a desperate struggle for survival. They harvested the palm heart when they ran low on food supplies, and used its leaves to build temporary whare.

The unripe green berries are edible. The ripe red berries are so dense they have been used as ammunition for shooting birds. *(Matthew Cattin)*

The tentacle-like projections bearing the fruit display some similarity to the arms of an octopus. *(Edin Whitehead)*

CULTURAL ICON

Today, the nīkau's distinctive shape and appearance lend a unique tropical aesthetic to the New Zealand bush. Nīkau has been recognised by the New Zealand public as a cultural icon, featuring prominently in artwork and sculptures, and is planted in our major gardens and cities. It holds an important place in the hearts and minds of many New Zealanders, including children, who have been known to use the discarded fronds as natural toboggans to race down grassy slopes.

Pink flowers emerging from the nīkau trunk. *(Jacqui Geux)*

Illustration of nīkau for *Curtis's Botanical Magazine*, by Walter Hood Fitch, 1868. *(Biodiversity Heritage Library)*

PĪNGAO

The eyebrows of Tāne Mahuta

Before it was displaced by introduced species and modern development, pīngao would have crowded the shore of every sandy beach from Northland to Stewart Island/ Rakiura. The curly golden leaves were much admired as a weaving material and were used to make hats, bags, mats, headbands, belts and rain capes, and pretty putiputi flowers. South Island Māori were even known to make body armour with the leaves, which was worn into battle. Pīngao was also eaten, the tender growing tips being chewed by travellers or cooked as a relish with fish.

Pīngao was such an important part of the lives of coastal iwi that it is said the spirits of the dead carried the plant along the pathway to the underworld. On the long journey back to Hawaiki they would drop pīngao to mark their passage, which accounts for its distribution along the coast.

THE ORIGIN OF PĪNGAO

All of the most prestigious plants had legendary origins, and the little pīngao is no exception. In the Far North it is believed that pīngao began her life as a seaweed on the shore of the ocean. From her watery home she spied the slender, handsome kākaho — the long flower stalks of the toetoe — his long, blond hair blowing in the wind. Driven mad with love, she left the ocean and crawled across the hot sand to meet the tall stranger. However, she became stranded on the dry, sandy dunes, and she called out to her father, Tangaroa, to help, but all he could do to ease her suffering was shower her with sea spray. There she remains to this day, with the salty spray of Tangaroa covering the plant on the incoming tide. However, the two lovers do occasionally meet, as pīngao is often woven together with the kākaho to form tukutuku panels on the marae.

In another telling, pīngao was created by the gods during a terrible battle. Tangaroa — lord of the ocean — was waging a violent war against his brother Tāne — lord of the forest. Tāne wished to end the war, so he plucked off his golden eyebrows and gave them to Tangaroa as a peace offering. But Tangaroa could not find it in his heart to forgive his brother, and cast the eyebrows back on the shore. There they remain to this day as pīngao, forever marking the boundary between land and sea.

In another story, pīngao was taken from the ocean and placed on the sand dunes so she could nurture her whānau, the toheroa. This seafood delicacy was once found in huge abundance around New Zealand's west coast and was considered a national delicacy, being made into a greenish soup and sold internationally. The tiny larvae or spat look similar to the seeds of pīngao, and it is believed that the sea foam of the high tides deposits the toheroa larvae among the leaves. Here they grow, protected by the leaves of pīngao, until they are carried back to the oceans and streams by riding along on the tumbling seed heads of spinifex.

TAXONOMY

Pīngao (*Ficinia spiralis*) was once widespread, found on coastal sand dunes throughout the North, South, Stewart and Chatham Islands. It is now classified as at.risk and in decline. There is one other member of the genus in New Zealand, the knobby club rush (*F. nodosa*). The centre of diversity for the *Ficinia* genus is in South Africa, where there are 70 species. The group belongs to the sedge family, Cyperaceae, which includes the popular garden plant genus *Carex*.

Pīngao by Sydney Parkinson. (*Te Papa, 1992-0035-2353/2249*)

PĪNGAO AND FAUNA

It is not only toheroa that love pīngao, though; a number of native birds and insects thrive in pīngao dunes. The New Zealand pipit, the Australasian harrier and the New Zealand dotterel all nest among its leaves.

It is also home to the critically endangered katipō spider, which is in serious decline, as it has a highly specialised lifestyle, living among sand dunes. Pīngao is its preferred plant of choice for spinning its webs, as the individual plants are spaced apart with open sand in between. This means the katipō can spin a disorganised tangle of webs over the sand to catch crawling insects.

Pīngao lives a fluid existence, and thrives in coastal environments where dunes are constantly shifting and moving over time. However, after the arrival of Europeans, coastal areas were extensively burned and browsed by stock and possums, rabbits and goats. The dunes were also planted with introduced species, such as marram grass, tree lupins and pine trees. These species stabilise the sand dunes and completely smother and outcompete pīngao. The situation has not got much better, with extensive coastal development, mining for sand, damage from cars and foot traffic, and over-harvesting.

ETYMOLOGY

The name *Ficinia* honours the 19th-century German botanist Heinrich David August Ficinus. The species name *spiralis* means 'spiralling' or 'coiling', and may refer to the spiralling seed heads. The common English name is 'golden sand sedge', but this is less commonly used nowadays. The name 'pīngao' does not have any clear links with the Pacific, where sand dune systems and plants are rare. The word 'pī' in Māori can sometimes refer to the flow of the tide, and across the Pacific the word carries meanings relating to splashing or sprinkling with water, so perhaps its name references its habitat at the border between the realms of Tāne and Tangaroa.

Today, pīngao has experienced a massive decline, and only a few remnant populations remain scattered around the coast. However, the future of pīngao is far from over, and a range of programmes are underway to protect pīngao and replant it in sand dunes throughout the country.

The leaves of pīngao are beautifully flecked with green, yellow and orange.
(Edin Whitehead)

A seed head of pīngao in sand dunes in the Far North. The plants here grow larger than anywhere else and are much sought after by weavers.
(Robert Vennell)

TOETOE

*The blond-haired beauty
of the coast*

Toetoe is the lovechild of Tāne Mahuta, lord of the forests, and Ngaore, a particularly beautiful deity known as 'the tender one'. Toetoe retains a spark of that divine beauty, and its long, delicate, feathery plumes have captivated and enchanted people ever since. The sand sedge pīngao was said to have crawled out of the ocean, driven mad with love for the beautiful toetoe, only to become stranded on the shore. Unfortunately, toetoe is said to be well aware of his own beauty and is incredibly vain, always tossing his hair back and forth in the breeze.

Other stories suggest that the feather plumes are a symbol of shame. Toetoe was a witness to the actions of Rātā, who attempted to cut down a tree without performing the correct karakia. Filled with embarrassment, toetoe forever more bowed his flowery head in shame.

The resemblance of toetoe to a flowing head of hair was even noted by the American author Mark Twain on his travels, who wrote in his journal:

> And there was a ten foot reed with a flowing suit of what looked like yellow hair hanging from its upper end. I do not know its name but if there is such a thing as a scalp-plant, this is it.[47]

CEREMONIAL USES

Toetoe was used in a wide range of ceremonies. When students were learning from an expert tohunga, they would carry out a symbolic ritual using the toetoe stalk. The tohunga would drip water from the stalk onto the ears of the students, symbolising the transfer of knowledge from the teacher to the pupil. Once the student had learned all this secret knowledge, he would chew on the kākaho, which was said to prevent him from sharing these secrets.

In some mourning ceremonies, a line of toetoe grass was tied to the hand of the deceased, while the mourning family would hold on to the other end and encourage the spirit of their loved one to climb higher into the realm of Heaven.

Tohunga also used toetoe to help cast out evil spirits or curses. When it was determined that a patient was insane, the tohunga would cut out a lock of their hair and tie it to a stalk of toetoe. This was then drifted down a river while the tohunga prayed to the gods to forgive the patient.

TAXONOMY

Toetoe is used to refer to the five species of native *Austroderia* that are all endemic to New Zealand. *Austroderia fulvida* is found only in the North Island, *A. splendens* is found only in the upper North Island, *A. toetoe* is found in the lower North Island, *A. richardii* is found only in the South Island, and *A. turbaria* is present only on the Chatham Islands. They belong to the grass family Poaceae, which also contains the world's most important crops – wheat, maize, rice, millet and barley.

TOETOE TREATMENTS

The feathers or stalk of toetoe provided a range of traditional remedies, particularly for wounds. The soft part of the stalk was commonly applied to burns or bleeding wounds, or burned and the ashes rubbed into the afflicted area. The stem could be boiled in water, and the liquid applied to serious wounds from spears and lances, and other sores and ulcers. Sometimes this stem infusion was mashed up with the roots of bush lawyer and supplejack and drunk in order to treat parasites.

The stem could be chewed to treat diarrhoea and kidney complaints, and the juice that exudes out of it was applied to the tongues of babies suffering from yeast infections. One rather unpleasant medicinal remedy made with toetoe was a natural enema for those suffering constipation. The roots of harakeke were crushed into a potion which produces violent diarrhoea. A stalk of toetoe was filled with the potion and inserted into the patient's anus. Someone would then need to blow on the other end of the toetoe so that the potion spurted into the rectum. It is said that the problem was fixed very rapidly after this.

Toetoe tosses its flowerheads back and forth in a sea breeze. (*Matthew Cattin*)

BUILDING AND WEAVING

The kākaho stalks provided Māori with an excellent building material, as they are long and straight with a consistent and even width. A lot of time was spent finding stalks that were just the right size and colour, and the stalks were used to line the insides of walls and roofs of houses, marae and storehouses, and are still seen today in tukutuku panels. They have been made into straws, pipes and frames for kites.

The flowers had an important role as a sieve to filter out the deadly seeds of the poisonous tutu when making juice and wine. The leaves also had their uses, although care needed to be taken to remove the sharp leaf margins, which can easily draw blood. Once these were dealt with, the leaves could be woven into mats and baskets.

INVASIVE PAMPAS

Many people are unaware of an invader in our midst. South American pampas grass closely resembles toetoe, and was first introduced into New Zealand in the 1800s as a fodder species for cattle. Pampas soon escaped into the wild and went rampant, outcompeting the native toetoe and covering vast swathes of the countryside. One of the biggest problems is that many people are unaware of the difference between the plants, and this exotic grass is often referred to as toetoe as well. The invasive pampas is even seen in photos depicting pristine, natural New Zealand landscapes.

Once the difference is learned, however, the pair can be easily distinguished, even at a distance. Toetoe has waxy leaves with drooping white, creamy flowers that often become yellowish in early summer. The invasive pampas has non-waxy leaves that build up in big brown chunks at the base of the plant, and erect white, pink or purple flowers that stand up straight like spears.

ETYMOLOGY

The New Zealand species were until recently included in the *Cortaderia* genus, from the Spanish word *cortadera*, which refers to a sharp knife or cutting instrument. The new genus name *Austroderia* adds the term *Austro*, meaning 'southern'. The species names of the group refer to various characteristics, *fulvida* meaning 'yellow', and *splendens* meaning 'shining'. The name 'toetoe' can also mean 'to shred or divide into strips', and seems to come from an older word in the Pacific for splitting *Pandanus* into strips. It is possible that the appearance of the feathery plumes or the splitting of the plant for weaving may have been in the minds of those who named it, but regardless as a plant name in New Zealand it is unique. The name 'kākaho' for the stalk is used for the culm of *Chionochloa* tussock grass in the South Island, and similar words are used across Polynesia to describe the Pacific Island silvergrass (*Miscanthus floridulus*). Toetoe is also known as 'cutty grass', due to the sharp edges of the leaves, which can draw blood.

BOTANICAL ODDBALLS

The weird and the wonderful

TREE FUCHSIA

A tasty fruit, and blue lipstick

When it comes to New Zealand's native plants, the tree fuchsia — kōtukutuku — stands apart. Most New Zealand native plants produce small, pale, inconspicuous flowers, but the tree fuchsia erupts with a dazzling display of purple flowers with bizarre blue pollen. Where most native plants will keep their leaves year-round, the tree fuchsia not only drops its leaves, but appears to shed its bark as well, leaving a skeleton of ragged branches. It is also far larger than it has any right to be. Fuchsia species are usually shrubs or small trees, but in New Zealand they have grown to gigantic proportions, reaching up to 12 metres in height, making this the largest fuchsia in the world.

TAXONOMY

Tree fuchsia (*Fuchsia excorticata*) is found throughout the North, South and Stewart Islands, and even grows on Auckland Island in the subantarctic. There are two other species of native fuchsia: one is a climbing shrub (*F. perscandens*), and the other creeps along the ground and is thought to be the smallest fuchsia in the world (*F. procumbens*). They all belong to the evening primrose family, Onagraceae, which includes many popular garden plants.

THE TASTY KŌNINI

This strange plant was a favourite food source for Māori. The edible purple berry tastes like a tamarillo, and was so valued that it was given its own name — kōnini. Berries were typically collected by Māori men, who would either climb the branches with baskets in hand, or shake the branches so the kōnini fell onto mats laid out below.

Kōnini berries were also relished by European settlers, who made them into jam, stewed them with honey or baked them into puddings. Kōnini were one of the very few native plant foods that European settlers were happy to unreservedly endorse, and even the most homesick settlers, with little positive to say about the New Zealand bush, had to admit that the fuchsia flowers were pretty and the berries didn't taste too bad. The missionary Henry Williams, generally regarded as fairly cool and calm-headed, even got into a brawl over them. He had bought and paid for a basket of kōnini from a local seller, who suddenly decided to raise the price. The two men came to blows, and Williams knocked the man on the head with a metal key concealed in his hand.

FOOD FOR THE BIRDS

The sweet berries are irresistible to birds also, particularly the kererū. This made the trees good places for hunting, as the politician Alfred Saunders wrote in 1868:

> I have seen a man shoot eighty fine pigeons on one fuchsia tree, as fast as he could load and fire, often killing three at a shot.[48]

Tree fuchsia (Fuchsia excorticata) by Fanny Osborne. *(Auckland War Memorial Museum, CCBY)*

While this particular statement is more than a little hard to believe, large flocks of birds certainly frequent the plant. The tree fuchsia seems to do quite well out of the bargain, with its seeds growing exceptionally well after being consumed and dispersed by birds. One study looking at bird diets found that a single dropping from an introduced blackbird produced a whopping 178 tree fuchsia seedlings.[49] Birds such as tūī and bellbird are important pollinators for fuchsia flowers as well, and are known to colour their faces blue with pollen as they drink nectar from the flowers. Evidence from coprolites (fossilised animal dung) show that the upland moa (*Megalapteryx didinus*) also fed on tree fuchsia nectar,[50] so presumably moa, too, wandered around the prehistoric Southern Alps with their faces stained blue.

ADDING COLOUR

As well as being an excellent food source, the tree fuchsia had a number of other important uses. The leaves were used along with bush lawyer and mangeao in a bath for pregnant mothers to help ease childbirth, and were also said to relieve fever and bruises.

The timber is strong and durable, but it was not used frequently as it is difficult to find a straight length of it, for the tree often grows twisted and convoluted. When enough suitable wood was found, it was used to make house blocks, posts, strainers and cabinets.

With their striking hues of pink, purple and blue, the colourful flowers are unlike anything else in the forest.
(*Edin Whitehead*)

Whalers in the South Island even experimented with the bark as a substitute for tobacco, although it is hard to imagine this was very effective.

The kōnini berry was also used to make purple dyes and inks, and the blue pollen of the flower was used as a type of makeup. Young girls would colour their cheeks red using other flowers, and then cover their lips with the brilliant blue pollen.

WHEN THE LEAVES FALL

In the North Island, the tree fuchsia flowers in September, and was an important event in the Māori calendar, signalling that it was time to begin the early spring planting of crops such as kūmara. If someone wished to help themselves to a large feed of kūmara but had not been willing to help out during this critical time of planting, one might proclaim:

> *I whea koe I te ngahorotanga o te rau o te kōtukutuku?*
> Where were you when the fuchsia leaves fell?[51]

This was said with a bitter sarcasm that struck the recipient with shame — in other words, 'Where were you when there was work to be done?' It has also been suggested that the falling leaves had another meaning, and were used to symbolise fellow warriors falling in battle. In this instance, it was used in a similar way: 'Where were you when your comrades were falling in battle?'

Fuchsia trees are often seen hanging over forest streams, as in this painting by Nicholas Chevalier from the 1860s. *(Te Papa, 1919-0002-8)*

LANCEWOOD

A camouflaged plant with thorny armour

Lancewood, or horoeka, is one of the oddest plants anywhere on earth. As it grows, it goes through a series of radical morphs in colour and shape. Plants with different growth stages are unusually common in the New Zealand bush, but none is quite as unusual as lancewood. The difference between the young and the adult form is so striking that early botanists classified lancewood as two separate species.

From the very moment its leaves burst out of the soil, lancewood is immediately interesting. Unlike the green seed leaves of most plants, lancewood's first leaves are brown and splotchy, making them difficult to spot on the forest floor. But it does not remain this way for long, as once it is a little bit taller it arms itself, growing stiff, narrow leaves studded with thorny edges and coloured with glowing, bright spots like dabs of paint. Then, after it has reached several metres in height, it undergoes another morph, spreading out and producing broad, green leaves that blend in with the rest of the forest canopy.

One theory for the lancewood's radical growth is that it evolved as a defence against moa species, which were once the dominant herbivores in a variety of environments across New Zealand. The 'moa browse hypothesis' often generates heated debate in the scientific community, however, and theories of plant coevolution with moa are difficult to confirm conclusively, given that the birds died out around 600 years ago. But the case for lancewood seems a little more compelling than most.

SHIFTING STRATEGIES

The tiny mottled brown seedlings have been proposed as one of the first examples of plants using camouflage to hide from their predators. Spectrographic analyses of the leaves have shown that moa, and birds in general, would struggle to identify the leaves against a background of brown leaf litter.[52] Intriguingly, however, once the plants grow up and arm themselves with long, narrow leaves with thorny projections, they appear to change their strategy entirely. The same spectrographic analysis showed that the colour patches along the spines of the leaves would have been glaringly obvious to birds, whose vision is highly sensitive to bright visual signals. It appears that once lancewood has developed its thick, thorny leaves, it gives up its strategy of hiding, and makes it clear that it is well defended and would make a difficult meal. Producing a signal like this has a cost, as less chlorophyll — the photosynthetic substance that allows plants to produce their food — is produced. But whatever the reason for the signal, it is presumably worth it.

Lancewood, as depicted by Martha King, 1842. (Alexander Turnbull Library, A-005-036)

The thorny spines of the juvenile lancewood may have deterred browsing moa. *(Edin Whitehead)*

In adulthood the tree changes again, which typically happens around 3 metres in height, which would put it beyond the reach of the tallest species of moa. From this point lancewood begins to act like any other tree of the forest, producing ordinary green leaves that can make the most of the available sunlight.

While the moa defence theory is captivating, it is also possible that the trees are responding to some other variable, such as changing climatic effects from the forest floor to the sub-canopy. It is interesting to note, however, that a close relative of lancewood growing on the Chatham Islands (*Pseudopanax chathamicus*), where moa were never present, has a fairly normal growth pattern, with typical green seedlings, green oblong leaves without thorns, and no obvious change as an adult.

MULTIPLE USES

This extraordinary plant also had an impact on the human inhabitants who arrived in New Zealand. Lancewood leaves made a good substitute for bootlaces, and when a bridle or harness broke the leaves could be used to mend them. The supple, flexible trunks could be used as whips; sometimes, when other wood was scarce, they were used as timber, particularly in the south around Otago. One account

ETYMOLOGY

The generic name *Pseudopanax* means 'false panax', and refers to its similarity to the genus *Panax*, which includes ginseng. The species name *crassifolius* means 'thick-leaved', and refers to the leathery leaves. The name 'horoeka' is thought to derive from an ancient Polynesian word 'soroeka', but it is unclear to which plant it refers. The three-leaved lancewood hybrids have been called 'tara-a-Māui' or 'spikes of Māui'. The common name 'lancewood' refers to its use as bird lances by Māori, and it was once also known as 'the fishbone tree' on account of the odd appearance of the leaves branching out, like ribs from a spine.

suggests the bark was chewed for its gum-like fluid, which helped to soothe the bowels after a bout of diarrhoea.

Māori used the sturdy trunks to construct spears for hunting birds, as referenced in its common name in English. These spears required no tip; the wood was simply sharpened to a point and burned. During stormy weather, kererū stay low in the forest to keep dry, and so this was the ideal time for spearing them.

As well as spears, the trunks make fine walking sticks, valued by Europeans and Māori, the twisting, grooved pattern of the wood giving a unique visual pattern to each cane.

The tough, leathery leaves also provided Māori in the South Island with a type of paintbrush. The leaves were pounded and lengths of fibrous hairs extracted to make the brush; animal fats, gums, soot and red ochre were combined to make paint. Some lancewood paintings depict extinct moa and the giant Haast's eagle, indicating that the artworks may date to over 500 years ago, before these species disappeared. Other paintings depict European ships, writing and horses, suggesting this painting technique lasted for centuries.

Watercolour painting of a lancewood branch, by Martha King, 1842. *(Turnbull Library, A-005-039)*

NEINEI

A tree of many names

Neinei is such a strange-looking plant that no one seems to be able to decide what to call it. One of its common names is 'the grass tree', as its long leaves look like tufts of grass on top of a branching wooden candelabra. Others have labelled it 'the pineapple tree' for its spiky, pineapple-like projection of seeds in the summertime. This lends the plant a distinctly tropical appearance, which is made even more unusual when it is seen gracing the tops of mountains or growing up alongside snow and glaciers.

Early Pākehā bushmen referred to the plant as 'kerosene wood', as it is supremely effective at promoting fire. It was commonly recommended as a survival tool for bushmen and travellers as they explored the new country, and it burns well even when wet and green.

They also called the plant 'spider wood', as when a transverse section is cut into the wood it reveals a beautiful web-like pattern. Māori appear to have made a similar connection, as the tree is sometimes regarded as sacred to Tāwhaki, who it is said ascended to the heavens on magical vines or spiders' webs to find his wife. Within the web-like pattern in the wood, the tree contains a record of this magical act of Tāwhaki climbing into the sky.

Neinei leaves often contain abundant red pigments, which make the plant stand out. (*Robert Vennell*)

Neinei (*Dracophyllum latifolium*) by Sarah Featon, c. 1885. (*Te Papa, 1992-0035-2277/22*)

Today, a common colloquial name is the 'Dr Seuss tree', as the plant's other-worldly appearance makes it look like one of the Truffula trees in the children's book *The Lorax*.

Neinei timber was valued by both Māori and Pākehā for making walking sticks and staffs, with curious twists and grooves in the trunk giving these sticks an intriguing pattern. Māori used them to craft toko wānanga, the staff of authority carried by a tohunga when teaching students. To preserve the beautiful spider's-web pattern in the wood, a green *Dracophyllum* trunk was suspended over a fire and beaten with a stick to remove the bark without damaging the heartwood. Occasionally the trunk was hollowed out and the wood made into a type of flute.

The long, stiff leaves were also useful, and were a speciality item for weavers, used for decorative features, such as tags to adorn the edges of cloaks. An edging of neinei leaves was woven into rain capes to help funnel water away from the body.

Neinei like this one are commonly spotted along mountain ridges. (*Robert Vennell*)

QUICK TO ADAPT

New Zealand is the world centre of diversity for *Dracophyllum*, with the vast majority of the species found here and only a few found in Australia and New Caledonia. DNA studies suggest *Dracophyllum* plants originated in Australia sometime during the Miocene, around 20 million years ago when the continent's temperate forests were transforming into dry desert. Only a few species of *Dracophyllum* persisted in cooler areas of Australia on mountain tops and further south in Tasmania.

One theory for their current distribution is that some *Dracophyllum* species were able to disperse seed to New Zealand, where the plants occupied a diverse landscape, with new habitats carved out by glaciers and other geological processes. By adapting to this wide range of environments, *Dracophyllum* was able to split into many different species.

Dracophyllum belong to the same plant family as heath, the Ericaceae, which are experts at dealing with poor soil environments. Many of the species in New Zealand live in poor soil, such as in the acidic podzols created by kauri trees or in rugged alpine environments. They produce thousands of seeds from their pineapple-like seed cones,

Hundreds of seeds are released by each of the neinei's spectacular seed heads. (Robert Vennell)

but very few germinate. They make up for this by being extremely long-lived — once their seeds take in an area, they will persist there for a very long time.

Another species of *Dracophyllum*, found further south, is known as 'inanga', and amazingly, despite its small size, it can grow to well over 200 years old. It was also called the 'kerosene plant' as it ignites rapidly, and Māori hunting tītī off Stewart Island/ Rakiura used inanga to build small whare to shelter in during the harvest.

ETYMOLOGY

The name *Dracophyllum* means 'dragon leaf', and refers to the similarity this group shares with the dragon tree (*Dracaena draco*) of the Canary Islands. The species name *latifolium* means 'broad leaf', while *traversii* honours the 19th-century naturalist William Travers. The word 'neinei' is used in Rarotonga for *Fitchia speciosa*, a tree in the daisy family that is restricted to the mountainous cloud forest. It is difficult to find common ground between the two trees, and it may have been a rather abstract connection that led to them sharing the same name. Two other plants in the New Zealand bush are known by the name 'neinei-kura': the native brooms *Carmichaelia grandiflora* and *C. odorata*. Both are equally as strange-looking as *Dracophyllum*, but it is difficult to see what their shared characteristics are beyond that.

REWAREWA

A glow-in-the-dark honeysuckle

Rewarewa looks somewhat out of place in the New Zealand forest. The lanky trunk emerges above the canopy to wave its spiky, leathery leaves and bundles of strange red and yellow flowers. These flowers are often found littered all over the forest floor — weird, colourful cylinders of spiralling tubes that look unlike anything else in the bush.

The reason behind rewarewa's strange appearance is that it is one of only two species in New Zealand that belong to the protea family, the Proteaceae. This group includes the sugar bushes of Africa, and the waratah, macadamia and banksia of Australia. The fossil and pollen record shows that New Zealand had a much more colourful flora in the past, with a diverse array of protea plants, but almost all became extinct during the ice ages. Rewarewa and toru (*Toronia toru*) are the only remaining proteas left.

The seed pods are a curious shape as well, and look like a small curved boat. In Māori tradition, they were said to be the inspiration for the shape of waka. One tale focuses on a young boy, Tautiniawhitia, whose father left to live in another land when he was just a baby. As Tautiniawhitia grew up, he was filled with shame at being abandoned and decided to seek out his father. He had heard a rumour that his father now resided on a faraway island, and to get there he would need to find a way to cross the ocean. Heading into the forest for materials to build a boat, he stumbled upon a seed pod of rewarewa. When he placed it on the water, it floated well and didn't rock from side to side. Using the pod as his blueprint, Tautiniawhitia took trees from the forest and fashioned a waka, which he used to sail to the faraway island. The craft was a success and he made it across the sea to the island, where he was briefly captured and enslaved, but was ultimately reunited with his father once more.

The sweet nectar produced by the flowers is thoroughly enjoyed by native birds, insects and humans alike. Māori collected the nectar and used it in the same way as harakeke, although the height of the tree must have made that a tricky task. After the nectar was collected in gourds, it could be slurped out using a long, hollow reed as a drinking straw. Today, rewarewa honey is one of the most popular native honeys; it is described as dark, malty and complex with a sweet finish. It contains a relatively high proportion of antioxidants and plant phenolics.

TAXONOMY

Rewarewa (*Knightia excelsa*) is the sole species in the *Knightia* genus, although other *Knightia* species are known from the New Zealand fossil record. It belongs to the protea family, Proteaceae, the only other member of which in New Zealand is toru (*Toronia toru*).

FIRE AND PHOSPHORESCENCE

Rewarewa wood has gained a bad reputation over the years. Pākehā settlers dubbed it the 'bucket of water wood', as it is often damp and rotten and not much use for starting fires. But despite this it has a beautiful, variegated, mottled wood, which has been made into furniture, axe handles, wheel spokes, cabinets and picture frames. Māori employed rewarewa wood as posts in rivers, and used it to build palisade walls. Although it is difficult to burn, once ignited it will stay lit for a long time, and these burning logs were used to hollow out the centres of trees when crafting waka.

A tall rewarewa tree, holding aloft bundles of bizarre-looking red flowers. *(Edin Whitehead)*

Intriguingly, there are reports that, under the right conditions, rotten rewarewa wood emits a phosphoric glow. This is most likely not an attribute of the wood, but the activity of some type of wood-decay fungus, possibly a species of *Armillaria*. While the phenomenon has been observed in other trees and the stipes of tree ferns, Māori appear to have singled out rewarewa for this quality.

One intriguing report suggests that glowing rewarewa wood was used on occasion to light houses. Some Māori speaking to Elsdon Best said they avoided using rewarewa in cooking, because glow-worms inhabited the wood. Glow-worms were believed to be the offspring of a mischievous deity called Tangaroa-piri-whare, and it was said that it was best to avoid the wood, otherwise crops might fail. Few accounts of this phosphoric phenomenon exist, but a tantalising report from the explorer Ernst Dieffenbach may refer to rewarewa trees. While exploring the Taranaki region his party was beset by rain for several days and could not light a fire:

ETYMOLOGY

The genus was given the name *Knightia* in honour of Thomas Andrew Knight, a president of the Royal Horticultural Society of London. The species name *excelsa* means 'tall' or 'elevated'. Europeans gave rewarewa the name 'New Zealand honeysuckle' on account of its delicious, edible nectar. The Māori name, 'rewarewa', is most likely derived from the Polynesian words 'reva' and 'leva', names for the suicide tree (*Cerbera odollom*), which contains toxic kernels that have been used in homicides and suicides. Although not closely related, both trees have long leaves, edible nectar and are used for the treatment of sore throats. The word 'rewa' in te reo Māori also carries the meaning 'elevated', and it may be that the emergent rewarewa inspired this lofty term.

During these nights the forest assumed a beautiful appearance: the fallen trees and almost the whole surface of the ground sparkled in a thousand places with the phosphorescence of the decayed matter; we seemed to have entered the illuminated domain of fairy-land.[53]

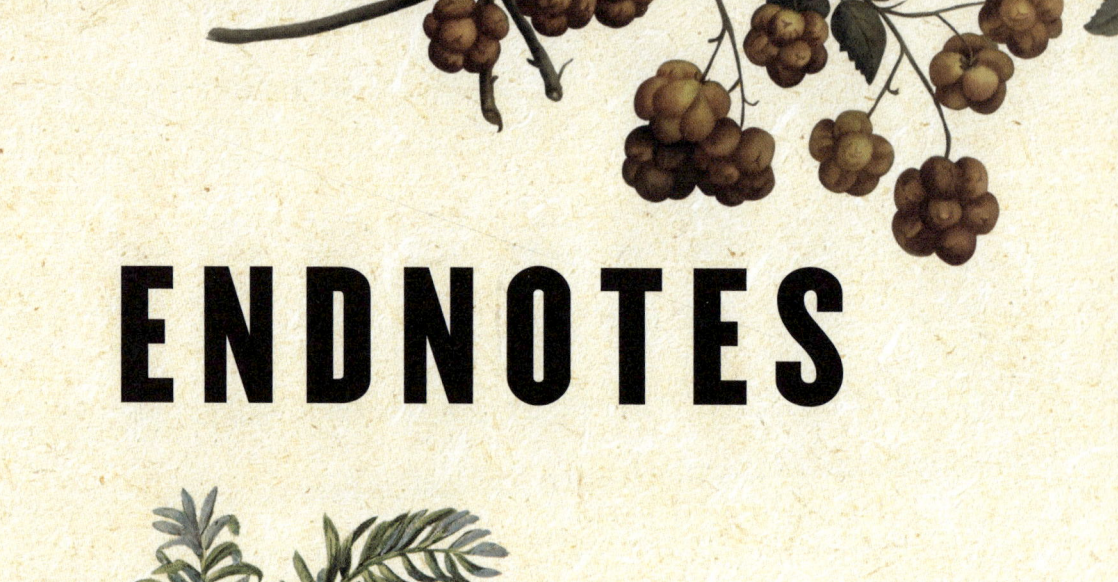

ENDNOTES

1. Interestingly, cytisine has a long history of helping people stop smoking, and four systematic reviews have concluded it is better than a placebo for getting people to quit in both the short and long term. See: Prochaska et al. (2013).

2. Shortland, E. (1851). *The Southern Districts of New Zealand: A journal, with passing notices of the customs of the Aborigines.* London: Longman, Brown, Green, & Longmans. NZETC.

3. Colenso, W. (1881). 'Contributions towards a better knowledge of the Maori race.' *Transactions and Proceedings of the Royal Society of New Zealand*, 14, 33–48.

4. Mair, G. (1895). 'The ancient tribe Te Panenehu.' *Transactions and Proceedings of the New Zealand Institute*, 28, 36–40.

5. Best, E. (1977b). *Forest Lore of the Maori.* Wellington: E.C. Keating. NZETC.

6. Georg Forster quoted in Best, E. (1977b).

7. Thomas Edgar quoted in Best, E. (1977b).

8. Harcourt Aubrey quoted in Best, E. (1977b).

9. Best, E. (1977b).

10. Best, E. (1977b).

11. Hursthouse, C. (1849). *An Account of the Settlement of New Plymouth, in New Zealand: From personal observation, during a residence there of five years.* Retrieved from: www.enzb.auckland.ac.nz/document/?wid=633&action=null

12. May, J. (1869). *Guide to Farming in New Zealand.* Retrieved from: www.enzb.auckland.ac.nz/document/?wid=2902&action=null (page 70)

13. Best, E. (1977b).

14. Angas, G.F. (1847). *Savage Life and Scenes in Australia and New Zealand, Vol. II.* Retrieved from www.enzb.auckland.ac.nz/document/?wid=607&action=null

15. Taylor, R. (1868). *The Geography of New Zealand. The past and present of New Zealand: With its prospects for the future.* London: W. Macintosh. NZETC.

16. Hursthouse, *An Account.*

17. The flute, named Murirangaranga, now resides in Rotorua Museum, Ethnology no. 69.

18. Best, E. (1977b).

19. Colenso, W. 'Contributions …'.

20. Selwyn, G. (1847). *Annals of the Diocese of New Zealand.* Retrieved from: www.enzb.auckland.ac.nz/document/?wid=1652&action=null

21. Pike, M. (2015). 'I ate tutu … and lived to tell the story.' *Wilderness Magazine NZ.* Retrieved from: www.wildernessmag.co.nz/ate-tutu-lived-tell-story

22. Von Hochstetter, F. (1867). *New Zealand: Its physical geography, geology and natural history, with special reference to … the provinces of Auckland and Nelson.* Retrieved from www.enzb.auckland.ac.nz/document/?wid=433&action=null

23. Best, E. (1924). *The Maori As He Was: A brief account of Maori life as it was in pre-European days.* Wellington, Dominion Museum.

24. Banks, J. (2005). '*The Endeavour journal of Sir Joseph Banks.*' Project Gutenberg. Retrieved from http://gutenberg.net.au/ebooks05/0501141h.html

25. Clout, M.N., & Hay, J.R. (1989). 'The importance of birds as browsers, pollinators and seed dispersers in New Zealand forests.' *New Zealand Journal of Ecology*, 12, 27–33.

26. Best, E. (1977b).

27. Hunt, F. (1866). *Twenty-five Years' Experience in New Zealand and the Chatham Islands.* Retrieved from: www.enzb.auckland.ac.nz/document/?wid=2079&action=null (page 137)

28. Grey, G. (1857). *Ko nga whakapepeha me nga whakaahuareka a nga tipuna o Aotea-roa: Proverbial and popular sayings of the ancestors of the New Zealand race.* Cape Town: Saul Solomon.

29. Taylor, R. (1855). *Te Ika a Maui, or New Zealand and Its Inhabitants.* London: Wertheim & Macintosh. NZETC.

30. Lindsay Buick, T. (2013).

31. Cook, J. (1768). *Captain Cook's Journal During His First Voyage Round the World Made in HM Bark "Endeavour".* London: Elliot Stock. Project Gutenberg, retrieved from www.gutenberg.org/files/8106/8106-h/8106-h.htm

32. Bear Grylls, *Man vs. Wild* (Season 7, Episode 5).

33. Anon. (1860, 19 September). [War Correspondent, Taranaki]. *Nelson Examiner and New Zealand Chronicle,* Volume XIX, Issue 77.

34. Grey, *Ko nga whakapepeha.*

35. Haynes, S.L. (1868). *A Ramble in the New Zealand Bush.* Retrieved from: www.enzb.auckland.ac.nz/document/?wid=4633&page=0&action=null (Page 194)

36. Guinness World Records (2016). *Guinness World Records 2017.* Guinness World Records.

37. Lovell-Smith, M. (2005, 3 December). 'Sting of native nettle.' *The Press.*

38. Buenz, E.J., Parry, G.J., Bauer, B.A., Howe, C.L., Hammond-Tooke, G., Tsuchihara, T., ... & Peacey, M. (2017). 'A potential therapeutic for chronic pain from the New Zealand native stinging nettle *Urtica ferox* (ongaonga).' *Journal of Neurology, Neurosurgery and Psychiatry;* 88 (5), e1.

39. Thorsen, M. J., Seddon, P. J., & Dickinson, K.J. (2011). 'Faunal influences on New Zealand seed dispersal characteristics.' *Evolutionary Ecology,* 25 (6), 1397–1426.

40. Colenso, W. (1891). 'Vestiges, reminiscences, memorabilia of works, deeds, and sayings of the ancient Maoris.' *Transactions and Proceedings of the New Zealand Institute,* 12, 445–467.

41. Von Hochstetter, F. (1867). *New Zealand: Its Physical Geography, Geology and Natural History, with Special Reference To . . . the Provinces of Auckland and Nelson.* Retrieved from http://www.enzb.auckland.ac.nz/document/?wid=433&action=null

42. Banks, J. (2005 [1768–1771]). 'The *Endeavour* journal of Sir Joseph Banks.' Project Gutenberg Australia. Retrieved from http://gutenberg.net.au/ebooks05/0501141h.html

43. Monckton, F. (1885, 4 February). '*Phormium tenax* and its therapeutic value.' *The West Coast Times,* Issue 4833.

44. Grey, *Ko nga whakapepeha.*

45. Cook, J. (1777.) *A Voyage Towards the South Pole and Round the World, Volume 2.* London: Strahan & Caddell. Project Gutenberg, retrieved from: www.gutenberg.net.au/ebooks/e00045.html

46. Colenso, W. (1880). 'On the vegetable food of the ancient New Zealanders before Cook's visit.' In *Transactions and Proceedings of the New Zealand Institute,* 13, 3–38.

47. Twain, M. (1897) *Following the Equator; A journey around the world.* Project Gutenberg. Retrieved from: www.gutenberg.org/files/2895/2895-h/2895-h.htm.

48. Saunders, A. (1868). *New Zealand: Its climate, soil, natural and artificial productions, animals, birds and insects, aboriginal and European inhabitants etc.* Retrieved from: www.enzb.auckland.ac.nz/document/?wid=4568&action=null

49. Beveridge, A.E. (1964). 'Dispersal and destruction of seed in central North Island podocarp forests.' *Proceedings of the New Zealand Ecological Society*, 11 (11), 48–55.

50. Wood, J.R., Wilmshurst, J.M., Wagstaff, S.J., Worthy, T.H., Rawlence, N.J., & Cooper, A. (2012). 'High-resolution coproecology: using coprolites to reconstruct the habits and habitats of New Zealand's extinct upland moa (*Megalapteryx didinus*).' *PloS one*, 7 (6), e40025.

51. Colenso, W. 'Contributions …'.

52. Fadzly, N., Jack, C., Schaefer, H.M., & Burns, K.C. (2009). 'Ontogenetic colour changes in an insular tree species: signalling to extinct browsing birds?' *New Phytologist*, 184 (2), 495–501.

53. Wells, B. (1878). *The History of Taranaki: A standard work on the history of the province.* Retrieved from: www.enzb.auckland.ac.nz/document/?wid=745

PICTURE CREDITS

Pages 6–7: Fruit of the supplejack, *Ripogonum scandens* by Martha King (Alexander Turnbull Library, A-005-034), *The taua, a large forest-tree* by Martha King (Alexander Turnbull Library, PUBL-0011-13-2), *Coprosma australis*/Kanono by Sarah Featon (Te Papa, 1992-0035-2277/45)

Page 12: Wharariki (*Phormium cookianum*) by Fanny Osborne (Auckland War Memorial Museum, CCBY), Poroporo by Sarah Featon (Te Papa, 1992-0035-2277/87), Warangi [Rangiora] by Martha King (Alexander Turnbull Library, A-005-017), Manuka (*Leptospermum scoparium*) by Fanny Osborne (Auckland War Memorial Museum, CCBY)

Page 242: Bush lawyer (*Rubus schmidelioides*) by Fanny Osborne (Auckland War Memorial Museum, CCBY), Miro/Kawaka by Sarah Featon (Te Papa, 1992-0035-2277/64), Hinau (*Elaeocarpus dentatus*) by Fanny Osborne (Auckland War Memorial Museum, CCBY).

BIBLIOGRAPHY

KEY SOURCES

Alexander Turnbull Library — National Library of New Zealand — Te Puna Mātauranga o Aotearoa, https://natlib.govt.nz/collections/a-z/alexander-turnbull-library-collections

Benton, R. (2018). *Te Māra Reo; The Language Garden*. Retrieved from www.temarareo.org/

Best, E. (1977b). *Forest Lore of the Maori*. Wellington: E.C. Keating Early New Zealand Books — University of Auckland Libraries and Learning Services. www.enzb.auckland.ac.nz

Biodiversity Heritage Library BHL, www.biodiversitylibrary.org

Greenhill, S.J., & Clark, R. (2011). 'POLLEX-Online: The Polynesian Lexicon Project Online.' *Oceanic Linguistics*, 50(2), 551–559.

Manaaki Whenua Landcare Research. (2018). Ngā Tipu Whakaoranga database. Retrieved from: www.maoriplantuse.landcareresearch.co.nz

Moorfield, J.C. (2005). *Te Aka: Māori–English, English–Māori Dictionary and Index*. Auckland: Pearson Longman.

New Zealand Electronic Text Collection — Te Pūhikotuhi o Aotearoa — Victoria University of Wellington, www.nzetc.victoria.ac.nz

Papers Past — National Library of New Zealand www.paperspast.natlib.govt.nz

Puke Ariki, www.pukeariki.com/Heritage-Collections

Riley, M. (1994). *Māori Healing and Herbal: New Zealand Ethnobotanical Sourcebook*. Paraparaumu: Viking Sevenseas NZ.

Tāmaki Paenga Hira — Auckland War Memorial Museum, http://www.aucklandmuseum.com/discover/collections

Taylor, M., Bieleski, R.L., & Allan, H.H. (2002). *Meanings and Origins of Botanical Names of New Zealand Plants*. Auckland: Auckland Botanical Society.

The Museum of New Zealand Te Papa Tongarewa, www.collections.tepapa.govt.nz/

OTHER SOURCES

Adams, O. (1945). 'Maori medicinal plants'. *Auckland Botanical Society*, Bulletin 2.

Allen, R.B., Payton, I.J., & Knowlton, J.E. (1984). 'Effects of ungulates on structure and species composition in the Urewera forests as shown by exclosures.' *New Zealand Journal of Ecology*, 7, 119–130.

Allingham, B. (2018) 'Ngā toi ana — Who were the rock artists?', *Te Ara — the Encyclopedia of New Zealand*. Retrieved from http://www.TeAra.govt.nz/en/nga-toi-ana/page-1

Angas, G.F. (1847). *Savage Life and Scenes in Australia and New Zealand, Volume II.* Retrieved from http://www.enzb.auckland.ac.nz/document/?wid=607&action=null

Anon. (1860). [War Correspondent, Taranaki]. *Nelson Examiner and New Zealand Chronicle*, Volume XIX, Issue 77.

Anon. (1863). 'The bush and bush scourers.' *The New Zealander*, Volume XIX, Issue 1945.

Anon. (1870). 'A new fruit.' *The New Zealand Herald*, Volume VII, Issue 1994.

Anon. (1884). 'Tawhiao in England'. *The Otago Daily Times*, Issue 7047.

Anon. (1888). [Advertisement for Koromiko Cordial]. *Daily Telegraph*, Issue 5140.

Anon. (1916). [Koromiko in the First World War]. *Taihape Daily Times*, Volume 8, Issue 113.

Anon. (1919). 'Māori fish trap.' *Ohinemuri Gazette*, Volume CCC, Issue 4034.

Anon. (1942). 'The Empire's war activities: value of koromiko treatment for dysentery.' *Bay of Plenty Beacon*, Volume 6, Issue 6.

Baber, J. (1886). 'The medicinal properties of some New Zealand plants.' *Transactions and Proceedings of the New Zealand Institute*, 19, 319–322.

Bagnall, L.J. (1886). 'Kahikatea as a building timber.' *Transactions and Proceedings of the New Zealand Institute*, 19, 577–580.

Balance, A. (2010). *Kakapo: Rescued from the brink of extinction.* Nelson: Craig Potton Publishing.

Banks, J. (2005 [1768–1771]). 'The *Endeavour* journal of Sir Joseph Banks.' Project Gutenberg Australia. Retrieved from http://gutenberg.net.au/ebooks05/0501141h.html

Barber, I.G., Maxwell, J.J., & Petchey, F. (2016). 'A radiocarbon investigation of Moriori forest use on Rēkohu (Chatham Island), southwestern Polynesia.' *Journal of Archaeological Science: Reports*, 10, 96–109.

Bathgate, A. (1874). *Colonial Experiences, or Sketches of People and Places in the Province of Otago, New Zealand.* Retrieved from www.enzb.auckland.ac.nz/document/?wid=2804&action=null

Beattie, H. (1920). 'Nature-lore of the southern Maori.' *Transactions and Proceedings of the New Zealand Institute*, 52, 53–77.

Beattie, H. (1994 [1954]). *Our Southernmost Maoris.* Christchurch: Cadsonbury Publications.

Beever, J. (1981). 'The origin of the name cabbage tree for *Cordyline* species in New Zealand.' *Wellington Botanical Society Bulletin*, 41, 50–58.

Bennett, G. (1860). *Gatherings of a Naturalist in Australasia.* Retrieved from www.enzb.auckland.ac.nz/document/?wid=4732 (original held by Auckland Museum)

Bentley, T. (2010). *Cannibal Jack: The life and times of Jacky Marmon, a Pākehā-Māori.* Auckland: Penguin.

Benton, R. (2018). *Te Māra Reo; The Language Garden.* Retrieved from www.temarareo.org/

Best, E. (1896). *In Ancient Maoriland.* The Pamphlet Collection of Sir Robert Stout, 74, retrieved from: www.nzetc.victoria.ac.nz/tm/scholarly/tei-Stout74-t18.html

Best, E. (1899). 'The art of the whare pora.' *Transactions and Proceedings of the New Zealand Institute*, 31, 625–658.

Best, E. (1907). 'Maori forest lore.' *Transactions and Proceedings of the Royal Society of New Zealand*, 40, 185–253.

Best, E. (1913). 'Tuhoe: the Children of the Mist.' *The Journal of the Polynesian Society*, 22 (87), 149–165.

Best, E. (1924). *The Maori As He Was: A brief account of Maori life as it was in pre-European days.* Wellington,: Dominion Museum.

Best, E. (1976). *Māori Religion and Mythology.* Wellington: A.R. Shearer. NZETC.

Best, E. (1977a). *Fishing Methods and Devices of the Māori.* Wellington: E.C. Keating. NZETC.

Best, E. (1977b). *Forest Lore of the Maori*. Wellington: E.C. Keating. NZETC.

Beveridge, A.E. (1964). 'Dispersal and destruction of seed in central North Island podocarp forests.' *Proceedings of the New Zealand Ecological Society*, 11(11), 48–55.

Bidwill, J.C. (1841). *Rambles in New Zealand*. Retrieved from www.enzb.auckland.ac.nz/document/?wid=1186&page=1&action=null

Biggs, B. (1991). 'A linguist revisits the New Zealand bush.' *The Journal of the Polynesian Society*, 48, 67–72.

Blair, W.N. (1879). 'The building materials of Otago.' *Transactions and Proceedings of the Royal Society*, 9, 134–176.

Bond, W.J., Lee, W.G., & Craine, J.M. (2004). 'Plant structural defences against browsing birds: a legacy of New Zealand's extinct moas.' *Oikos*, 104(3), 500–508.

Brock, J.M., Perry, G.L., Lee, W.G., Schwendenmann, L., & Burns, B.R. (2018). 'Pioneer tree ferns influence community assembly in northern New Zealand forests.' *New Zealand Journal of Ecology*, 42 (1), 18–30.

Brooker, S.G., Cambie, R.C., & Cooper, R.C. (1981). *New Zealand Medicinal Plants*. Auckland: Heinemann.

Brooker, S.G., Cambie, R.C., & Cooper, R.C. (1988). *Economic Native Plants of New Zealand*. Champaign, Ill.: Balogh Scientific Books.

Brunner, T. (1850). *Journal of an Expedition to Explore the Interior of the Middle Island of New Zealand*. Christchurch: Pegasus Press. NZETC.

Buenz, E.J., Parry, G.J., Bauer, B.A., Howe, C.L., Hammond-Tooke, G., Tsuchihara, T., ... & Peacey, M. (2017). 'A potential therapeutic for chronic pain from the New Zealand native stinging nettle *Urtica ferox* (ongaonga).' *Journal of Neurology, Neurosurgery and Psychiatry*; 88 (5), e1.

Burns, K.C. (2010). 'Is crypsis a common defensive strategy in plants? Speculation on signal deception in the New Zealand flora.' *Plant Signalling and Behavior*, 5(1), 9–13.

Cambie, R.C., & Ferguson, L.R. (2003). 'Potential functional foods in the traditional Māori diet.' *Mutation Research/Fundamental and Molecular Mechanisms of Mutagenesis*, 523, 109–117.

Carpenter, J.K., Wood, J.R., Wilmshurst, J.M., & Kelly, D. (2018). 'An avian seed dispersal paradox: New Zealand's extinct megafaunal birds did not disperse large seeds.' *Proceedings of the Royal Society B*, 285(1877), 20180352.

Clout, M.N., & Hay, J.R. (1989). 'The importance of birds as browsers, pollinators and seed dispersers in New Zealand forests.' *New Zealand Journal of Ecology*, 12, 27–33.

Cockayne, L. (1919). *New Zealand Plants and Their Story*. Wellington: John Mackay.

Colenso, W. (1844). *Excursion in the Northern Island of New Zealand in the Summer of 1841–2*. Retrieved from: www.enzb.auckland.ac.nz/document/?wid=3721&action=null

Colenso, W. (1880). 'On the vegetable food of the ancient New Zealanders before Cook's visit.' *Transactions and Proceedings of the New Zealand Institute*, 13, 3–38.

Colenso, W. (1881). 'Contributions towards a better knowledge of the Maori race.' *Transactions and Proceedings of the Royal Society of New Zealand*, 14, 33–48.

Colenso, W. (1891). 'Vestiges, reminiscences, memorabilia of works, deeds, and sayings of the ancient Māoris.' *Transactions and Proceedings of the New Zealand Institute*, 12, 445–467.

Connor, H.E. (1977). *The Poisonous Plants in New Zealand*. Wellington: Government Printer.

Connor, H.E., & Fountain, J.S. (2009). *Plants that Poison: A New Zealand guide*. Lincoln: Manaaki Whenua Press.

Cook, J. (1768). *Captain Cook's Journal During His First Voyage Round the World Made in HM Bark "Endeavour"*. London: Elliot Stock. Project Gutenberg, retrieved from www.gutenberg.org/files/8106/8106-h/8106-h.html

Cook, J. (1777.) *A Voyage Towards the South Pole and Round the World*, Volumes 1 & 2. London: Strahan & Caddell. Project Gutenberg, retrieved from: www.gutenberg.net. au/ebooks/e00044.html

Cooney, L.J., Van Klink, J.W., Hughes, N.M., Perry, N.B., Schaefer, H.M., Menzies, I.J., & Gould, K.S. (2012). 'Red leaf margins indicate increased polygodial content and function as visual signals to reduce herbivory in *Pseudowintera colorata*.' *New Phytologist*, 194(2), 488–497.

Cowan, J. (1925). *Fairy Folk Tales of the Māori*. Auckland: Whitcomb and Tombs.

Cowan, J. (2006 [1934]). *Tales of the Māori Bush*. Auckland: Raupo.

Cowan, P.E., & Waddington, D.C. (1990). 'Suppression of fruit production of the endemic forest tree, *Elaeocarpus dentatus*, by introduced marsupial brushtail possums, *Trichosurus vulpecula*.' *New Zealand Journal of Botany*, 28(3), 217–224.

Cranwell, L. (1931). 'Food and medicine.' *The Northern Advocate*.

Cranwell, L. (1933). 'Native wild flowers.' *The Auckland Star*, Volume LXIV, Issue 261.

Crawford, J.C. (1876). 'On New Zealand coffee.' *Transactions and Proceedings of the New Zealand Institute*, 9, 545–546.

Crayon (1842). 'Character of the natives — value of the soil and climate.' *The New Zealand Journal*, 3, 278–280.

Crowe, A. (1990). *Field Guide to the Native Edible Plants of New Zealand*. Auckland: Hodder and Stoughton.

Crowe, A. (2003). *Which Native Forest Plant?* Auckland: Penguin Books.

Crowe, A. (2009). *Which Native Fern?* New Ecology Edition. Auckland: Penguin Books.

Dawson, J., & Lucas, R. (2012). *Field Guide to New Zealand's Native Trees*. Nelson: Craig Potton.

Dawson, J.W. (1986). 'The vines, epiphytes and parasites of New Zealand forests.' *Tuatara*, 28(2), 43–70.

Dawson, M. (2014). 'On distant shores: New Zealand's natives as weeds abroad.' *New Zealand Garden Journal*, 17(1), 10–24.

Dendy, A. (1901). 'On some relics of the Moriori race.' *Transactions of the New Zealand Institute*, 34, 123–134.

Dieffenbach, E. (1843). 'Letter to the editor of the *Chemical Gazette* on *Phormium tenax* as a substitute for sarsaparilla.' *The New Zealand Gazette and Wellington Spectator*. Volume IV, Issue 274.

Dieffenbach, E. (1843). *Travels in New Zealand (Vol. 1)*. Retrieved from: www.enzb.auckland.ac.nz/document/?wid=210&action=null

Eldred-Grigg, S. (1984). *Pleasures of the Flesh: Sex and drugs in Colonial New Zealand, 1840–1915*. Wellington: Reed.

Fadzly, N., Jack, C., Schaefer, H.M., & Burns, K.C. (2009). 'Ontogenetic colour changes in an insular tree species: signalling to extinct browsing birds?' *New Phytologist*, 184(2), 495–501.

Fraser, C.I., Spencer, H.G., & Waters, J.M. (2012). *Durvillaea poha* sp. nov. (Fucales, Phaeophyceae): a buoyant southern bull-kelp species endemic to New Zealand.' *Phycologia*, 51(2), 151–156.

Gillies, S. (2015). 'Kiwi's death bolt out of the blue.' Radio New Zealand. Retrieved from: www.radionz. co.nz/news/regional/285042/kiwis-death-bolt-out-of-the-blue

Goldie, W. (1905). 'Maori medical lore.' *Transactions of the New Zealand Institute*, 37, 1–120.

Greenhill, S.J., & Clark, R. (2011). 'POLLEX-Online: The Polynesian Lexicon Project Online.' *Oceanic Linguistics*, 50(2), 551–559.

Greenwood, R.M., & Atkinson, I.A.E. (1977). 'Evolution of divaricating plants in New Zealand in relation to moa browsing.' *Proceedings of the New Zealand Ecological Society*, 24, 21–33.

Grey, G. (1853). *Ko Nga Moteatea: me nga hakirara o nga Maori*. Retrieved from http://nzetc.victoria.ac.nz/tm/scholarly/tei-GreKong.html

Grey, G. (1857). *Ko nga whakapepeha me nga whakaahuareka a nga tipuna o Aotea-roa: Proverbial and Popular Sayings of the Ancestors of the New Zealand Race.* Cape Town: Saul Solomon.

Guinness World Records (2016). *Guinness World Records 2017.* Guinness World Records.

Harper, A.P. (1896). *Pioneer Work in the Alps of New Zealand: A record of the first exploration of the chief glaciers and ranges of the Southern Alps.* London: T.F. Unwin.

Hay, J. (1915). *Reminiscences of Earliest Canterbury and Its Settlers.* Christchurch: Christchurch Press.

Haynes, S.L. (1868). *A Ramble in the New Zealand Bush.* Retrieved from: www.enzb.auckland.ac.nz/document/?wid=4633&page=0&action=null

Heenan, P.B., De Lange, P.J., & Wilton, A.D. (2001). 'Sophora (Fabaceae) in New Zealand: taxonomy, distribution, and biogeography.' *New Zealand Journal of Botany*, 39(1), 17–53.

Hildreth, B. (1979). *How to Survive in the Bush, on the Coast, in the Mountains of New Zealand.* Wellington: Government Printer.

Hiroa, T.R. [Sir Peter Buck] (1910). 'Medicine amongst the Maoris, in ancient and modern times.' Unpublished thesis for the Doctor of Medicine, New Zealand.

Hiroa, T.R. [Sir Peter Buck] (1921). 'Maori food-supplies of Lake Rotorua, with methods of obtaining them, and usages and customs appertaining thereto.' *Transactions of the New Zealand Institute*, 26, 429–451.

Hiroa, T.R. [Sir Peter Buck] (1949). *The Coming of the Maori.* Wellington: Maori Purposes Fund Board.

Hokotehi Moriori Trust (2014). *Rakau momori (Moriori memorial trees) Fact Sheet.* Retrieved from: www.moriori.co.nz/_w/_w/wp-content/uploads/2014/09/Ra%CC%84kau-Momori-fact-sheet-aug-2014-final.pdf

Horrocks, M., D'Costa, D., Wallace, R., Gardner, R., & Kondo, R. (2004). 'Plant remains in coprolites: diet of a subalpine moa (Dinornithiformes) from southern New Zealand.' *Emu*, 104(2), 149–156.

Huang, W. (2012). 'Development of a novel alcoholic spirit from the New Zealand native plant *Cordyline australis*.' Unpublished doctoral dissertation, Auckland University of Technology.

Hunt, F. (1866). *Twenty-five Years' Experience in New Zealand and the Chatham Islands.* Retrieved from: www.enzb.auckland.ac.nz/document/?wid=2079&action=null

Hursthouse, C. (1849). *An Account of the Settlement of New Plymouth, in New Zealand: From personal observation, during a residence there of five years.* Retrieved from: www.enzb.auckland.ac.nz/document/?wid=633&action=null

Hutt, M., & Andrews, P. (1999). *Te Iwi Maori me te Inu Waipiro: He Tuhituhinga Hitori / Māori and Alcohol: A history.* Wellington: Health Services Research Centre/ALAC.

Indigena (1908). 'Maori burial customs.' *The New Zealand Herald*, Volume XLV, Issue 13769, Supplement.

Indigena (1908). 'Some wahitapu in the north.' *The New Zealand Herald*, Volume XLV, Issue 13775, Supplement.

Invercargill City Council (2013) *Sandy Point Management Plan.* Retrieved from: https://icc.govt.nz/wp-content/uploads/2014/10/Sandy-Point-Domain-Management-Plan-July-2013.pdf

Jaishankar, A., Wee, M., Matia-Merino, L., Goh, K.K., & McKinley, G.H. (2015). 'Probing hydrogen bond interactions in a shear thickening polysaccharide using nonlinear shear and extensional rheology.' *Carbohydrate polymers*, 123, 136–145.

Janssen, P.L., & Hollman, M. (2011). *Trees of New Zealand: Stories of beauty and character.* Auckland: Hodder Moa.

Kerridge, D. (2017). 'Mamaku: the native ingredient in the best green smoothie yet.' *The Spinoff*. Retrieved from www.thespinoff.co.nz/atea/08-12-2017/mamaku-the-native-ingredient-in-the-best-green-smoothie-yet/

Knox, J. (2013). *A Forager's Treasury: A New Zealand guide to finding and using wild plants.* Auckland: Allen and Unwin.

Leach, H. (2003). 'Fern consumption in Aotearoa and its Oceanic precedents.' *The Journal of the Polynesian Society*, 112(2), 141–155.

Lindsay Buick, T. (2013 [1914]). *The Treaty of Waitangi: Or how New Zealand became a British Colony*. Project Gutenberg Australia. Retrieved from: www.gutenberg.org/files/41800/41800-h/41800-h.htm

Locke, S. (1882). 'Historical traditions of the Taupo and East Coast tribes.' *Transactions and Proceedings of the New Zealand Institute*, 15, 433–459.

Lorrey, A. M., Boswijk, G., Hogg, A., Palmer, J. G., Turney, C. S., Fowler, A. M., … & Woolley, J. M. (2018). 'The scientific value and potential of New Zealand swamp kauri.' *Quaternary Science Reviews*, 183, 124–139.

Lovell-Smith, M. (2005). 'Sting of native nettle.' *The Press*.

McGlone, M.S., Wilmshurst, J.M., & Leach, H.M. (2005). 'An ecological and historical review of bracken (*Pteridium esculentum*) in New Zealand, and its cultural significance.' *New Zealand Journal of Ecology*, 165–184.

McLauchlan, G., & Ross, H. (2009). *The Story of Beer: Beer and brewing, a New Zealand history*. Auckland: Penguin.

Mair, G. (1870). 'Notes on the Chatham Islands and their inhabitants.' *Transactions and Proceedings of the New Zealand Institute*, 3, 311–313.

Mair, G. (1895). 'The ancient tribe Te Panenehu.' *Transactions and Proceedings of the New Zealand Institute*, 28, 36–40.

Manaaki Whenua Landcare Research. (2018). Ngā Tipu Whakaoranga database. Retrieved from: www.maoriplantuse.landcareresearch.co.nz

Mancall, P.C., Robertson, P., & Huriwai, T. (2000). 'Māori and alcohol: a reconsidered history.' *Australian and New Zealand Journal of Psychiatry*, 34(1), 129–134.

Matthews, R.H. (1910). 'Reminiscences of Māori life fifty years ago.' *Transactions and Proceedings of the New Zealand Institute*, 43, 598–605.

Maxwell, J.J., Howarth, J.D., Vandergoes, M.J., Jacobsen, G.E., & Barber, I.G. (2016). 'The timing and importance of arboriculture and agroforestry in a temperate East Polynesia Society, the Moriori, Rekohu (Chatham Island).' *Quaternary Science Reviews*, 149, 306–325.

May, J. (1869). *Guide to Farming in New Zealand*. Retrieved from: www.enzb.auckland.ac.nz/document/?wid=2902&action=null

Mead, H.M., & Grove, N. (2004). *Ngā Pēpeha a Ngā Tīpuna: The sayings of the ancestors*. Wellington: Victoria University Press.

Menzies, I.J. (2013). 'Do foliar anthocyanin pigments in horopito (*Pseudowintera colorata*) function as visual signals to deter insect herbivores?' Unpublished doctoral dissertation, Victoria University of Wellington.

Miller, D. (1952). 'The insect people of the Maori.' *The Journal of the Polynesian Society*, 61(1/2), 1–61.

Monckton, F. (1885). '*Phormium tenax* and its therapeutic value.' *The West Coast Times*, Issue 4833.

Moorfield, J.C. (2005). *Te Aka: Māori–English, English–Māori Dictionary and Index*. Auckland: Pearson Longman.

Nepia, G., & Mclean, T.P. (2002). *I, George Nepia: The autobiography of a rugby legend*. London: League Publications.

O'Connor, S.J., & Kelly, D. (2012). 'Seed dispersal of matai (*Prumnopitys taxifolia*) by feral pigs (*Sus scrofa*).' *New Zealand Journal of Ecology*, 36(2), 228–231.

Orbell, M. (1995). *The Illustrated Encyclopedia of Māori Myth and Legend*. Christchurch: Canterbury University Press.

Ortiz, J., Romero, N., Robert, P., Araya, J., Lopez-Hernandez, J., Bozzo, C., … & Rios, A. (2006). 'Dietary fiber, amino acid, fatty acid and tocopherol contents of the edible seaweeds *Ulva lactuca* and *Durvillaea antarctica*.' *Food Chemistry*, 99 (1), 98–104.

Park, G. (1995). *Ngā Uruora: The Groves of Life — Ecology and history in a New Zealand landscape.* Wellington: Victoria University Press.

Patel, M. (2009). 'The potential for a novel alcoholic drink prepared from the New Zealand native plant *Cordyline australis* (ti kōuka).' Unpublished doctoral dissertation, Auckland University of Technology.

Perry, G.L., Wilmshurst, J.M., & McGlone, M.S. (2014). 'Ecology and long-term history of fire in New Zealand.' *New Zealand Journal of Ecology*, 38 (2), 157–176.

Pike, M. (2015). 'I ate tutu … and lived to tell the story.' *Wilderness Magazine NZ.* Retrieved from: www.wildernessmag.co.nz/ate-tutu-lived-tell-story/

Polack, J.S. (1840). *Manners and Customs of the New Zealanders (Volume 2).* Retrieved from: www.enzb.auckland.ac.nz/document/?wid=155&action=null

Pond, W. (1997). *The Land With All Woods and Waters.* Rangahaua Whanui Series. Wellington: Waitangi Tribunal.

Prochaska, J.J., Das, S., & Benowitz, N.L. (2013). 'Cytisine, the world's oldest smoking cessation aid: growing evidence for its use as an affordable treatment globally.' *BMJ*, 347, f5198

Riley, M. (1988). *Māori Vegetable Cooking: Traditional and modern methods.* Paraparaumu: Viking Sevenseas NZ.

Riley, M. (1994). *Māori Healing and Herbal: New Zealand ethnobotanical sourcebook.* Paraparaumu: Viking Sevenseas NZ.

Riley, M. (2018). *Māori Healing Remedies: Rongoā Māori.* Paraparaumu: Viking Sevenseas New Zealand Limited.

Ross, P.M., Beentjes, M.P., Cope, J., de Lange, W.P., McFadgen, B.G., Redfearn, P., … & Te Tuhi, J. (2018).' The biology, ecology and history of toheroa (*Paphies ventricosa*): a review of scientific, local and customary knowledge.' *New Zealand Journal of Marine and Freshwater Research*, 52(2), 196–231.

Royal, C., & Kaka, J. (2010). *Cooking with Charles Royal.* Wellington: Huia.

Salmond, A. (1992). *Two Worlds: First Meetings Between Māori and Europeans, 1642–1772.* Honolulu: University of Hawaii Press.

Salmond, A. (1997). *Between Worlds: Early Exchanges between Māori and Europeans 1773–1815.* Auckland: Viking.

Salmond, A. (2017). *Tears of Rangi: Experiments across worlds.* Auckland: Auckland University Press.

Scheele, S., & Sweetapple, P. (2018). *Weaving Plants — Fact Sheets.* Manaaki Whenua Landcare Research. Retrieved from: www.landcareresearch.co.nz/science/plants-animals-fungi/plants/ethnobotany/weaving-plants/information-sheets

Shortland, E. (1851). *The Southern Districts of New Zealand: A journal, with Passing Notices of the Customs of the Aborigines.* London: Longman, Brown, Green, & Longmans. NZETC.

Simpson, P. (2000). *Dancing Leaves: The story of New Zealand's cabbage tree, Ti Kouka.* Christchurch: Canterbury University Press.

Simpson, P. (2004). *Pōhutukawa and Rātā: New Zealand's iron-hearted trees.* Wellington: Te Papa Press.

Simpson, P. (2017). *Tōtara: A natural and cultural history.* Auckland: Auckland University Press.

Taylor, M., Bieleski, R.L., & Allan, H.H. (2002). *Meanings and Origins of Botanical Names of New Zealand Plants.* Auckland: Auckland Botanical Society.

Taylor, R. (1848). *A Leaf from the Natural History of New Zealand.* Wellington: Robert Stokes NZETC.

Taylor, R. (1855). *Te Ika a Maui, or New Zealand and Its Inhabitants.* London: Wertheim & Macintosh. NZETC.

Taylor, R. (1868). *The Geography of New Zealand. The past and present of New Zealand: With its prospects for the future.* London: W. Macintosh. NZETC.

Te Papa (2018). *Traditional Māori Food Gathering.* Wellington: Museum of New Zealand Te Papa Tongarewa. Accessed from: www.tepapa.govt.nz/discover-collections/read-watch-play/Māori/traditional-Māori-food-gathering

Te Rūnanga o Ngāi Tahu (2015). *Ngāi Tahu Mahinga Kai, Season 1*. Accessed from: www.ngaitahu.iwi.nz/culture/mahinga-kai/

Thomson, C., & Challies, C. N. (1988). 'Diet of feral pigs in the podocarp-tawa forests of the Urewera Ranges.' *New Zealand Journal of Ecology*, 11, 73–78.

Travers, W.T.L. (1875) 'Notes on the extinction of the moa, with a review of the discussion on the subject.' *Transactions of the New Zealand Institute*, 8, 58–83.

Tregar, E. (1904). *The Maori Race*. Wanganui: Archibald Dudingston Willis. NZETC.

Twain, M. (1897). *Following the Equator; A journey around the world*. Project Gutenberg. Retrieved from: www.gutenberg.org/files/2895/2895-h/2895-h.htm.

Von Hochstetter, F. (1867). *New Zealand: Its physical geography, geology and natural history, with special reference to … the provinces of Auckland and Nelson*. Retrieved from www.enzb.auckland.ac.nz/document/?wid=433&action=null

Wade, W.R. (1842). *A Journey in the Northern Island of New Zealand*. Hobart: George Rolwegan. ENZB.

Wagstaff, S.J., & Breitwieser, I. (2004). 'Phylogeny and classification of *Brachyglottis* (Senecioneae, Asteraceae): an example of a rapid species radiation in New Zealand.' *Systematic Botany*, 29 (4), 1003–1010.

Wagstaff, S.J., Dawson, M.I., Venter, S., Munzinger, J., Crayn, D.M., Steane, D.A., & Lemson, K.L. (2010). 'Origin, diversification, and classification of the Australasian genus *Dracophyllum* (Richeeae, Ericaceae) 1.' *Annals of the Missouri Botanical Garden*, 97 (2), 235–258.

Wagstaff, S.J., & Garnock-Jones, P.J. (1998). 'Evolution and biogeography of the *Hebe* complex (Scrophulariaceae) inferred from ITS sequences.' *New Zealand Journal of Botany*, 36 (3), 425–437.

Walsh, R.S. (1978). *Nectar and Pollen Sources of New Zealand*. National Beekeepers Association of New Zealand.

Wee, M.S.M., Lentle, R.G., Goh, K.K.T., & Matia-Merino, L. (2017). 'The first of the viscoceuticals? A shear thickening gum induces gastric satiety in rats.' *Food and Function*, 8 (1), 96–102.

Wells, B. (1878). *The History of Taranaki: A Standard Work on the History of the Province*, pp. 23–42. Retrieved from: www.enzb.auckland.ac.nz/document/?wid=745

White, J. (1875). 'Letter to W. Travers. In "Notes on the extinction of the moa, with a review of the discussion on the subject".' *Transactions of the New Zealand Institute*, Volume 8.

White, J. (1887). *The Ancient History of the Maori. His Mythology and Traditions. Volumes I–VI*. Wellington: Government Printer.

Wood, J.R., & Wilmshurst, J.M. (2017). 'Changes in New Zealand forest plant communities following the prehistoric extinction of avian megaherbivores.' *Journal of Vegetation Science*, 28 (1), 160–171.

Wood, J.R., Wilmshurst, J.M., Wagstaff, S.J., Worthy, T.H., Rawlence, N.J., & Cooper, A. (2012). 'High-resolution coproecology: using coprolites to reconstruct the habits and habitats of New Zealand's extinct upland moa (*Megalapteryx didinus*).' *PloS one*, 7 (6), e40025.

Worthy, T.H., & Holdaway, R.N. (2002). *The Lost World of the Moa: Prehistoric life of New Zealand*. Bloomington: Indiana University Press.

Wyse, S.V., Burns, B.R., & Wright, S.D. (2014). 'Distinctive vegetation communities are associated with the long-lived conifer *Agathis australis* (New Zealand kauri, Araucariaceae) in New Zealand rainforests.' *Austral Ecology*, 39 (4), 388–400.

Yager, K.G., Schaefer, H.M., & Gould, K.S. (2016). 'The significance of shared leaf shape in *Alseuosmia pusilla* and *Pseudowintera colorata*.' *Botany*, 94(7), 555–564.

GLOSSARY

aruhe the starchy rhizome of bracken, also known as fern root

atua spiritual ancestor, divine being

aute paper mulberry (*Broussonetia papyrifera*)

hakuturi mysterious creatures that act as guardians for the forest

hāngī earth oven, and the food cooked in it

hapū kin group or subtribe

Hawaiki the spiritual homeland of the Māori people

hīnaki eel pot

inanga whitebait (*Galaxias* spp.) or *Dracophyllum longifolium*

iwi tribe

kahu cloak or garment

kai food

kaitiaki guardian

kākā native parrot (*Nestor meridionalis*)

kākaho long flower stalk of the toetoe

kākāriki New Zealand parakeet (*Cyanoramphus* spp.)

karakia prayer, chant or incantation

kāuru edible tap-root of the cabbage tree

kekeno fur seal

kererū native woodpigeon (*Hemiphaga novaeseelandiae*)

kina sea urchin (*Evechinus chloroticus*)

kinaki relish

kiore Polynesian rat (*Rattus exulans*)

koata fleshy heart of the cabbage tree from which new shoots emerge

kōauau flute

kōiwi human remains

komeke hīnau hīnau cake

kōrari flower stalk of the flax

kōtaha throwing spear

kōura freshwater crayfish (*Paranephrops* spp.)

kūmara sweet potato (*Ipomoea batatas*)

kūpapa Māori Māori who fought for the British during the 19th-century New Zealand Wars

kurī an extinct breed of Polynesian dog

mana spiritual power, status, authority

marae meeting house or meeting area

mauri life force

mōkehu bracken fern frond

mōkihi waka or raft made from raupō

pā fortified village or settlement

paikaka home-brew beer

pānukunuku toboggan

pāraerae sandal

parāoa sperm whale (*Physeter macrocephalus*)

patupaiarehe fairy folk

pōhā bag made of bull kelp

pou upright post

pounamu greenstone, jade

pūkāea long trumpet

pungapunga sweet, light cake made from
the pollen of raupō

rāhui temporary ban or restriction

rākau tree

rākau rangatira chiefly tree

rākau tapu sacred tree

rangatira high-ranking chief or leader

rārahu bracken

rerepe a type of porridge made from raupō
pollen and mashed mānuka beetles
(*Pyronota festiva*)

rito the heart of the nīkau palm

rongoā medicine

rōria harp, musical instrument played with
the teeth

tā moko traditional Māori tattooing,
involving carving into the skin and applying
dye; often on the face

taiaha long club used in warfare

taniwha powerful creature that lives in water and
takes on many forms

taonga treasure, or anything highly valued

tapu sacred or forbidden

tāwhara large, fleshy flower bract of the
kiekie

tāwhiti makamaka portable rat trap

Te Ao Māori the Māori world

te ira tangata the essence of humanity

te reo Māori the Māori language

tī cabbage tree (*Cordyline* spp.)

tītī muttonbird (*Ardenna grisea*)

toa warrior

tohunga priest or expert

tōī mountain cabbage tree (*Cordyline
indivisa*)

toko wānanga the staff of authority

tuākana older siblings

tukutuku ornamental woven panels in
the marae

tūtae ruru mānuka beetle (*Pyronota festiva*)

umu earth oven

ureure fruit of the kiekie

wai water

waka canoe

waka huia ornately carved container for
storing precious taonga

waka kererū drinking trough to help snare
kererū

waka kōrari wash-through sailing canoe
made from bull kelp and flax flower stalks

whakapapa genealogical tree

whakataukī proverb

whare house, building, hut, shelter

whenuapua fruitful land

DEITIES, AND MYTHICAL AND LEGENDARY FIGURES AND PLACES

Aituā figure of death

Haumia-tiketike atua of wild food crops

Kōpūwai giant with a dog's head and a
man's body

Papatūānuku earth mother, primordial
divine being

Ranginui sky father, primordial divine being

Rongo-mā-Tāne atua of cultivated foods

Tāne Mahuta atua of the forest and birds

Tangaroa atua of the oceans

Tāwhaki demigod with powers of
lightning

Te Wao Nui o Tāne great forest of Tāne

Tūmatauenga atua of war

Tunaroa atua of eels

Wainui mother of the waters

ACKNOWLEDGMENTS

Firstly, a huge thank you to Alex Hedley, Scott Forbes and all of the team at HarperCollins Publishers. I am immensely grateful for the opportunity, and incredibly stoked for your help in making this book a reality.

Huge thanks to the talented Edin Whitehead, the magical Matthew Cattin and citizen-scientist extraodinaire Jacqui Geux for their brilliant photos. A massive thanks to my colleagues at Auckland War Memorial Museum, in particular Vasiti Palavi, Sarah Berry and Tom Trnski, who all provided support while I completed the book, and Dhahara Ranatunga, Ewen Cameron, Yumiko Baba and Bethany Edmunds who provided images and advice. Thanks to Richard Benton for our entertaining discussions about the origin of native plant names, and to Wayne Petera and Betsy Young for our chats at Kapowairua on the stories and uses of native plants.

I also owe a huge debt of thanks to fans of the blog, and the many people who have supported it along the way. There are too many to name everyone, but special thanks to Hone Ropata, the crew from SBS Tuakana, Rochelle Constantine, Margaret Stanley and Cheryl Krull.

I could not have completed the book without the work of previous researchers in the area. In particular, I am indebted to Murdoch Riley's *Māori Healing and Herbal*, the Ngā Tipu Whakaoranga Database put together by Sue Scheele at Landcare Research Manaaki Whenua, and the writings of Elsdon Best. For the taxonomic information, I relied on the New Zealand Plant Conservation Network Database, and fact sheets prepared by Peter de Lange. For the etymology section, Te Māra Reo, the POLLEX-Online database, Te Aka online Māori dictionary, and Taylor, Bielski and Allan's book on New Zealand botanical names were essential sources.

For the many quotes, illustrations and background research, I am grateful for the contributions of the Alexander Turnbull Library, the Museum of New Zealand Te Papa Tongarewa, Puke Ariki, Auckland War Memorial Museum Tāmaki Paenga Hira, the Biodiversity Heritage Library, Project Gutenberg, Papers Past, the New Zealand Electronic Text Collection Te Pūhikotuhi o Aotearoa at Victoria University of Wellington, and the Early New Zealand Books Collection at the University of Auckland.

I am grateful for the support of my family and friends, to Oketi, Kerry and Johnny, and to Nana, Mum, Chris and Dad. And finally, to my best friend, Lizzy.

This publication was proudly supported by the Auckland War Memorial Museum Tāmaki Paenga Hira.